With the .45 automatic pistol nestled inside his belt, Hayer sat quietly and thought about the crime he was about to commit. "I didn't know what to expect [at the Audubon]," he admitted. "You know. I didn't come with any expectations about this, that or the other thing. I didn't know what to expect. This was it, man." Hayer had a certain amount of fear as he sat there and waited for the event that would define the rest of his life. But the fear was overcome with a sense that he was doing what he thought was right. He was striking a blow for justice and carrying out the will of Allah and His Messenger Elijah Mohammad. "I don't want to sound like any kind of hero," Hayer said, "because in my life—I've been through some changes with this whole thing, y'know? I don't know. You just do what you have to do, and that's all I can say, man. You know. And that's what I did...."

MALCOLM X

The Assassination

Michael Friedly

ONE WORLD BOOKS
BALLANTINE BOOKS • NEW YORK

A One World Book
Published by Ballantine Books

Copyright © 1992 by Michael Friedly

All rights reserved under International and Pan-American Copyright Conventions. Published in the United States by Ballantine Books, a division of Random House, Inc., New York, and in Canada by Random House of Canada Limited, Toronto. Originally published by Carroll & Graf Publishers, Inc. in 1992.

Library of Congress Catalog Card Number: 92-35822

ISBN 0-345-40010-0

This edition published by arrangement with Richard Gallen and Company, Inc.

Manufactured in the United States of America

First Ballantine Books Edition: February 1995

10 9 8 7 6 5 4 3

Acknowledgments

I would like to thank a number of people who have contributed greatly to this book. The first is Clayborne Carson, professor of history at Stanford University and senior editor of the Martin Luther King, Jr., Papers Project. Clay was my advisor when this book was my honors thesis at Stanford, and his advice was a great asset. His endless belief in the abilities of his students sets him apart from other professors at Stanford.

Duvid Gallen, author of *Malcolm X: As They Knew Him*, was also invaluable. He helped furnish me with a book contract and then oversaw the project to the end. His continual encouragement guided me through the writing process. He kept up with the details of the project and provided me with expanded resources that I could not have done without. David's only motivation was his enormous respect for Malcolm X.

I also want to thank a number of others who also contributed to this book. Lindsey Pedersen provided me with important advice and criticism from the beginning. Lydia Park conducted some of the research for this book in New York City while I was in California. Peter Goldman, author, of *The Death and Life of Malcolm X*, provided me with transcripts of some of his important interviews. Laura Selznick and the Undergraduate Research Opportunities office at Stanford offered me funding for my project. Stanford History Professor George Fredrickson read my manuscript and offered me advice on how to improve it. The staff at

Stanford's Green Library answered all of my many questions and were always willing to help. And the staff of the King Papers Project, most notably Karl Knapper, also helped me out a great deal.

And, finally, I would like to thank Chuck Sparnecht, who piqued my interest in the first place.

Contents

CHAPTER ONE

The Crime

"Violence is as American as apple pie."
—*H. Rap Brown, Former Chair,*
Student Nonviolent Coordinating Committee

Malcolm X always knew he would die a violent death. His entire life, like those of many African-Americans, had been plagued by violence. According to his autobiography, only one of his six uncles died of natural causes; many of the others were killed by whites. His father died in 1931, when Malcolm was only six years old. Earl Little's body was mangled, his leg severed after being run over by a streetcar. Although the actual circumstances remain unknown, Malcolm X always believed that his father had been attacked by racist whites and then laid across the streetcar tracks to simulate an accident. "It has always been my belief that I, too, will die by violence," he wrote in his autobiography, which was completed within weeks of his assassination. "I have done all that I can to be prepared."[1]

As he came of age in the ghettos of Boston and New York, Malcolm X, who was born and raised under the name Malcolm Little, almost guaranteed that his prediction of violent death would come true, as the gun-toting teenager involved himself in the criminal underworld where death by natural causes was the exception and not the norm. He cultivated the reputation of a crazy, trigger-happy punk who cared no more for his own life than he did for those he threatened to kill. At one point he loaded his pistol with a single bullet, put the gun to his head and pulled the trigger in an attempt to show his fellow burglars that they must not be afraid to die. Only many years later did he reveal that he had palmed the bullet. After a few close calls in which he was nearly killed either by his criminal friends or by the police, "Big Red" Little was arrested for burglary and sentenced to prison. He spent the next seven years of his life distancing himself from his criminal past and remodeling himself into a Muslim minister for the Nation of Islam who would adopt the name Malcolm X.[2] The unfortunate irony, however, is that by removing the threat of the drug-infested underworld from his life, he replaced it with an even larger threat that would eventually prove to be his undoing.

Malcolm X's bold prediction of a violent death finally came to fruition three months before his fortieth birthday, as he addressed several hundred of his followers at the Audubon Ballroom in Harlem. He spent the night before his death in a room at the New York Hilton Hotel; his house had been firebombed the week before, and he and his family did not yet have permanent lodgings. He and his wife Betty had picked out a house on Long Island, but his austere life left him with no money to purchase the house. Even that night before his death, his life was apparently in danger; a number of unknown men approached the Hilton's bellboy, asking for Malcolm X's room number. Although the bellboy did not reveal the information, extra security was quickly added outside his twelfth-floor room.

His final week had pushed Malcolm X to the limits of his own sanity. It was the culmination of a year-long battle with his former associates in the Nation of Islam, in which they had come frighteningly close to killing him on a number of occasions. His enormous stress was evident as he told a meeting of his Organization of Afro-American Unity (OAAU), which he founded in June 1964, "I've reached the end of my rope."[3] Within days of his death, he told writer Alex Haley, with whom he was collaborating on his autobiography, "Haley, my nerves are shot, my brain's tired."[4]

Malcolm X knew his death was imminent. It was a fact of life with which he claimed to be familiar, but his actions show that he was still not comfortable with the idea. "Deep down, I actually believed that after living as fully as humanly possible, one should then die violently," he wrote in his autobiography about his days of living on the edge in the criminal underworld. "I expected then, as I still expect today, to die at any time."[5] But despite his public pronouncements, he still seemed as ill-at-ease with his impending death as anyone would have been in his position.

Malcolm X's eventual assassination was anything but unpredictable. He had spent the past year outrunning armed Muslims who had been ordered to kill him after he had broken from the Nation of Islam in March 1964. He had barely escaped assassination attempts in New York, Boston, Chicago, and Los Angeles. And his luck was quickly running out. In his last week, he said he was given the names of five Muslims who had been dispatched from Chicago to kill him once and for all. He was prepared to reveal those names in a public meeting such as the one on Sunday, February 21. But he never got the chance.

One telling conversation during Malcolm X's final days demonstrates his realization of his plight. Dr. C. Eric Lincoln, a scholar who wrote the first major book on the Nation of Islam, called Malcolm X in the week before his death and asked him to come to Brown University to address some students on Tuesday, February 23, 1965. According to Lincoln, Malcolm X told him:

"I tell you, Professor Lincoln, I may be dead on Tuesday." I said, "Come on, Malcolm, cut the bullshit; come on up and talk to these kids," and he said, "You know I'll come, but I want you to hear me: I may be dead on Tuesday. . . . But, okay, tell your kids that I'll be up there on Tuesday if I am alive."[6]

Malcolm X had good reason to fear for his life. For the past year, he had been chased by members of the Nation of Islam who had both the ability and the desire to kill him. For twelve years, Malcolm X had been the most prominent member of the Nation, serving as the National Minister and the minister of the New York Mosque Number Seven, the largest in the country. But Malcolm X broke from the Nation of Islam on March 8, 1964, at the end of a ninety-day suspension from the Muslim group. His punishment came as the result of his biting comment the previous year at a public rally that the assassination of President John F. Kennedy was a case of "chickens coming home to roost." Malcolm X's apparent pleasure over Kennedy's death initiated a fire-storm of criticism and allowed Nation of Islam leader Elijah Muhammad to discipline his independent-minded protégé, with whom he had clashed on a number of issues the previous year.

The most nagging issue was Muhammad's ongoing adultery, which had been covered up for the previous ten years in an attempt to shield the self-styled "Messenger of Allah," a title that Muhammad had taken for himself. The disciplined New York Muslim took the opportunity of his silencing to break away from the Nation of Islam, with which he had become disillusioned, and he soon founded his own black-nationalist organizations that would be more action minded than the xenophobic Nation of Islam. He spent much of the next year either running from Black Muslim assassins, who had been sent to eliminate any potential rivalry, or traveling in Africa and the Middle East. There he went on a pilgrimage to Mecca and converted to orthodox Islam, a religion that was far different from the modified Islam he had been taught by Elijah Muhammad.

Despite the religious empire that he built gradually for himself, Elijah Muhammad had modest beginnings. He was born in 1897 in Sandersville, a small town in Georgia, and named Elijah Poole. Like Malcolm X, he had a limited education, reaching only eighth grade but, unlike Minister Malcolm, he never transformed himself into a self-educated, articulate man, and he retained his ungrammatical speech his entire life.[7] Also like Malcolm X, his father was a Baptist minister, but religion was not a part of young Elijah's life until he went to Detroit and met a mysterious man named W. D. Fard. Fard appeared in the ghetto of Detroit in the summer of 1930, selling silks and spreading his gospel to disenchanted African-Americans who were caught in the midst of the Depression. He said he "came from the East" and told numerous parables from the Bible in an attempt to get the ghetto residents to cleanse themselves morally and spiritually. As he gained followers, Elijah Poole among them, he finally revealed himself as a Muslim from Mecca who had come to give guidance to the "so-called Negroes" who were trapped in the "wilderness of North America."[8] Fard disappeared in 1934 as mysteriously as he had appeared, and the newly-named Elijah Muhammad emerged as the leader of Fard's followers.[9] Upon his succession to the modest throne, Muhammad declared Fard to be "the person of Allah" who had visited the Lost-Found American Negro, and Muhammad named himself the "Messenger of Allah."

Although Elijah Muhammad called the religion that he espoused in his organization Islam, his version of the faith bore little resemblance to the Islam of the Arabic-speaking countries of the Middle East. Instead, the Messenger taught a religion that was based on the issues of race and the power relations between different racial groups. According to the philosophies of the Nation of Islam, the black race was descended from the original tribe of Shabazz, which ruled the known world. This "black race" actually encompassed all non-whites, the Messenger taught. The white race appeared only because of the experiments of an evil scientist named Yacub, who bleached a segment of the black race of its color by interbreeding only the lightest of the people for thousands of years. Eventually, with all of the pigment removed from these experimental people, a new race of whites was created, a people without morals or compassion. Soon the whites took over the world, and dominated the entirety of the "darker world."[10]

But, as Allah communicated to the Messenger, the reign of the white race was soon to end after a short grace period. When the whites' time was up, the darker majority in the world would rise up and exterminate the evil race of European whites and return the power to the descendants of the original tribe of Shabazz. In the meantime, Elijah Muhammad—who was always referred to by his followers with respectful names such as the Messenger, the Honorable Elijah Muhammad, Mr. Muhammad, or the Holy Apostle—taught the doctrine of separation of the races. Since the white race was a race of "devils," blacks should avoid them at all costs, or else they would be tricked by their evil ways. Muhammad taught the "back to Africa" rhetoric that black nationalist Marcus Garvey had espoused earlier in the century. Muhammad, however, would also settle for the division of America into black and white states. The integrationist sentiments of Dr. Martin Luther King, Jr., and his fellow civil rights leaders were particularly anathema to the Muslims, and they took every opportunity to downgrade the efforts of the "so-called Negro leaders."

The doctrine of nonviolence preached by these civil rights leaders also inspired the anger of the Nation of Islam. As Muslims, the followers of Elijah Muhammad lived by the Islamic code of "an eye for an eye and a tooth for a tooth." The concept of not retaliating against violence inflicted by "white devils" was incomprehensible to the Muslims, and anyone who followed such a philosophy was a fool. Armed self-defense was the proper approach. Muslims would never instigate violence against others but, if attacked, maximum physical retaliation would be in order. This was the official policy of the Nation of Islam, and although it was not followed in many instances, it allowed Elijah Muhammad to demonstrate that his followers were law-abiding citizens who would only resort to violence if absolutely necessary.

In order to protect the faithful Muslims from the onslaught of police harassment that Muhammad had expected to follow from the creation of a militant black organization, he established the Fruit of Islam, the paramilitary wing of the Nation of Islam. The FOI was composed of the men of the individual Muslim mosques around the country, with a special detail assigned to protect the Messenger with elaborate security precautions. The Fruit of Islam was also charged with being the front line of defense in the upcoming War of Armageddon, in which blacks would finally take power from their white oppressors. A tertiary role that the FOI adopted was the internal enforcement of the rigid discipline that the Islamic code imposed. Members of the Nation of Islam were punished for violating rules against drinking, taking drugs, eating more than one meal a day, overindulgence, and other offenses.

When Malcolm X first became a Muslim, Muhammad had been in charge of the Nation of Islam for fewer than twenty years. He was a tiny man—quite short and frail—and it was far from obvious that this physically weak man was in charge of such a powerful movement. He always wore a suit in public, generally gray, with a proper bow tie around his feeble neck. Usually covering his bald head was a jewel-encrusted fez, garnished with gems in the shape of stars and the Islamic crescent. His voice was weak and even squeaky, particularly in his later years when his health deteriorated. His speech was halting and ungrammatical. His words, however, inspired thousands of African-Americans, Malcolm X among them, to purify themselves and work for the liberation of blacks across America.

Elijah Muhammad and the Nation of Islam had been the inspiration and the lifeblood for Malcolm X since he became a Muslim, around 1948. At the time, Malcolm X was serving a seven-to-ten year prison sentence in Massachusetts for burglary, and his original conversion to Islam changed him from a drug-running, carefree Harlem ruffian to an austere and disciplined Muslim minister. The Nation of Islam found enormous success in taking its black nationalist, anti-white teachings to the urban masses and to the prisons, where it recruited thousands of blacks such as Malcolm X, who had lost hope in other religions and in other forms of politics. Malcolm X rose quickly in the organization, vigorously preaching the philosophy that the white race is a race of devils. He converted thousands to the Nation's unique form of Islam and transformed the Nation of Islam from a small cult in a few cities to a nationwide movement that attracted the attention of the entire country. His eloquence was unequaled in the movement, and his rapid rise to fame brought him far greater name recognition than even his leader could claim. His fame also inspired the jealousy of other Muslim officials, many of whom had closer proximity to Muhammad's Chicago-based organization and greater access to the Messenger. The ear of the Messenger was a crucial factor in an organization that was run dictatorially by Muhammad and his family, and the closeness of Malcolm X's enemies to Muhammad allowed them to sway his loyalty away from the New York minister. The animosity between Malcolm X and other Muslim officials was a major factor in the break between him and the Nation of Islam and spurred the ensuing conflict between Malcolm X's followers and those of Elijah Muhammad.

In February 1965 the animosity had reached a fevered peak, as many members of the Nation of Islam were convinced that Malcolm X needed to be killed. His continuing presence in the African-American struggle for liberation was a constant threat to the very survival of the Nation of Islam, or so the Muslims thought. Malcolm X had tremendous power of persuasion over his followers and threatened to extend his powers over those who still remained loyal to Elijah Muhammad after Malcolm X left the Muslims. Muslim membership had already declined markedly because of the split, although Muhammad actually claimed that his followers had increased in number after Malcolm X left. Malcolm X's new black nationalist group, the Organization of Afro-American Unity, was in direct competition with the Nation of Islam for membership, and few seriously believed that the Nation could compete with the oratory abilities of Malcolm X.

Even if Malcolm X did not threaten to seriously diminish the Nation's membership by direct competition, he was still a threat in other ways. As an important official for the Nation of Islam for twelve years, Malcolm X knew many of the inner secrets of the Nation with which the Muslim membership was not familiar. Many of these secrets would have compromised the militant stance of the Muslims, and would have called into question the morality of their supposedly divine leader, Elijah Muhammad. These secrets, if publicized, could destroy the nation of Islam and everything that it stood for, and Malcolm X had the ability to make that come true. Backed into a corner by the hostility of the Muslims, Malcolm X began revealing the secrets during his final year in a futile attempt at self-defense, but his revelations only increased the anger of the swarming Muslims. For the Muslims, the conclusion was simple: Malcolm X had to be killed.

Malcolm X woke up on the morning of Sunday, February 21, 1965, to the sound of a ringing phone. "Wake up, brother," the voice on the other end of the line told him before hanging up. Malcolm X, who prided himself on being able to distinguish between voices of white men and black men, knew that this voice was white. He soon called Betty who, along with his four daughters, was staying with friends after the bombing. He asked his dutiful wife to dress the kids and bring them to the Audubon Ballroom that afternoon, where he was scheduled to speak to his followers. The request was unusual, since he had indicated earlier that he didn't want them to come, but she readily agreed. Betty Shabazz had guided her husband through the trauma that he had faced in the previous year, and she had suffered greatly watching the plight of her husband. Betty Shabazz was a strong woman, strong enough to tolerate her husband's insistence that she stay in the home and take care of the children rather than work outside the home, as she had always wanted to do.[11] Their marriage had not always been stable; she admitted recently that she had left him three different times, always because he refused to allow her to work outside the home. But she always came back to him; although it was generally unspoken, there was a strong love between them and for their growing family.[12]

Malcolm X finally left his hotel room at about one o'clock in the afternoon, checked out, and drove his familiar blue Oldsmobile to the Audubon Ballroom, the usual site for meetings of his Organization of Afro-American Unity. Rather than finding a parking place near the ballroom, he instead chose a site almost twenty blocks from his destination. It is still unclear why he did not drive straight to the Audubon; the police guessed that he didn't want to appear in a car that everyone—particularly the Black Muslims—knew to be his. Another theory is that he had resigned himself to die and that he wanted to provide the Muslims with an open shot away from his family and friends, who might be caught in the cross-fire. "You can run and run and run," he told Percy Sutton, his lawyer. "But when the time comes, you are going to die."[13]

As he began walking, he was hailed by a passing car driven by Fred Williams, with Charles X Blackwell, one of Malcolm X's lieutenants, in the back seat. Malcolm X first saw Williams, who was unknown to him, but his instinctual fear dissolved when he saw Blackwell's familiar face. Both men were on their way to the ballroom as well, so Malcolm X jumped in the back of the car and was driven the rest of the way.

The Audubon had been fully prepared for his speech by the time he arrived. Some 400 chairs faced a lonely podium on the stage in the front of the room, and a number of audience members were already present, eager to get a good seat for the show. Unlike Muslim events, there was no security check at the entrance to the room. Black Muslims were searched thoroughly and efficiently before they entered any of the Nation of Islam's many events. Guns and knives were confiscated, along with more mundane objects that were banned by the Nation, such as cigarettes, alcohol, and cosmetics. When he set out on his own, Malcolm X had kept this tradition, in large part to ward off any assassination attempts that might be planned for his gatherings. But the security checks had eventually fallen out of his favor as he began to realize the inevitability of his death. Besides, many of his followers, especially those who were not accustomed to the rigid discipline of the Muslims, had become irritated by the custom and offended that they were not above suspicion. Several weeks before his death, he ordered the searches stopped, arguing that "if I can't be safe among my own kind, where can I be?"[14] The only apparent security precaution was the questioning of an audience member who was wearing the pin of the Fruit of Islam, the paramilitary wing of the Nation of Islam. The Muslim was allowed to stay, but was forced to take off the pin. Malcolm X's reasons for stopping the security checks were sound, but such security measures would have prevented his assassination—or at least the attempt that particular day at the Audubon.

Malcolm X arrived at about two o'clock and made his way backstage as his aides made last-minute preparations. The guest speaker of the day was the Reverend Milton Galamison, a Presbyterian minister with a congregation in Brooklyn. The radical Reverend had made a name for himself by organizing school boycotts in Brooklyn to protest the continued segregation of the city's schools. No one really knew whether Galamison would actually show up, since he had never officially confirmed that he would.

As he waited for the program to begin, Malcolm X seemed especially ragged, moving clumsily, rather than with his usual elegant gait. He seemed preoccupied. He sat in a folding chair in his dressing room backstage at the Audubon, getting up occasionally to see how large the crowd had become. Finally, a message came from Galamison's secretary that the Reverend would be unable to attend because of his busy schedule in Brooklyn; Malcolm X responded to the message with a flash of misdirected anger.

Malcolm X seemed fed up. A number of times that final day he allowed his anger to get the best of him. At one point, he screamed at a Muslim cleric who had tried to show some sympathy for him. "Get out of here!" he shouted, prompting both the sheik and Malcolm X's chief aide, Benjamin Goodman, to leave the room.[15] He verbally attacked another of his aides for passing the message that Galamison was a no-show to a female follower. "You gave that message to a woman? You should have known better than that!"[16] He drooped over his chair, uninvolved in the preparations that were going on around him, unable to take charge as he usually did because of his own preoccupations.

"He was more tense than I'd ever seen him," Goodman reported later, "and I'd seen him for seven years. He just lost control of himself completely. I never saw him do that before."[17]

Finally, two o'clock rolled around, and it was time to start the event. Because of the last-minute changes, there was no set schedule, and Malcolm X asked Goodman to speak first. As Goodman began his rambling diatribe, Malcolm X sat backstage and tried to concentrate on what was being said.

This was not the first time that Goodman had been asked to give the warm-up speech. In many similar events, Goodman had filled the role that Ralph Abernathy performed for Martin Luther King, Jr., playing the crowd and priming them for the main event. Goodman, who later changed his name to Benjamin Karim, was one of Malcolm X's most trusted aides, and when the OAAU leader left on his eighteen-week trek to Africa and the Middle East in 1964, he appointed Goodman as the interim leader. On this particular day, Goodman spoke for about half an hour before finally introducing Malcolm X. Meanwhile, backstage, Malcolm X became increasingly nervous as he prepared to speak to the faithful. "The way I feel, I ought not to go out there today," he said.[18] At one point, he turned to the sister who was in charge of booking Reverend Galamison for the event and castigated her for not following through on her responsibility. Earlier, he attacked her for asking him whether Goodman could be the first speaker, while Goodman stood by and watched. "You know you shouldn't ask me right in front of him!" he barked before relenting to the request.[19]

As he prepared to mount the stage after Goodman's introduction, Malcolm X turned to the assistant and apologized. "You'll have to forgive me for raising my voice to you—I'm just about at my wit's end," he explained. Applause from the audience began to rise as Goodman wrapped up his introduction. "And now, without further remarks, I present to you one who is willing to put himself on the line for you, a man who would give his life for you—I want you to hear, listen, to understand—one who is a Trojan for the black man." Malcolm X moved slowly to the podium, and gave the traditional Muslim welcome. "As-salaam alaikum," he intoned in his deep, growling voice. May peace be with you. "Wa-alaikum Salaam," the audience replied. And unto you.

But before Malcolm X could utter another word, a disturbance arose in the crowd. In the middle of a row about midway back in the audience, a man jumped out of his seat, screaming at his neighbor, "Hey man, get your hand out of my pocket!" As the audience turned to watch the scuffle, Malcolm X moved to the side, out from behind the wooden podium, calling, "let's be cool, brothers." His bodyguards left the front of the audience and began moving down the ballroom to settle the scuffle, leaving their leader open and unguarded.

The sound of the shotgun rocked the room. One shot from a man near the front was all that was necessary to kill Malcolm X. The former Black Muslim reeled from the explosion of the shrapnel entering his body. The shot was aimed perfectly, as twelve pieces of hot metal imprinted a bloody circle through his chest. He fell backward from the immense force, falling over a set of chairs that were to seat the guests that never came, and his head thudded painlessly on the ground. As he lay on the ground dying, the man with the shotgun fired again, and the shrapnel tore through the wooden podium that was too flimsy to protect Malcolm X. Two more black men armed with pistols ran to the stage, firing into Malcolm X's motionless body, adding insult to injury. Their shots hit the slain Muslim mostly in his legs, which were draped over a chair facing the audience. Members of the crowd began to scream, panicking from the sound of the gunfire. Despite the Muslim rhetoric of armed self-defense, very few in the audience had actually witnessed such violence, and they piled on top of each other, desperately trying to run from the room or to take cover. In the back of the room, a homemade bomb that was tucked into a sock exploded, adding to the immense confusion. The pandemonium played right into the hands of the conspirators, who melted into the crowd and began to make their escape.

Their job complete, the three gunmen turned to flee, along with their cohorts, who had started the initial commotion. One of them, the gunman with the Luger, was sent sprawling down the stairs by one of Malcolm X's followers, but he picked himself up quickly and ran out of the building. The man with the .45, who later identified himself to police as Talmadge "Tommy" Hayer, began to run, waving his gun at the crowd to clear a path for himself, but ran right into Gene Roberts, one of Malcolm X's bodyguards. Roberts instinctively grabbed a chair to protect himself, and Hayer pumped a round in Roberts' direction, but the bullet slipped through his suit jacket without injuring him. Roberts threw the chair at the assassin, who fell under the force of the blow. As he got up to run again, limping this time, a bullet ripped through his leg. The shot was fired by Reuben Francis, one of the few of Malcolm X's bodyguards who had responded effectively to the violence. Many of the other guards, including the man who would become the star witness for the prosecution against the alleged assassins, hid under the chairs and tables or became lost in the crowd.

As Hayer fought his way through the crowd, Betty Shabazz emerged from her hiding place under the tangle of chairs, where she had been trying to protect her children, and ran to her husband. "They are killing my husband!" she shrieked, ignoring the hordes of people that were desperately trying to flee from the ballroom. Several of Malcolm X's friends and followers surrounded him, loosening his tie and trying to see what could be done to save his life. Roberts, who later revealed himself to be an undercover New York City policeman who had infiltrated the OAAU, tried in vain to resuscitate Malcolm X's graying body.[20] But the damage was already done.

Meanwhile, Hayer hopped as quickly as he could down the stairs and out of the building, still carrying Francis' bullet in his leg, but the crowd soon realized that he was one of the gunmen. With vicious force, the mob began to pummel him, breaking one of his legs before Patrolman Thomas Hoy, the first police officer on the scene, pulled him from the swarming mob. As the crowd began to descend on Hayer again, two other officers, Alvin Aronoff and Louis Angelos, came to the suspect's aid. With great difficulty, the three policemen managed to push the suspect into a waiting police car. After the officers finally managed to separate the angry crowd from their police car, Hayer was immediately driven to the 34th Precinct in Harlem. By this time, a force of policemen, stationed at the Columbia Presbyterian Medical Center across from the Audubon, had descended on the scene. The police had been at the medical center in case of just such an incident, but they had been ordered to stay out of the Audubon to avoid a confrontation with Malcolm X's followers. As it was, they were far away enough to prevent a scene, but also too far away to save Malcolm X or capture his killers. In fact, Thomas Hoy, who pulled Hayer from the crowd, just happened to be passing by the Audubon when he heard the commotion, unaware that Malcolm X was even in the area. According to Deputy Police Commissioner Walter Arm, a special detail of police, which included two sergeants and eighteen uniformed officers, was stationed at the medical center. He also emphasized that it was "normal procedure" to keep uniformed policemen away from Malcolm X's meetings. Gene Roberts, however, later testified that he had never seen so few officers attend one of Malcolm X's OAAU meetings.[21]

As the police finally entered the scene and tried to calm the crowd, several brothers made their way across the street to the medical center and grabbed a stretcher to transport Malcolm X across the street. They ran back to the Audubon and carefully placed Malcolm X across the gurney, his head tilted far back and his teeth exposed in a twisted gnarl. His composure was gone. The man that one woman once compared to an elegant black panther had now become a bloody mess, his face contorted with the intense pain that he felt in his final moments; it was the final disgrace that he died in such agony in front of his friends and followers. As the brothers and policemen crossed the street carrying the stretcher, a photographer captured the picture that would make many of the front pages the next morning, an agonizing shot that highlighted Malcolm X's protruding teeth, his pained expression, and his final humiliation.

"The person you know as Malcolm X is dead," the hospital spokesperson announced after surgeons attempted to revive him by cutting through his chest and massaging his heart.[22] At first, there was no question about who was responsible for Malcolm X's death. Regardless of who had pulled the triggers, it was Elijah Muhammad and his followers in the Nation of Islam who had initiated the escalation of rhetoric and violence that ended with the murder of the Messenger's chief rival. Malcolm X's followers immediately vowed revenge and reportedly formed a group of brothers who would travel to Chicago to seek the head of Elijah Muhammad, the man who had instigated the war within the Muslims.

The call for retribution against Muhammad and the Nation of Islam is further testimony to the bitterness of the battle between Malcolm X and his former leader. The Islamic rule is an eye for an eye and a tooth for a tooth, Malcolm X always reminded his listeners when it came to white violence against blacks. This violence should be no different, many of his followers reasoned. Malcolm X had always taught the philosophy of maximum physical retaliation, arguing once that a white man who killed a black man should be executed at once, without a trail or other resorts to the white criminal-justice system. Malcolm X generally talked tougher than he acted, as he often tried to stop violence among his own Muslim followers. But now his restraining voice was gone, leaving his lieutenants with no guidance on how to respond to this ultimate act of violence.

As Malcolm X's followers tried to decide how to act without their leader, Harlem went about the solemn business of mourning its lost leader and arranging his funeral. Malcolm X's body was put on display at the Unity Funeral Home in Harlem over the objections of an orthodox Muslim cleric, who argued that the family should observe the Islamic rule that the body must be buried before the setting of the second sun. After several bomb threats forced the police to search the funeral home twice, the body was finally shown to the public on Monday evening, February 22. Malcolm X's supporters and friends, as well as Harlemites who had respected what he stood for, waited outside the funeral home in the freezing cold for hours to get a chance to say farewell to their symbolic leader. The line outside the viewing area stretched for blocks and was often stalled as police closed the building at almost regular intervals to search for bombs. Security was tight, and at least two men were arrested for carrying concealed rifles outside the funeral home. By the end of the week, an estimated 30,000 people had passed through the funeral home to see Malcolm X's body; testimony to his strong support in the community despite his small number of core followers.

On Friday night, February 26, the viewing was stopped, and Sheik Ahmed Hassoun Jaaber, an orthodox Muslim who had been a consultant to the American Muslim, stripped Malcolm X of his Western suit in favor of the flowing white garment of traditional Islamic burials. He was draped from head to foot, with only his peaceful face poking through the binding cloths. His funeral was held the next morning at the Faith Temple Church of God as 1,000 people jammed inside the building and 3,000 more waited outside under heavy security to catch one more glimpse of their fallen hero. The emotional eulogy was performed by actor Ossie Davis, who had befriended Malcolm X, along with his wife, actress Ruby Dee. Davis saluted Malcolm X as "our manhood, our living black manhood" and called him "our own black shining Prince!—who didn't hesitate to die, because he loved us so."[23]

After the performance of Islamic rites, Malcolm X was taken to Ferncliff Cemetery in Westchester County to be buried under the name of El-Hajj Malik El-Shabazz, which was given to him upon his original conversion to Islam and his pilgrimage to Mecca. In a final salute to their fallen leader, several of his followers, mournfully dressed in their black suits and ties, began scooping dirt over his coffin rather than allowing the white gravediggers to have the honor. Realizing the emotions involved, the whites quickly surrendered their shovels and allowed Malcolm X's supporters to cover the grave, which symbolically pointed due east toward Mecca.

CHAPTER TWO

The Suspects

"Was Malcolm on the way to becoming not extreme enough for the ultra-extremists? Was he, as some have declared, the victim of an 'international conspiracy?' Where did the narcotics peddlers, whom Malcolm hated, fit in, if at all? How about the Communists, the white, the red and the Negro hangers-on? . . . Harlem, the country and the world will never be able to piece together any answers if avengers cloud the thinking and cover the trails with attempts at counter-assassination."

—*Roy Wilkins[1]*

The ensuing physical war between the Black Muslims and the followers of Malcolm X never reached the fever peak that the rhetorical war had attained, although there were a small number of potentially dangerous moments. One of the first blows in the war came in Chicago, when a fire blazed out of control at Muhammad Ali's apartment house while the world heavyweight champion was not at home. Ali, formerly Cassius Clay, announced that he was a member of the Nation of Islam after his 1964 championship bout with Sonny Liston, and was one of the key prizes in the fight between Malcolm X and Elijah Muhammad. Despite Malcolm X's efforts to woo Ali into his camp, the boxer refused to abandon the "Messenger of Allah" in order to follow the discredited former Muslim leader, who was branded the "chief hypocrite" of the Muslim movement. Although he stayed far from the conflict between the two black nationalist Muslim leaders, Ali was the most visible Black Muslim after Malcolm X's departure, so his residence seemed to be a natural target for revenge seekers. The fire devastated the second and third floors of the South

Side Chicago building where Ali lived, although there were no reported injuries. The police eliminated arson as a possible cause the next day, but the incident nevertheless heightened the tensions between the two groups, and the assumption remained that the fire was set by some of Malcolm X's people who sought revenge for their leader's death.

Elijah Muhammad immediately tried to distance himself from the conflict, announcing at a press conference the next day that the Nation of Islam had nothing to do with the killing at all and that he did not know who would try to kill the Muslim leader. "I don't have any knowledge of anyone trying to kill Malcolm," he announced. "We have never resorted to such a thing as violence."[2] Muhammad appeared at the news conference in the living room of his luxurious Chicago mansion, flanked by his son Herbert, who was also Muhammad Ali's manager; John Ali, the Nation's National Secretary; and minister James Shabazz. Chicago policemen surrounded the house to prevent assassination attempts against Muhammad, but none came, despite the warning that six of Malcolm X's followers were on their way from Chicago to avenge their leader's death. Muhammad publicly dismissed the threat to his life. "I don't feel disturbed about that in the least. We are innocent of Malcolm's death. It doesn't matter if there are 600 or 6,000" followers of Malcolm X who would try to kill Muhammad.[3]

Even after Malcolm X was dead, Muhammad remained on the offensive against his former protégé, as he tried to blame Malcolm X for his own death. "I hoped Allah would chastise him and bring him back on his knees," Muhammad told the assembled media in his typically ungrammatical speech. "I am the man who taught Malcolm. I didn't teach him what he went for himself. As for what he had gone for himself, I didn't teach him that." But Muhammad ironically also emphasized that his organization did not want to see Malcolm X killed, despite pronouncements in his movement's newspaper stating that Malcolm X deserved death for his actions against the Nation of Islam. "Malcolm died of his own preaching. He preached violence, and violence took him away," declared the Messenger of Allah.[4] But he also emphasized that the Nation of Islam would not resort to violence, despite the growing public awareness that violence was a tool that they used with increasing regularity. "A hypocrite is not to be killed," Muhammad intoned. Rather, the hypocrite, Malcolm X, should be shunned by the rest of his Muslim brethren and cast into "spiritual isolation." However, Muhammad's political double-talk did nothing to diminish his responsibility for creating the violent climate in which Malcolm X was killed. Pronouncements in *Muhammad Speaks*, the movement's newspaper, did everything short of ordering the Muslim faithful to kill Malcolm X, as they branded the former minister of the New York mosque the "chief hypocrite" who was only "worthy of death."

Malcolm X's followers vowed revenge against the Black Muslim murderers. His half-sister, Ella Mae Little Collins, was one of the many Muslims who initially had been recruited into the Nation of Islam by Malcolm X. Collins joined her brother's Organization of Afro-American Unity in 1964 and assumed command of the divided organization upon his death. "He will be avenged," she declared, openly threatening those who were responsible for her half-brother's death. "We are going to repay them for what they did to Malcolm," announced Leon Ameer, a member of the Nation of Islam who broke from Elijah Muhammad only a couple months earlier to join forces with Malcolm X.[5] Ameer was beaten viciously by several Black Muslims from the Boston mosque two months earlier on Christmas Day, 1964, for leaving the Nation. The attack left him in a coma for three days. As Ameer vowed revenge, another of Malcolm X's lieutenants, James Shabazz,[6] tried to turn the anger of Malcolm X's followers into a healthier pursuit of black equality:

If this becomes a war of black man against black man, Muslim against Muslim, who benefits? The followers of

Mr. Muhammad do not, nor do the loyal supporters of Malcolm. The only ones who benefit are those elements who have enslaved us, kept us in slavery and who seek to perpetuate us in slavery. I, respecting the thinking, accomplishments and determinations of Malcolm X, am concerned with the unification of all people of African origin in America and the rest of the world with a unification of the Muslims throughout the world.[7]

The most dramatic shot in the war between the Muslims was the torching of the Nation of Islam's Harlem mosque, over which Malcolm X had ruled for so many years before his defection from the Muslims. The four-story mosque on the corner of Lenox Avenue and 116th Street had been Malcolm X's power base from the time that he took over the small temple in 1954 until he was cast from the Muslim membership ten years later. The fire began at 2:25 on Monday morning, February 22, only eleven hours after Malcolm X was killed. Although police patrols in the area had been stepped up due to the increased tension in Harlem over Malcolm X's death, the arsonists were unseen as they lit the fire through an upper window. The three-alarm blaze gutted the building, and although no one was in the building at the time, six firefighters were injured, two of them seriously, when a section of a burning wall collapsed on them. As the firefighters eventually contained the flames, icicles began growing from the edifice during the cold winter night, creating a startling contrast of fire and ice. "It was a vicious sneak attack," charged Joseph X, a member of the Harlem mosque. "The worst thing a man can do is tamper with your religious sanctuary."

Another Harlem resident reacted more calmly to the news of the mosque fire. "I would say we expected something like this. . . . I would say these cats are going to be scratching until there's not but one of them left."[8] The followers of Malcolm X and Elijah Muhammad were teetering on the edge of an all-out war that threatened the survival of both groups. Already, one of the generals, Malcolm X, had been killed in the battle, and the remaining hatred promised a future of further violence and death.

"Steady Eddie!" the *New York Amsterdam News*, a Harlem newspaper, blared in a front-page editorial of its February 27 edition in an attempt to head off the escalating war between the Muslim forces and Malcolm X's followers. The editorial came after another Black Muslim mosque, this one in San Francisco, was destroyed by fire and an apparent bombing attempt, this time unsuccessfully, was made on the Rochester, New York mosque. Tensions were running high, and every attempt was being made by the leaders of New York's black community to avert a possible riot, such as the one that had devastated Harlem the summer before.

> None of these . . . emotions [from Malcolm X's death] can be, or should be used, as an excuse to set off disorder and rioting such as took place in our community a few months ago. Despite what has been said about him, Malcolm X had a great respect for law and order and no one can truthfully say that he ever precipitated a riot, or was ever known to lead one. . . . Let's give Malcolm the warmth and respect that is due him. But let's be cool about it![9]

While the *Amsterdam News* treated Malcolm X with tremendous respect after his death, other newspapers showed their contempt for the black nationalist. *The New York Times*, for example called Malcolm X a "bearded extremist" in its coverage the day after his assassination. *Time* magazine went even further, calling the Muslim "a disaster to the civil rights movement."[10] The varied responses to the murder demonstrated the polarization that Malcolm X created as he defined his version of black nationalism; thousands flocked to hear him speak and sing his praises, while an equal number condemned him for his supposed professions of hatred and violence. But the immediate flow of reactions from across the globe to Malcolm X's assassination simply demonstrated the Muslim's prominence in the

African-American battle for liberation and the significance of that fight to the rest of the world.

Malcolm X clearly meant more to the African-American struggle for freedom than can be expressed in terms of the number of followers that he could claim. In fact, his followers were few, in large part because the radical changes that he was undergoing did not allow for a stable following. Many of those who left the Nation of Islam with Malcolm X were unable to explain the changes he was undergoing, and many drifted away from him when he began his process of moderating his opinions away from those of the Nation of Islam.

But Malcolm X was the voice for millions of African-Americans who still lived under the name "Negro." He appropriated the anger that resided in the urban black population and screamed his resentment for all the world to hear. He made certain that those blacks in the Northern cities who were being forgotten by the Southern civil rights movement would still have a voice. His bitterness toward American society was real and uncompromising, and his ability to express his angry emotions made him the obvious leader for African-Americans across the country. For every person who actually claimed to be a follower of Malcolm X, a vast number of others agreed with him and experienced silent delight when he castigated the "white devils" for their immoral behavior against the black population of America. Malcolm X was the one black leader in America who would stand toe-to-toe with the white oppressors without flinching, compromising, or backing down out of fear of white retaliation.

But Malcolm X's passionate rhetoric did not just benefit the black community. Malcolm X was also the conscience of white society in America. He nagged them and cajoled them for their inhumane actions against African-Americans. He tormented them when four innocent black children were killed in a Birmingham church bombing in 1963, and he reminded them on the occasion of President John F. Kennedy's death that the American leader did not do enough to support the blossoming civil rights movement. As America mourned the assassination of their president, and celebrated his accomplishments, Malcolm X refused to allow the African-Americans to be forgotten. He was the uncompromising critic of white society who jolted many white listeners to the conclusion that he was right, that America's rigid racial hierarchy had to be abolished. His assassination removed a thorn in the side of white America, but the anger that he represented lived on in the ghettos of American cities.

Reactions to the assassination poured in from around the globe, most of them from radical nations who saw in Malcolm X a champion of the oppressed. According to the *Lagos Daily Times*, "Malcolm X fought and died for what he believed to be right. He will have a place in the palace of martyrs." Even the Chinese Communist government responded to the killing, as it charged the United States government with an imperialist conspiracy to murder Malcolm X. No doubt the Chinese had been impressed with the black nationalist leader the previous year, when he called the Chinese acquisition of nuclear weapons the greatest advancement yet for blacks in the upcoming war between the white race and the darker majority in the world.[11] "Their murder of Malcolm X indicates that [the American imperialists] are prepared to use any despicable means to intimidate American Negroes and quell their struggles," the Chinese government charged.[12] Carl Rowan, the director of the United States Information Agency and vocal critic of Malcolm X, told the press that news of the assassination was "grossly misconstrued in some countries where the people did not know what Malcolm represented."[13]

Closer to home, major civil rights leaders, including some who had been openly hostile to the fiery New York Muslim, lamented his death. James Baldwin, speaking at a press conference in London, called Malcolm X's death a "major setback for the Negro movement." Baldwin, who throughout his life demonstrated his sympathy with the philosophies of Malcolm X, blamed the killing on the climate of racial hatred that had been brewing between blacks and whites. "You did it," he cried to the news reporters present. "Whoever did it was formed in the crucible of the Western world, of the American republic."

Roy Wilkins, executive director of the NAACP, tried to ease the tensions of a high-strung Harlem community in an editorial for the *Amsterdam News*. Under the headline "No Time for Avengers," he wrote that "the police blotters and hospital records all over the country are full of Negroes killing and maiming Negroes. . . . But in the Malcolm X case it is to be hoped that there will be no revenge murders." Wilkins even tried to defend the Black Muslims by introducing some conspiracy theories that befuddled the facts of the assassination. "Was he, as some have declared, the victim of an 'international conspiracy?' Where did the narcotic peddlers, whom Malcolm hated, fit in, if at all? How about the Communists, the white, the red and the Negro hangers-on?"[14]

James Farmer, the national director of the Congress of Racial Equality, warned in a press conference that Malcolm X's assassination most likely had nothing to do with the war between his supporters and the Nation of Islam. Although he refused to elaborate further during his February 23, 1965 press conference, Farmer declared that he had "grave suspicions that it will go deeper" than a mere squabble between the black nationalists. Instead, the assassination "will have international implications."[15] Martin Luther King, Jr., executive director of the Southern Christian Leadership Conference, addressed the assassination at a press conference at the Los Angeles airport on February 24, 1965:

The assassination of Malcolm X was an unfortunate tragedy and it reveals that there are still numerous people in our nation who have degenerated to the point of expressing murder, and we haven't learned to disagree without being violently disagreeable. . . . I think one must understand that in condemning the philosophy of

Malcolm X, which I did constantly, that he was a victim
of the despair that came into being as a result of a society that gives so many Negroes the nagging sense of
"nobodyness." And just as one condemns the philosophy,
he must be as vigorous in condemning the continued existence in our society of the conditions of racial injustice,
depression and man's inhumanity to man.[16]

As reactions to Malcolm X's death flowed in from
around the world, the Nation of Islam held its annual convention in the Chicago Coliseum. Most of the attention was
understandably diverted to the potential war between the
Malcolm X camp and the Muslims. Security was omnipresent as the Chicago Police Department quintupled the
number of officers who were normally present, and the Nation of Islam's own security organization, the Fruit of Islam, was represented in force. A phalanx of FOI members
protected the Messenger at all times, putting a physical bar-
rier between him and any would-be assassin. The tall, muscular FOI practically smothered the tiny, frail leader in
protection, even as Muhammad stood onstage speaking to
his followers; a potential assassin would have had a difficult job getting a bullet past the wall of bodyguards.
Muslims, as well as members of the media, were searched
not once but twice at the door, just to ensure that the war
between the Muslims did not erupt at the Coliseum. In his
speech before the convention, Elijah Muhammad escalated
the war of words between the rival groups, telling the thousands of faithful Muslims that "we will fight" to protect the
Nation of Islam from attack by Malcolm X's supporters.
The main purpose of the meeting, ostensibly, was to unify
the Muslims around an anti-Malcolm X position, in case
any of them had become disenchanted by the whole affair.
"I didn't harm Malcolm, but he tried to make war against
me," Muhammad preached. "We didn't want to kill Malcolm. His foolish teaching would bring him to his own
end." The convention featured endless attacks on Malcolm X from all sides, including from his two brothers,

who remained as ministers in the Nation of Islam even after their brother left.

Philbert X, Malcolm X's oldest full brother, explained to the faithful that he had attempted in vain to show his brother the path back to the Nation of Islam and to help him avoid the "dangerous course" on which he had embarked. "Now that he is dead there is nothing I can do—or anybody else," he lamented. But he warned the Muslims that they should not allow the war between them and their rivals to divert them from their main goal. "Do not let the white man come between us," he warned. Malcolm X's younger brother Wilfred, the minister of the Nation's Detroit mosque, told the story of how he had first recruited his brother into the ranks of the Muslims. But, he reported, his brother chose a "reckless path [that] no doubt, is what brought him to his early death." One of the highlights of the convention was the public return of Wallace Muhammad back into the Muslim ranks. Wallace, Elijah Muhammad's son, had been the chosen successor to the movement until he broke from the Nation, charging his father with immorality and corruption. Although he did not join Malcolm X's new Muslim Mosque, Inc., Wallace openly showed his sympathy for the New York Muslim until, of course, he was assassinated. Before the crowd of Muslims, Wallace recanted his opposition and was formally reinitiated into the Nation of Islam.[17]

The vilification of Malcolm X served to unify the Muslims around a common cause. By defining an enemy, a group such as the Nation of Islam was able to define itself as something other than the enemy. By declaring themselves to be enemies of the white devils, they classified themselves and their allies as being non-white. By declaring themselves to be enemies of Malcolm X, the "chief hypocrite," they cast themselves as being above such hypocrisy. But, in defining the enemy, Elijah Muhammad also created a visible animosity that often went beyond the control of the Nation's leaders. Malcolm X was castigated in no uncertain terms for almost a year before he was killed, largely in order to unify the Muslim masses in a "holier-than-thou" exhibition of their faith. By creating an enemy in Malcolm X and by continually vilifying him in an effort to unify the Muslims, Elijah Muhammad and other leaders of the Nation of Islam created the climate in which the assassination of Malcolm X became inevitable. Although he escaped blame because of the inconclusiveness of the trial of the suspected killers, Muhammad was directly responsible for Malcolm X's death, regardless of whether he had specific foreknowledge of the actual killing. His continual verbal attacks on Malcolm X essentially constituted a call for his death, and the call did not go unheeded.

While the Muslims were busy attacking each other and assigning blame for the assassination, the police prepared themselves for the dual jobs of preventing further violence and finding Malcolm X's assassins. The first task was handled admirably. Although the incidents of arson at the Harlem and San Francisco mosques were regrettable, these were crimes of property rather than violent crimes, and the police were able to prevent additional deaths and injuries during the war of words. Throughout the entire tense period after Malcolm X's death, they were out on the streets in force, trying to ease the tension and deter violent activities by their presence. Hundreds of police officers attended Malcolm X's funeral not because they were lachrymose at his passing, but because they had their jobs to perform. A number of arrests were made for carrying concealed weapons, but there were no serious outbreaks of violence in New York or Chicago.

The police had less success in their second pursuit of tracking down the killers, although they made certain that the public got the opposite impression. One of the assassins had already been caught. Hayer was in custody—in traction because of the wounds to his leg—and there was no chance that the authorities would release him on bail. As expected, Hayer refused to divulge any information but his name, which got confused as he gave it to police. According to the arrested assassin, the police began to interrogate him even before he got to the police station. One of the police officers "asked me my name," the assassin told the court in his trial the next year.

> And I was telling him that I was shot; he didn't know that I was shot. And he was asking me a lot of questions and I was telling him that I was shot. So I finally told him my name was Thomas Hayer. Tommy Hayer. So he says, "Did you say Tommy Hagan?" So I just said yes. I'm shot, you know, I want to go—I need a doctor. So that's how my name got to be Thomas Hagan.[18]

So the police and the prosecution booked and prosecuted Hayer under the mistaken name of Hagan.

Finding physical evidence against Hayer was not difficult. While in the police car that took Hayer away from the Audubon, Sergeant Aronoff had discovered a .45 cartridge in Hayer's pocket, which matched one of the murder weapons perfectly. Hayer originally claimed ignorance, saying he did not know how the cartridge could have gotten into his coat. Analysis of the homemade bomb in the back of the auditorium also revealed Hayer's fingerprint, although he still pleaded innocent when faced with this evidence. Police also arrested Reuben Francis, Malcolm X's bodyguard, and charged him with felonious assault for shooting Hayer in the leg as he tried to escape.

Convinced that they had captured one of the three or more assassins, the police set out to find the rest, or at least as many as they could given the limitations under which they had to work. Before all the witnesses dispersed from the scene of the crime, police made every attempt to interview as many of them as possible, extracting information as to how many shots were fired, how many assassins were involved, and what they looked like. The difficulty with this approach was that few of the witnesses had any burning desire to talk to white police officers. Many in the audience were former Black Muslims, whose dislike for anything white was renowned. White police officers were particularly anathema, since it was they who were responsible for so much of the tension in black communities across the country.

An exacerbating factor was the attitude of some of the more cynical Muslims that the police were actively involved in planning the assassination, or at least that they had foreknowledge of the crime, and were only putting up the pretense of conducting an investigation. The patrolmen and detectives on duty that day, who were unaware of what their superiors in the police department did or did not know, were thus forced to fight an uphill battle against what they saw as a groundless suspicion. Nevertheless, they persisted in interviewing as many of the faithful as would talk to them, but their picture of the crime was severely skewed from the beginning because of the tense relationship between them and the witnesses. According to one of the men in charge of the investigation, in an overly positive recollection of the investigation:

The problem was to try to piece together from this confusing mass of detail what had actually occurred. The murder took place in front of perhaps two hundred witnesses and, as you know, no two people ever see the same thing the same way. The second problem was that the prospective witnesses were people who were not partial to the authorities. The one saving grace was that, by and large, the people in the ballroom were absolutely devoted to Malcolm X. We received quite a lot of cooperation from his followers, who were sincerely interested in finding out who had killed him and bringing those responsible to justice.[19]

The detectives in charge of the assassination case were under the leadership of Herbert Stern of the district attorney's office and Joseph Coyle of the police department. Stern was a graduate of the University of Chicago Law School who took his bar exam in 1961, only four years before he was to lead the grand jury investigation in the Malcolm X case. After a brief stint in the New York National Guard as a two-and-a-half-ton-truck driver, Stern began his duties as an assistant district attorney in New York County at a beginning salary of $5,500 a year. He started out his prosecuting career in the unglamorous Complaint Bureau, but quickly moved his way up to more important casework. In 1964, he rose to arguing homicide cases before the New York Supreme Court, a position that he requested because that is "where you get the most trial work," he said. He was a 28-year-old divorcé and military veteran on February 21, 1965, when Malcolm X was killed and he found himself thrown into the lead of a complex investigation that would take almost a year to complete.[20] By that time, however, Stern had left his job with the district attorney in favor of being a federal prosecutor for the state of New Jersey.

On the other side of the spectrum, Joseph L. Coyle, the police department's assistant chief inspector, had almost forty years of experience at the NYPD. He joined the force in 1927, and was a 61-year-old veteran by the time the Malcolm X case came across his desk. Coyle, whose photographs bear a striking resemblance to William Frawley of the television show "I Love Lucy," said he originally became a cop mainly because he had nothing else to do, but his bravery in the line of duty soon distinguished him. He quickly made his way up the police department's hierarchy, moving from plainclothesman to sergeant, lieutenant, and then detective. In 1965 he was in charge of the Manhattan North district, which had more homicides the previous year than any other part of the city. It also, coincidentally, put him in charge of the Malcolm X slaying, which too often kept him from his home, his wife and four sons, one of whom was also a police officer.[21]

The police established a working theory of the crime almost immediately after it happened, bypassing the investigatory phase, during which a working theory is generally formed. The murder was perpetrated, they assumed, by members of the Nation of Islam. It wasn't difficult to figure that part out. After all, they knew that the Muslims had been trying to hunt down their former minister for almost a year now, and numerous attempts at his life had already been made. While the assumption was reasonable, the police took the unusual step of working entirely on this theory without stopping to consider other possibilities. In a recent interview, Stern admitted that he and the police never really considered alternative scenarios of the crime, mainly because of what they saw as the open-and-shut nature of the case. The main goal, according to the police, was to actually find the gunmen who killed Malcolm X, without deliberating the question of who was ultimately responsible for Malcolm X's death. Reminiscent of the police chief in *Casablanca*, the New York Police Department then began to "round up the usual suspects."

The first major break in the case, at least from the police department's perspective, was the connection made between the assassination of Malcolm X and the recent shooting of another Muslim defector, Benjamin Brown, the month before. Brown had left the Nation of Islam to found his own mosque in New York, but soon faced the ire of Harlem Muslims who began to regard him as a rival. After a tense discussion with three Muslims who had paid an unfriendly visit to his new mosque, Brown was hit from behind with a bullet from a .22-caliber Winchester rifle. Upon his recovery at the hospital, he named the three Muslims whom he thought were involved. The police quickly located the suspects and charged them with the crime. The police were confident that they had the right men when the offending rifle was found in one of their houses. The three arrested men were identified by the police as Willie 8X Gaines, Thomas 15X Johnson, and Norman 3X Butler, all members of the New York mosque's Fruit of Islam.[22]

Detective John Kilroy was one of those assigned to the Malcolm X murder case. He also happened to be one of the officers who had arrested Norman Butler for the Brown shooting. Apparently it was he who first recognized the similarities between the two cases: a defector from the Nation of Islam who was shot in order to discourage the eruption of any potential rivalries among the Muslims. Kilroy passed this linkage along to his boss, and the police began to make a photo file of the various suspects, including Gaines, Johnson, and Butler. Descriptions of the Malcolm X assassins taken from eyewitnesses pointed to the latter two—Johnson and Butler—since they matched many of the characteristics. But the descriptions from witnesses were vague and often contradictory, since the killers had been unnoticed until the assassination took place, at which time people were trying harder to get out of the killers' way than to get a good look at them. Both Johnson and Butler were out on bail when Malcolm X was killed, although Butler had been advised to stay off his feet because of an injury to his legs from a pistol whipping by the police when he was arrested for the Brown shooting. These two Muslims soon became the primary suspects, floating to the top of the pool of other known Muslim enforcers. "After that, eyewitness identifications began accumulating, and the net began to close."[23]

Butler was the first of the two to be arrested, as police came to his house on Thursday, February 25, 1965. Butler was 26 years old when the police came to arrest him that day. He had spent much of his brief adulthood in the military, serving aboard various ships in the U.S. Navy. He said he was first attracted to the Nation of Islam in 1959, when he happened upon a Muslim newspaper while away from his ship. "So I read the paper and I said, 'Wow! This is great!' And I wrote them," Butler said. "So the letter came back from [Nation of Islam] headquarters, 'If you still feel the same way when you get out of the military service, come to the mosque.' " Butler continued on in the navy, eventually forgetting the offer from the Muslims to join their organization. But two racial incidents in the military forced him to decide that the navy was not the place for him.

The first incident occurred during a shore leave in Louisiana, when a racially mixed group of sailors went to a bar looking for a good time. The sailors entered the bar and noticed a partition that ran down the middle of the room. Not realizing what the partition was for, the men chose a side and went to the bar to get a drink. But the bartender quickly intervened, telling the men, "No, y'all got to go over there and y'all got to go over there," indicating the white and black men, respectively. The sailors refused, and a brawl ensued in which the black and white soldiers fought together against the others in the bar. The incident affected Butler deeply and forced him to acknowledge the realities of race in America. "I started looking at things that I wasn't looking at before," he said. "On the ship, in the navy yard. Looking now, I wasn't looking before."

The second incident forced Butler out of the military just as he was on the verge of being promoted to a higher position. He was on commissary duty one day, chopping meat with a cleaver, when a cockroach jumped across the table. Reacting quickly, Butler smashed the roach with his cleaver, then got up and scrubbed it off. Unfortunately for Butler, one of the ship's officers was standing nearby and witnessed the event. The officer, disgusted by his unsanitary action, retaliated by blocking Butler's promotion in what seemed to be a racially motivated event. "I had made third class, right? And the officer that was in charge of my division didn't want to give it to me," Butler said. Despite the pleas of Butler's shipmates, many of them white, that he be promoted, the officer prevailed. "I was going to stay in [the navy]," Butler said. "But he made me change my mind. It was definitely my intention to stay, but that incident made me change my mind."

When he left the navy in 1962, Butler thought little about joining the Muslims until he ran across a copy of C. Eric Lincoln's book, *The Black Muslims in America*. He read the book, fascinated by the rigid discipline of the Muslims. He and his wife adopted the rules of the Nation of Islam, or as best as they could discern from the book. At that point in his life, he was "searching for some kind of structure in my life." They joined the Muslim temple in New York in late 1962, while Malcolm X was still the minister. Butler insisted that the leadership of Malcolm X was not what attracted him into the Muslim ranks. "People made him a whole lot of stuff that he didn't do," Butler said many years later. "Anything that he did, he was instructed to do." Like Hayer, he soon became fired up about his new religion and became an aggressive member of the Fruit of Islam.

> After I read how the FOI was and how the women were treated and how women acted, all that stuff was good to me, because that's what I was about, y'know? I was about discipline in the first place, been in the service for five years, and I was about certain things. My attitude was in a certain way. Not necessarily against whites but for black. Or for the elevation and the advancement of black. So that's how come I became a Muslim. Not because of Elijah Muhammad, and I had never *heard* of Malcolm X.[24]

Police were expecting a fight when they came to arrest Butler for the assassination of Malcolm X, since he had reportedly put his karate skills to use the last time he was arrested, but this time they found him sitting down watching television when they forced their way into his house. They took him to the station for questioning. When they arrived, they assembled a lineup with Butler and a number of black police officers. Two eyewitnesses, out of an unspecified number, were able to identify him as being present at Malcolm X's murder, so he was formally booked and charged with the assassination. Butler protested that he was incapable of the murder—the injuries to his legs had turned him into an invalid—but his pleas were to no avail. According to him, he had been home all day on Sunday, except for a trip to the doctor that morning to get treatment for his legs. Ironically, only two years earlier, Butler had applied for a job at the police department as a patrolman. He passed the entrance test, but then failed a character examination.[25]

The arrest of Norman Butler was a public-relations bonanza for the New York Police Department, always eager to show that they were on top of New York crime. News of the arrest captured the front pages of *The New York Times* and other newspapers across the country, demonstrating that the police were expertly conducting the investigation and justifying the *Times* front-page headline from two days earlier that declared. "Hunt for Killers in Malcolm Case on Right Track." Newspapers included an Associated Press picture of Butler that showed him wearing his tweed topcoat, similar to one which some witnesses had reported seeing one of the assassins wear. This added to the small pile of evidence that the police had against the suspect. According to the *Times*, the arrest "marked the first direct linkup of the Black Muslims to the assassination of Malcolm X. The police had almost instinctively worked on the theory that Malcolm's defecting from Elijah Muhammad's Black Muslims last spring lay behind the slaying."[26]

The police were given further evidence that Norman Butler was one of the killers when a mysterious check for $10,000 arrived for him soon after he was arrested. Enclosed with the check was a note congratulating Butler for "a job well done." The check was soon discovered to be a fake, but the suspicion that Butler was one of Malcolm X's assassins received further credence. The origin of the check is still not understood. The account number on the check led to the Harlem Progressive Labor Party (PLP), but that particular account had been closed in 1962, three years before the assassination, and it had not been used since. "I am positive," said defense attorney Joseph Williams, "that somebody wanted to harm either my client or the Progressive Labor Party or both."[27] Williams asked the district attorney and the grand jury to investigate the origin of the check, but nothing ever came of his request. One speculative answer to the mystery of the $10,000 check is that the FBI wrote it in an attempt to discredit both the PLP and Butler at the same time. They would certainly have the capability to discover the bank-account numbers of the PLP, although their information may have been out of date. There is no concrete evidence available to back up this theory, other than the FBI's history of performing similar stunts in order to discredit militant groups.

Thomas 15X Johnson was the next to be arrested. Police had slightly less evidence on him than they did on Butler, so they waited a couple of days until they could justify the arrest. The breakthrough came when Cary Thomas, one of Malcolm X's bodyguards, finally decided to talk. He identified all three men—Hayer, Butler and Johnson—as Malcolm X's slayers, just as the police had suspected. Finally, police believed they had enough evidence to arrest Johnson, and they visited him on March 3, 1965, ten days after Malcolm X was killed and four days after he was finally buried. Johnson joined the Harlem mosque in 1960 and rapidly ascended the ranks of the Fruit of Islam, becoming a lieutenant the next year. Ironically, he was initially attracted to the mosque by Malcolm X. "I used to listen to him on the radio—used to have him on those talk shows . . . and I used to get a lot of delight out of the way he used to handle himself," Johnson said later. Johnson quit his twelve-year drug habit, and he and his wife went down to the Harlem mosque and joined the Muslims. He even spent much of this time as a Muslim guarding Malcolm X, although he never really had an opportunity to talk to him and become friends. Even after Malcolm X broke from the Nation of Islam, Johnson still saw him almost every day when he hawked Muhammad's newspapers in front of the Hotel Theresa, where Malcolm X had his offices for the Organization of Afro-American Unity. Apparently, there was little animosity between the two. "I couldn't figure out why he would do something like that, y'know, against the teaching [of Elijah Muhammad]," Johnson said later. "It upset me. But I'm the type of person, man, that I don't get emotional. I think things out. . . . I don't become inflamed."[28]

In addition to detaining Johnson, the police also decided to hold Cary Thomas on $50,000 bail as a material witness. Although he had committed no crime and was only helping the police, he was placed in jail until the case came to trial to ensure that he would not leave the area or be killed by

Muslim enforcers. According to New York Supreme Court Justice Abraham J. Gellinoff, the year-long detention of Thomas was justifiable because he possessed "vital information concerning the identity of the perpetrators."[29] Thomas ultimately proved to be the most important witness in the entire case against Hayer, Butler, and Johnson.

Having found three suspects in the assassination of Malcolm X, the police decided not to pursue the investigation against other possible co-conspirators, although witnesses at the scene of the crime had reported seeing up to five assassins. Ballistics evidence showed the presence of three murder weapons, and the police worked their hardest to reconstruct the crime and place those weapons in the hands of the three men that they had arrested. The next ten months were consumed by the investigation of a grand jury, although the pace of investigation had dropped dramatically from the frenzy of the first few days. "The way these [investigations] are, they get very demanding in the beginning and then they begin to peter out," Stern reported.[30] When Stern took his position with the Justice Department, he was replaced by Vincent Dermody, who eventually argued the case in the trial during the next year.

Throughout the pretrial process, Peter L. F. Sabbatino, Hayer's private lawyer who was retained by Hayer's parents, continually made motions to the presiding judge asking him to reseat the three defendants at different tables. As it was, all three defendants were seated at the same table, although Hayer visibly avoided interacting with his co-defendants. One of the main defenses for Hayer was that he was not a member of the Nation of Islam and that he had no motive for killing Malcolm X. By seating the three defendants at the same table in the courtroom, Sabbatino argued, the jury would be given the incorrect impression that they knew each other and were indeed co-conspirators. Despite Sabbatino's continual plea that the seating arrangement would prejudice the jury, his motions were quickly denied as irrelevant. His pretrial motion to change the venue of the trial away from New York City, where tensions over the killing and prejudice against the Nation of Islam would unduly influence the jury, was also summarily denied by the court. The pretrial positioning of the various attorneys set the stage for what was to become one of the most confusing—and least illuminating—assassination trials in history.

CHAPTER THREE

The Trial

Dermody: "Did you get a look at [the assassin's] face?"

Shabazz: "I couldn't see his face. I saw the back profile."

Dermody: "Could you tell from what you saw of this man whether he was a white man or a Negro?"

Shabazz: "He was Afro-American."

—*Exchange between Malcolm X's widow, Betty Shabazz, and Assistant District Attorney Vincent Dermody during the 1966 Malcolm X assassination trial*

The trial of the assassins of Malcolm X was finally launched on January 12, 1966, after a number of delays, including a citywide transit strike that forced a postponement of nine days. Jury selection began in front of the presiding judge, Charles Marks, and George S. Carter, a chemist, was accepted by both sides as the foreman of the jury. The three defendants, charged with first degree murder, were represented by a total of six attorneys, two for each man. Although Butler's and Johnson's lawyers were appointed by the court with a salary of $2,000 each, Hayer's family was able to afford two of his own lawyers, Sabbatino and Peter Yellin, both of whom were white. Sabbatino, in another effort to maintain the separation of his client from the other two defendants, disputed the process of selecting jury members. Ordinarily, both the prosecution and the defense were allowed to reject twenty prospective members of the jury after examining them. But since three defendants were being tried instead of one, Judge Marks ruled that the entire defense team would be allowed to challenge twenty jurors, rather than twenty for each defendant. Although Sabbatino argued consistently that Hayer should get twenty challenges of his own, since his defense was not connected with the defense of the other two, Judge Marks denied the motion, a pattern that would be repeated regularly throughout the trial. After the jury had been selected, the trial got started in earnest on January 25, 1966, as Dermody, the assistant district attorney, began the opening arguments against the three defendants.

The prosecution's case against Hayer was virtually locked up, even though Hayer insisted on pleading innocent to the charges. The physical evidence was almost overwhelming. He was caught at the scene with a bullet in his leg that was fired to stop him from getting away. A .45 cartridge was found in his pocket that matched the murder weapon, his fingerprint was on an incendiary device that set up a distraction for the assassins, and a number of eyewitnesses attested to the fact that they saw him shooting Malcolm X. But the case against the other two was fragmentary, at best. There was not a shred of physical evidence that suggested that they were even within miles of the crime scene on the day Malcolm X was killed. The only real evidence against them was the testimony of a handful of witnesses, many of whom were able to finger one or another of them, but not both. Furthermore, much of the testimony was muddled, with such witnesses as Cary Thomas testifying one thing in front of the grand jury and another in the trial, thus undermining their own recollections and the prosecution's case.

From the outset, the point of the trial was not to determine the responsibility for the murder of Malcolm X or to elucidate the hidden answers as to why the black nationalist was killed. Rather, the point of the trial was to determine the guilt or innocence of the three men who had been arrested for the crime. The prosecution had no need for proving the motives of the three defendants; trying to prove that they were members of the Nation of Islam who acted either on their own or under the orders of superiors was irrelevant. In fact, they were unable to even convincingly establish that Talmadge Hayer was a member of the Black Muslims. He denied membership in the organization, and all the police could come up with were two innocuous pictures of someone who looked like Hayer at a karate session with some fellow Muslims.[1] But all that was necessary for the prosecution was to prove that all three had been at the Audubon Ballroom that day and that they each carried one of the murder weapons.

Dermody began the opening arguments with a brief sketch of Malcolm X's rise within the Nation of Islam, the break between him and Elijah Muhammad, and some of the reasons that the Nation of Islam would conspire against their former minister. The assistant district attorney then sketched the events on the day of the assassination, at least as far as the prosecution could determine. According to Dermody, Hayer and Butler sat in the middle of the auditorium that day and, as Malcolm X began to speak, Hayer jumped up, complaining about Butler picking his pocket. As soon as the guards were distracted, Johnson, who was sitting in the first row, revealed his sawed-off shotgun and opened fire at the Muslim leader. The other two proceeded to charge the stage, Hayer with his .45 and Butler with his Luger, and finish the job. Then, when it was clear that Malcolm X was dead, they each ran to the exit and the back of the auditorium. Butler and Johnson escaped; Hayer was shot in the leg and attacked by the crowd.

Hayer's initial defense was unspirited. He went to the Audubon Ballroom that day only as a spectator, his lawyer, Sabbatino, pointed out in his opening statements. He had no contact with the Nation of Islam and had no reason to want to see Malcolm X killed. The only reason he was arrested, he contended, was because a mob had accidentally mistaken him for one of the murderers. Reuben Francis's bullet in Hayer's leg was also a coincidence, an errant shot that happened to hit him. However, Sabbatino could not refute the physical evidence, and chose instead to raise procedural questions about how Hayer was allegedly not allowed to see a lawyer or any family members for several weeks after he was arrested. Sabbatino argued that his client, Hayer, "was taken to a hospital, and from there he was taken to the prison ward of another hospital, and he was kept there until some time in March without arraignment before any court, without any attorneys, until some time in March, with a denial of any privilege of having any member of his family see him while he was incarcerated."[2] Lawyers for the other two defendants chose to make their opening statements after the conclusion of the prosecution's case, but Judge Marks ruled that this constituted a waiver of their right to an opening defense.

The first witness for the prosecution was a civil engineer who submitted diagrams of the Audubon Ballroom into evidence. The next to be called to the stand was Cary Thomas, the prosecution's star witness, who was certainly only too happy to get out of jail and testify. Thomas was born on June 24, 1930 in New York City, where he spent most of his life. At the time of the trial, he was married and had four children, although he had not lived with them for some time before the trail in 1966. Under cross-examination, he testified that he had acquired a heroin habit in 1959 and had used and sold the drug for three years before joining the Nation of Islam. In 1961 he had been convicted of possession of narcotics in Boston and given a two-year suspended sentence and probation. He became a Muslim in December 1963, in large part because of the influence of Malcolm X. After receiving his "X" from Chicago, Thomas soon adopted the Islamic name Abdul Malik.

Of all the witnesses, Thomas was the only one who could provide a comprehensive indictment of all three defendants. The rest of the witnesses provided what the prosecution believed to be a patchwork of testimony that gave an accurate account of the crime. Thomas gave a brief description of the crime scene that matched almost perfectly with the one presented by the prosecution. Thomas identified the three defendants as members of the Nation of Islam and said that Hayer belonged to the mosque in Jersey City, although he admitted that he had never been to the Jersey City mosque. Although Thomas performed admirably as the most important witness for the prosecution, his testimony came under intense scrutiny and suspicion when it was compared to the testimony that he gave to the grand jury almost a year earlier. Then, he had told the police that Butler and Johnson had been the ones that started the scuffle while Hayer shot Malcolm X with the shotgun. This contradicted his later testimony, in which he upheld the prosecution's argument that Johnson carried the shotgun while Hayer and Butler started the disturbance. Thomas also failed to remember simple facts about himself, such as when he became a Muslim and whether Malcolm X was still the minister of the Harlem mosque at that time.

Thomas' testimony was spotty, at best, as he gave vague responses to the leading questions of the prosecutor. He said that he sat in the nineteenth row of the ballroom that day and covered himself when the shooting started. Hayer, he said, sat several rows in front of him, with the back of his head facing Thomas. But Thomas insisted, during the direct examination by Dermody, that he got a clear look at Hayer's face and recognized him as a Muslim from the New York—not the Jersey City—mosque. Only later did he say that Hayer was from the Jersey City mosque. He also testified that he saw Hayer and Butler rushing to the dying body of Malcolm X, pumping more rounds of ammunition into his prone body. But he told the jury that he did not actually see pistols in their hands; all he saw (from beneath the booth that he had used for cover during the shooting) was the pumping motion of the two men's hands and the shells being ejected from their guns. Even though he said that he had seen and recognized all three assassins, he did not go to the police. Only after the police came to him did he tell his story to the prosecution.

But despite Thomas' obvious flaws as a witness, his testimony constituted the bulk of the evidence that the prosecution had against Butler and Johnson. Thomas had given one account to the grand jury and another to the jury. His testimony during the trial was also rife with contradictions, although most of them went by without being questioned by the defense attorneys. His motivation for changing his testimony to match that of the prosecution is still unknown, although the State did have a stick that it could use to ensure Thomas' cooperation if necessary. While in prison as a material witness the year before, Thomas had set fire to his own bed and had been arraigned on a charge of arson. His cooperation in the trial of Malcolm X's supposed assassins would almost certainly engender some leniency on the part of the prosecutors in his own trial. It is, however, pure speculation whether Dermody used this tactic to change Thomas' testimony.

The remaining witnesses for the prosecution attempted to reconstruct the events of the crime from their limited perspectives. A number of them reported seeing Hayer in the auditorium, and many of them pinpointed either Johnson or Butler as being present. One of them, George Whitney, a former member of the Black Muslims, testified that he had known Butler for three years and would have been able to recognize him if he had seen him in the ballroom that day. But Whitney testified under oath that he did not see Butler. Instead, he, along with a number of other witnesses, identified only Hayer as being one of the assassins.

Over the next month, the prosecution called a total of twenty-four witnesses against the three defendants. All of them were either witnesses to the assassination who could finger Hayer, Johnson, or Butler as one of the killers, or else police officers who testified as to the sequence of the investigation that identified the latter two as the assassins. The police officers also presented the physical evidence against Hayer: the .45 clip that was found in his pocket and the smoke bomb with his fingerprint on it. Two of the witnesses testified secretly, with the courtroom cleared of observers. One of them was an eyewitness who desired secrecy because he said he feared for his life as a result of his testimony against Malcolm X's supposed assassins. The second round of secret testimony came from FBI special agent John

Sullivan, who had been given the .45 caliber murder weapon by Ronald Timberlake, who stumbled across it in the Audubon as the assassins fled the scene. Interestingly enough, Assistant District Attorney Dermody objected to almost all of Sabbatino's cross-examination questions that asked Sullivan whether the FBI had followed Malcolm X or had launched an investigation into his assassination. Judge Marks automatically sustained the objections.

In the case of Sullivan's testimony and that of every other witness, the basic goal of the prosecution was never to illuminate the facts behind the assassination. If so, Dermody would have allowed Sullivan to testify to Sabbatino's probing questions. Instead, the prosecution's goal was simply to obtain convictions of the three defendants. Dermody's questions to his witnesses aimed to establish the sequence of events during the assassination, rather then the motivation behind those events. One representative exchange in which Dermody sought to limit the amount of information that was released came during the testimony of Ronald Timberlake, a 31-year-old member of Malcolm X's OAAU who attended the Audubon rally on the Sunday of Malcolm X's assassination. Timberlake testified that he found Hayer's .45 automatic pistol sitting on the stairway leading to the street after Hayer had hopped down the stairs and been caught by the mob. Timberlake picked up the weapon, tried to fire it (not realizing that the safety catch was on), and put it in his pocket when it didn't work. Later that day, he called the FBI to tell them that he found the murder weapon.

Dermody: Mr. Timberlake, when did you call the authorities?
Timberlake: After it was announced on the radio that Malcolm had died.
Dermody: Will you tell us what authority you called?
Timberlake: Well, I thought the case had . . .
Dermody: No, no, don't give us any reason.

Timberlake: I called the Federal Bureau of Investigation.

Dermody: The FBI?

Timberlake: Yes.

Dermody: And did you have a telephone conversation with somebody from the FBI office? Just yes or no.

Timberlake: Yes.[3]

The examination of Timberlake was fairly representative of the style of Vincent Dermody's questions and his expectation of what the answers should be. His questions were designed to elicit the shortest possible answer, generally either yes or no. Such questions were exactly what the prosecution desired and needed to prove the guilt of the three defendants. By asking simple questions, Dermody could control the pace of the interview and stem the output of information. His questions generally led the witness to respond in a certain way, and despite the objections of the defense counsel, Judge Marks generally allowed the leading questions to continue.

Betty Shabazz provided some of the most emotional testimony during the trial, as she testified briefly on February 17, 1966. She told the jury that she had seen the scuffle from the back of the room as her husband began to speak. She then heard shots echoing from the front of the room, at which time she instinctively brought her four children—ages six years to six months—down under a bench to protect them from the hail of bullets. When she looked back at the stage, she could not see her husband, who had been standing there moments before. She ran to the stage to comfort her dying husband, then accompanied his body as it was taken across the street to the Medical Center, where Malcolm X was proclaimed dead. Her testimony did not elucidate any of the mysteries of the assassination, nor was she used to identify any of the defendants. Her role, rather, was to convey the poignancy of the emotions behind Malcolm X's death.

As she left the courtroom after her testimony, she wailed, "They killed my husband! They killed him! They had no right to kill my husband!" The defense attorneys immediately moved for a mistrial, arguing that Mrs. Shabazz had unduly prejudiced the case against the defendants. The judge, as was customary in this case, overruled the motion, saying that "she did not point to anyone. She did not face anyone; as she was walking out facing the rear of the courtroom she said audibly so that I could also hear, 'They killed my husband,' which could mean anyone."[4]

Hayer first got the opportunity to testify in his own defense on February 23, 1966. He denied a long series of allegations from the assistant district attorney that he was a member of the Nation of Islam, that he had sold *Muhammad Speaks* newspapers, that he was a karate expert in the Fruit of Islam, and that he had ever eaten in a mosque restaurant.[5] According to Hayer, he went to the Audubon Ballroom that day to hear Malcolm X on a whim; he told his wife that he would be at his father's house, but then decided spontaneously to take the bus from Paterson, New Jersey, up to New York City. When he got there, he had to "have a bowel movement," so he went to the bathroom and found a half-empty clip for a .45 automatic pistol lying next to the toilet. "I picked it up and looked at it. And out of curiosity—girls like dolls and boys like other things," he explained.[6] Not thinking much of it, he put the clip into his pocket and left to get a front-row seat in the ballroom. When the shooting began after Malcolm X came on stage, Hayer ducked under the chairs and re-emerged when the shooting subsided. He then joined the mob of people heading for the exit of the ballroom.

I fell over somebody as I was running, and as I was going out of the ballroom my leg went numb. I think I was shot. That's when I felt my leg go numb, caved in under me. I hopped—I hopped all the way out to the exit, to the stairs, I hopped. I fell on the stairs—I mean I fell on the railing that leads downstairs from the ballroom, and I slid down the railing. . . . When I went out the door, a whole swab of people came out behind me and they were kicking at me and grabbing at me, saying that "Stop him, stop him, he killed—he killed Malcolm X.[7]

Naturally, Hayer denied any knowledge of the smoke bomb in the back of the Audubon on which his thumbprint was found. He denied ever having anything to do with the device, but was unable to give a reasonable explanation for how his fingerprint got on it. "I didn't put it there, if it's on there," he said, in his best explanation to counter the evidence against him. He also denied ever having seen Johnson and Butler, his co-defendants, before they were all arrested. This piece of testimony was most likely true, but his inability to explain the physical evidence against him called the remainder of his testimony into question. The defense was generally half-hearted; little could be done to counter the physical evidence that the prosecution had against Hayer. But the defense made no attempt to bring up the procedural issues that Sabbatino had made in his introductory statements. Furthermore, there was no attempt by the defense to confuse the issue of the physical evidence, to contest the accuracy of the thumbprint matches, or otherwise to put some doubt into the minds of the jurors.

Butler finally had his chance to testify on March 1, 1966. He initially clashed with the bailiff who attempted to use the Bible—rather than the Koran—to swear him in, and he objected to the use of his "slave name" Butler. "Part of that name is mine and part of it is yours," he insisted. He also objected to the use of the term "Black Muslim," instead arguing that he was a "member of the Nation of Islam."[8] In his testimony, he swore that he was not at the Audubon on February 21 of the previous year; during the time of the murder, he had been at home, resting his infected leg.

Butler's doctor had been called to testify, as well, and Dr. Kenneth Seslove confirmed that he had diagnosed Butler with "a superficial thrombophlebitis," or an inflammation of the veins. "I gave him bandages and a shot of penicillin and told him to keep the leg elevated," he testified. Two corroborating witness also placed Butler at home at the time of the shooting. Two Muslim women both testified that Butler had been at home when they called to pass the news that Malcolm X had been shot, which they had just heard over the radio. Butler's biggest problem with his alibi, however, was that no one actually saw him at home. Although he was sent there by his doctor and called there by two women shortly after the shooting, this allowed the possibility—albeit slight—that he was able to murder Malcolm X, then rush home on his infected legs to answer the telephone.

On March 3, 1966, Johnson was allowed to testify in his own defense. He told the assembled members of the jury that he was at home with his pregnant wife on the day that Malcolm X was killed. The 30-year-old Johnson testified that he awoke at 5:00 A.M. that day in order to perform his first set of Muslim prayers for the day. After prayers, "my wife went back to bed and I read from the Holy Koran for an hour or so." Later in the day, "I fed the children and I started cleaning and vacuuming the house." Johnson said he did not learn of the murder until after 4:00 that afternoon, when some of their Muslim friends visited them and told them the news. Although he had an alibi, Johnson's case was somewhat undermined by his admission under examination by the prosecution that he had a heroin habit for ten years before joining the Nation of Islam. He furthermore admitted that he had a criminal record of five convictions in the six years before he became a Muslim.

But Talmadge Hayer provided the most colorful and shocking testimony during the two-month trial. On February 28, during his second stint on the stand, Hayer finally confessed his guilt in murdering Malcolm X. That he was guilty surprised no one, but his admission shocked the twelve-person jury. He told the court that he wanted the truth to be known, although he hedged on some of the most important information of how the assassination was carried out. Certain of his own guilt and virtually assured that he would be sent to prison, Hayer told the jury that he wanted to come forward to exonerate Butler and Johnson who, he maintained, had nothing to do with the assassination at all. In fact, he didn't even know them, a fact demonstrated by his marked aloofness from his co-defendants even when Butler and Johnson talked to each other during the trial. He urged the jury to let his co-defendants go, since they had no part in the assassination. "I just want the truth to be known that Butler and Johnson didn't have anything to do with this crime," he said under oath. "I was there, I know what happened, I know the people that did take part in it, and they (Butler and Johnson] wasn't any of the people that had anything to do with it. I want the jury to know."[9]

Hayer had a conversation with Butler and Johnson earlier that day before he took the stand to try to clear their names. "I told them that I was going to tell the truth, tell the jury and the Court what—what happened at the Audubon and that I took part in what happened, and that I was going to tell the truth that they wasn't there, they didn't have anything to do with it," he explained to the prosecutor.

"It's about time," Butler and Johnson responded to the news that Hayer was finally going to confess. "We was wondering when you was going to do this, tell the truth."[10] The prosecution, which still wanted to see all three suspects convicted of the assassination despite the new evidence, attempted to give the jury the impression that this conversation between Hayer, Johnson, and Butler was part of a conspiracy to have the charges dropped against the latter two defendants.

Hayer was noticeably vague in responding to questions about the assassination. He said that he was not a member of the Nation of Islam, nor did he or his fellow assassins have any established motivation for killing Malcolm X. He pointed to a conspiracy in which he was a hired gun, although he refused to name his co-conspirators, how much money he was paid, or who was ultimately responsible. Although he refused to answer the question of who hired him to kill Malcolm X, he specifically denied that it was the Nation of Islam that was behind the assassination. "I was offered some money for doing it from people that probably would have been revealed if Mr. Williams [an attorney for the defense] could have continued his interrogation," Hayer bitterly told the assistant district attorney. At the request of the prosecution, Hayer's response was quickly stricken from the record as unresponsive. Hayer also directly contradicted the events of the assassination as portrayed by the prosecution. He had actually not been one of the men involved in the scuffle that set up the killing. Rather, he had been sitting in the front row with his .45 caliber pistol, while a bearded man with the shotgun sat three rows behind him.

Dermody, speaking for the prosecution, desperately attempted to derail Hayer's testimony. Although his confession made his conviction a certainty, it jeopardized the convictions of the other two defendants. Dermody persuasively argued that the only reason that Hayer confessed was that he had wanted to save his fellow assassins, since he was already virtually assured of being convicted. "Is is not a fact that the reason you would not [tell the Court who fired the shotgun] is because if you told the truth you'd have to say it was Johnson?" Dermody demanded of Hayer. "No, sir," was the reply. "It's not true. You think I'm crazy or something?"[11] Even Hayer's lawyer, Sabbatino, tried to get the jury to ignore the confession, arguing that it was untrue and that Hayer had only tried to save his co-defendants by taking the entirety of the blame. "There was no reason for this lad to do what he did except a high sense of Christian charity," Sabbatino said, almost certainly inspiring the anger of the Muslim Hayer.[12]

The plan was simple, according to Hayer:

Four people, two people sitting in the front row, man with the shotgun, short dark man with the beard sitting around the fourth row from the front, man in the back, one man starts commotion, says, "Get your hand out of my pocket," guards from the stage goes after this man, man with the shotgun shoots Malcolm, two men on the front row shoots pistols.[13]

In his confession, Hayer did little to illuminate the issue of exactly who had killed Malcolm X. It was his intention that day to tell "the truth," but not to tell the whole truth, as Dermody insisted that he do. Even under the threat of punishment from the Court, Hayer still maintained that he knew who was responsible but would not tell the jury. "Got up here to tell the truth as of these two men [Butler and Johnson] didn't have anything to do with it," he argued. But his plea fell on deaf ears. The prosecution, which ordinarily would have welcomed the confession of a suspect in such a publicized assassination, tried to undermine Hayer's testimony in an attempt to show that all three suspects were guilty. Despite all available evidence, the assistant district attorney still sought to convict Johnson and Butler of a crime that they almost certainly didn't commit. They had alibis, there was no physical evidence to link them to the scene of the crime, and now they had the word of one of the confessed assassins that he had never seen them before in his life.

But, on the whole, the lawyers for the defense failed miserably in their quest to illuminate the facts of the assassination. Witnesses for the prosecution were unreliable, at best, as they forgot crucial details and contradicted themselves and each other. But the six defense lawyers were unable to go on the offensive during the entire two-month trial. They failed repeatedly to pursue contradictions in the testimony and were unable to present a coherent counterhypothesis that described the actual events around the assassination of Malcolm X. The testimony of Cary Thomas was at the same point some of the strongest and some of the weakest evidence introduced during the trial. Although he adequately corroborated the prosecution's version of the assassination, he also contradicted his earlier testimony on a number of points and demonstrated his inability to remember key facts. The defense, however, failed to capitalize on this weakness. William C. Chance, one of Butler's lawyers did try to exclude Thomas' testimony at the end of the trial, on the basis that the witness "suffered from an impaired mentality."[14] But he failed in this effort and in the easier effort to discredit Thomas' testimony.

It should not have been a difficult job to provide a credible defense for Johnson and Butler. One bit of available evidence that was never used in the trial was the testimony of such people as Benjamin Goodman, the man who gave the introductory speech at the Audubon Ballroom that day. Since the assassination, Goodman had always maintained that Butler and Johnson were innocent of the crime. Both of these men were known to him, and he said that he certainly would have recognized either of them if they had come to the Audubon on that Sunday afternoon, and he would have alerted security. Even if Goodman had not seen them, how would it have been possible for two well-known Muslim "enforcers," the men who had allegedly shot a former Black Muslim earlier that year, to attend one of Malcolm X's speeches without having been seen and detained? Although security was somewhat lax, most of the bodyguards were former members of the Nation of Islam and were on the lookout for Fruit of Islam members, such as Butler and Johnson, who would try to murder Malcolm X. Although this is such an obvious point in the defense of the two men, their lawyers failed to communicate this, as well as the other evidence in favor of the defendants, to the jury.

The defense attorneys, however, were greatly constrained by the actions of Judge Charles Marks, who consistently ruled in the favor of the prosecution and ignored the motions of the defense attorneys. As a general rule, the judge almost instinctively overruled the objections of the defense and sustained the motions of the prosecution, often without stopping to hear the grounds of the objections. One troublesome point of contention between the defense and the judge was the failure of the prosecution to provide the defense with enough relevant information on the People's case against the three defendants. First, Assistant District Attorney Dermody refused to provide the defense with a list of the witnesses he planned to call, thereby not giving the defense an opportunity to prepare their case. Although defense attorney Sabbatino consistently argued to the judge that this was a violation of his client's right to due process guaranteed by the Fourteenth Amendment to the Constitution, Judge Marks repeatedly ignored the objection.

Also, the defense attorneys were originally not given an adequate opportunity to review Cary Thomas' grand jury testimony before they began their cross-examination. When Sabbatino objected and asked for the court to reconvene the next day after he had a chance to read and analyze the testimony, Judge Marks again overruled. He did, however, reluctantly agree to recess for fifteen minutes to allow the defense to read the documentation. "Alright," Marks acquiesced. "Let the record show that the Court has read through the whole thirteen pages in three-and-a-half minutes, and digested it, as well, but counsel will have a multi-period of time. The Court will declare a recess for fifteen minutes."[15] The judge's apparent predilection for the prosecution became almost a personal battle between Marks and Sabbatino, who was the most forceful of the defense attorneys. At one point during Cary Thomas' testimony, the judge's anger boiled over when Sabbatino objected to the leading nature of the prosecution's questions.

Marks:	I told you already, no comment at all. Now these [objections] are being added up, you know, and it's not very good in a case of this sort, Mr. Sabbatino. Not with me. You ought to know that by this time. Not with this Court.
Sabbatino:	I didn't get you Honor's comment. Read it back.
Marks:	He will read it back to you later
Sabbatino:	I am entitled to know. If it is a rebuke I'm entitled to know the Court is rebuking me.
Marks:	It's not a rebuke; it's a statement of fact.[16]

But, ironically, the greatest blow to Butler's and Johnson's defense was the testimony of Talmadge Hayer when he tried to prove that his co-defendants were innocent of the charges against them. Hayer took the stand a second time because of his own feelings of guilt as he saw two Muslim brothers who were about to be convicted for a crime that they did not commit. Although he had noble motives for taking the stand, for a number of reasons, Hayer was unable to demonstrate that he was the only one charged who had actually killed Malcolm X. First, the prosecution and his own lawyers tried to portray the confession as a blatant lie that should be ignored by the jurors. Neither side of the conflict had any interest in seeing Hayer exonerate his co-defendants by indicting himself. Unfortunately for Johnson and Butler, their attorneys were successful in getting the jury to ignore the confession. Hayer instantly became an unreliable witness as soon as he took the stand to confess his guilt. After all, only a week before the confession, Hayer had taken the stand and perjured himself by asserting that he had nothing to do with the crime. It was impossible to determine whether Hayer was actually lying during his first stint on the witness stand in order to protect himself, or the second time in order to protect his fellow conspirators, or both. Hayer's double testimony put enough doubt in the minds of the jurors that they were forced to conclude that he was only trying to cover up the guilt of his fellow Muslims.

On March 10, 1966, the jury for the New York State Supreme Court found all three defendants in the assassination of Malcolm X guilty of first-degree murder. It took the racially mixed jury of nine men and three women more than twenty hours to come to the decision. As Hayer scanned the faces of the jurors and the other two defendants stared straight at the judge, the foreman of the jury, dressed in a brown suit and glasses, read the verdict to the court before an almost-empty courtroom. The charge carried with it an automatic sentence of life in prison, with the possibility of parole only after almost twenty-seven years. That sentence was ratified the next month as Betty Shabazz solemnly looked on from the back of the courtroom. At the sentencing, Sabbatino, who still contended that his client's confession was a fabrication, warned Judge Marks that "I don't think you have a solution here that history will support."[17]

Sabbatino's prediction that the trial would not be the end of the controversy over who killed Malcolm X has been far more correct than even he probably would have envisioned. The inconclusiveness of the trial has spawned endless variations of conspiracy theories, all of which purport to construct a more believable and probable version of events than the prosecution developed during the trial. This is not a formidable task, given the contradictions that are rife in the State's version. Little was proved during the Malcolm X assassination trial, beyond the basic fact that Talmadge Hayer had been one of the assassins. But Hayer's confession cast doubt on the rest of the prosecution's version of events, without illuminating the true nature of the assassination. Due to this confusion, conspiracy theorists have targeted everyone from the FBI and the CIA to the international drug cartel as the true assassins of Malcolm X. All present interesting theories, but none that can fully explain the facts of the assassination.

CHAPTER FOUR

The Theories

"This society, this violent and corrupt American society, this racist American society assassinated both Malcolm X and Martin Luther King, Jr. The men arrested may have pulled the trigger, but they by no means acted alone; American society was not only in concert with the assassins but there is every evidence that they were the hired killers."

—*Journalist Louis E. Lomax*[1]

Virtually any crime, whether it is a simple misdemeanor or a violent felony, will almost automatically elicit differing explanations that try to determine who actually should bear the responsibility for the crime. Assassinations of political figures, in particular, have been prone to alternative explanations from all sectors of society, in large part because of the complicated nature of assassinations, the wide range of individual motivations for wanting to see a public figure removed from power, and the political forces that impinge on a thorough investigation of the crime. The debate over who actually killed Abraham Lincoln still rages, and currently there is an attempt to secure the exhumation of the body of John Wilkes Booth to make sure that it is really he and not some unfortunate bystander who got in the way of federal guns. In 1991 conspiracy theorists convinced a federal judge to have the body of President Zachary Taylor exhumed in order to test a theory that he had been poisoned rather than dying of natural causes in 1850. As it turned out, this theory was false.

The early 1990s have been a virtual renaissance of conspiracy theories, many of them focusing on the string of American political assassinations of the 1960s. By far the most popular of these assassinations for conspiracy theorists has been the murder of President John F. Kennedy on November 22, 1963. Scores of books have been written and conferences have been organized and attended, all with the specific purpose of determining once and for all who killed JFK.[2] Numerous popular movies and television programs have focused on the assassination, as the American public has become obsessed not with who Kennedy was or what he did, but how he was killed. Theories have been posited that the CIA was involved, and others argue that it was the Cubans or the mob or the military. Some theorists, like Jim Garrison and Oliver Stone, argue that all of them had a hand in the master conspiracy that brought Kennedy to his death and Camelot to an abrupt end. Theories run from the plausible to the inane and occupy every middle point on that spectrum.

Although the JFK assassination remains the most popular ground—as well as the most fertile—for conspiracy theorists, other assassinations have also been the subject of intense debate. Paul Schrade, an aide to presidential candidate Robert F. Kennedy who was wounded in the 1968 assassination of the second Kennedy brother, has recently assembled a group of "former law enforcement officials, politicians and celebrities" to call for an investigation into the Los Angeles Police Department's conduct at the RFK slaying. The group has charged that the LAPD "suppressed and destroyed evidence, manipulated and coerced witnesses and failed to pursue obvious leads."[3] The 1968 assassination of Martin Luther King, Jr., also remains popular for conspiracy theorists. The most recent addition to this club is James Earl Ray, King's convicted killer, who recently wrote a book to show that he was actually not responsible for the murder. And new evidence in the assassination of Medgar Evers, a prominent Mississippi civil rights worker in the NAACP whose death was the first in a string of major assassinations in the 1960s, has brought back to trial

Byron de la Beckwith, a confirmed racist who had earlier escaped being convicted of the crime on two different occasions because of deadlocked juries.

The investigations into these assassinations all possess some common themes. Almost all of them profess an enormous disdain for the official version of the events in question. Rather than relying on the government's investigation of the assassination, these theorists have viewed these investigations as biased, political pieces of work without serious merit. In most of the assassinations, this perspective is quite justified. The government's version of events in the JFK killing, as represented by the Warren Commission, is entirely implausible, particularly its conclusion that a single bullet was responsible for the wounds to the president and Governor Connally, and that Lee Harvey Oswald acted alone in the killing. Similarly, there are serious questions concerning the conduct of the LAPD following Robert Kennedy's assassination, and about the long-standing contempt that the FBI harbored for Martin Luther King, Jr., before his confusing assassination. The various federal, state and local governments in this country are burdened by political considerations, which permeate even the organizations that are supposedly apolitical. The need for the government to adopt a "business as usual" posture after the death of John F. Kennedy did not permit government investigators to conduct a lengthy and costly probe of the killing, which would have preoccupied the nation and paralyzed the government at a critical time. Many conspiracy theorists, however, go beyond a simple dislike of the official explanation and actually implicate government agencies in the assassinations. The CIA killed JFK, the LAPD conspired against RFK, and the FBI murdered King, some argue.

Another similar thread that runs through conspiracy theories is the tendency to ask questions rather than to answer them. Particularly in the case of Malcolm X's assassination, proponents of alternate explanations have constructed a lengthy list of unanswered questions, which they string together in their attempt to prove that the government or some other force was ultimately behind the killings. Pointing out this lack of facts does not serve to discredit conspiracy theorists; raising unanswered (or unanswerable) questions is a valuable exercise and is necessary in any responsible investigation. However, their inability to answer many of these questions is a major shortcoming in many of these theories. But conspiracy theorists are necessarily hampered by a number of limitations. First, since many of the theorists are private individuals, they lack the time and resources to conduct a thorough investigation, as the federal government is more able to do. The government, however, is limited in other, sometimes more profound ways. Also, many of the questions asked by conspiracy theorists are simply unanswerable, and the allegations that they posit are as difficult to disprove as they are to prove.

The various investigations into—and theories about—the murder of Malcolm X are fairly typical in terms of comparison with other assassinations, although Malcolm X's death has not received the attention that some other prominent assassinations have attracted. But the death of Malcolm X brought with it a series of unanswered questions that the trial of the alleged assassins did not even begin to explain. The trial did not answer convincingly who killed Malcolm X, nor did it address the question of who, besides the actual gunmen, was ultimately responsible for the crime. Malcolm X's actions before he died reinforced the idea in the minds of many observers that the Muslims actually were innocent of the assassination, as he confided to his biographer, Alex Haley, that he was having doubts whether the Muslims could really be responsible for the havoc that had been caused shortly before his death. He had traveled to France, only to be barred from entering the country once he got there. He had seen his house go up in flames, almost killing himself and his family. "The more I keep thinking about this thing, the things that have been happening lately, I'm not all that sure it's the Muslims," he told Haley. "I know what they can do, and what they can't, and they can't do some of the stuff recently going on. Now, I'm going to tell you, the more I keep thinking about what happened to me in France, I think I'm going to quit saying it's the Muslims."[4] Conspiracy theorists have seized upon this statement as proof that the assassination was perpetrated by the federal government, and not by the Nation of Islam.

One of the hallmark studies of the assassination, Peter Goldman's *The Death and Life of Malcolm X*, which has been the most thorough examination of the assassination, is hampered by a faith in the abilities in the criminal justice system. In his book, Goldman adopted the persona of a detective investigating the murder case, and almost automatically reached the exact conclusion that they did, despite a plethora of contradicting evidence. In 1979, when evidence surfaced that made his original assertions seem incomplete, he revised his book and adopted the new prevailing theory. Another investigation, this time by Eric Norden, was published in 1967 in *The Realist*, the iconoclastic magazine that billed itself as "the magazine of wrongeous indignation." This piece is the classic statement of the white radical left of the 1960s, in which the author argues that it was the FBI, the CIA, and the NYPD that committed the murder, rather than members of the Nation of Islam.

Another interesting theory comes from James Farmer, one of the distinguished leaders of the civil rights movement, who argues that Malcolm X was killed not by the government or by the Muslims, but by the international drug cartel and its representatives in Harlem. His case is based mainly on personal recollections and meetings that led him to believe that it was Malcolm X's war on drugs—and not his war on the Nation of Islam—that led to his death.

James Farmer, an original founder of the Congress of Racial Equality who became its national director in 1961, called a press conference for Tuesday morning, February 23, 1965, after he was notified by his wife that Malcolm X had been killed. He told the media it was his belief that the Nation of Islam was not responsible for the murder, indicating that he had "grave suspicions that it will go deeper" than the dispute between Malcolm X and his former associates. Furthermore, Farmer said the crime was "a political killing with international implications," and told the press that he would ask President Lyndon B. Johnson for an official federal inquiry into the killing.[5] Rather than expanding on his thesis that the Muslims were uninvolved, he instead chose to leave the press guessing at the meaning of his statement. Speculation abounded at the time—and still persists—that Farmer somehow implied that the Communist Chinese government was ultimately responsible for Malcolm X's death because it sought to silence his antidrug rhetoric in Harlem, which lessened the demand for Asian narcotics. This interpretation of Farmer's statement was forwarded originally by the *New York Daily News*, but it was *The New York Times* that came to the correct conclusion, according to Farmer.

The New York Times wrote on February 24, 1965, that Farmer's cryptic statement meant that Malcolm X's death may have been a result of his preaching against the evils of narcotics and his professed belief that drugs were used as a weapon by white society against the blacks who were the primary users. As Malcolm X once said:

When trouble starts, if you are high and can't get yourself together, you'll hate yourself when you come to your senses and see you weren't here to help your brothers. Perhaps the brother who died might have been saved by you, had you been there. But you were high, too high to save his life. . . . That's just what the devil wants, that's why there are needles for you to jab into your arm and bottles to get you high.[6]

But instead of accusing the Chinese government of the assassination, *The New York Times* suggested that Farmer was referring to the drug lords in Harlem, who saw their business decrease at the hands of Malcolm X and the Muslims. In his autobiography, *Lay Bare the Heart*, Farmer indicates that this was precisely what he meant by his statement about "international implications" and said he "was not more explicit [in the press conference] because I was not in a position to prove my allegations."[7] Farmer began to feel more confident in his thesis that the killing was drug related when Percy Sutton, Malcolm X's attorney, supposedly confirmed his suspicions. "Jim, I don't know whether you realize how right you were in what you said about Malcolm's murder," Sutton reportedly told Farmer. "Furthermore, I understand the smart boys in Harlem are wondering how you could know so much from the outside." Farmer's thesis is dependent on a number of personal incidents that happened before and after the assassination that convinced him that more was going on than a simple rivalry between two disputing religious sects.

Farmer believed that the Muslims might not be responsible for the threats of violence against Malcolm X because of a meeting that he had in Accra, Ghana, with a former associate whom he had known in the United States. The woman was a Freedom Rider in 1961 who was a senior at Fisk University.[8] Alerted to his visit to Ghana in early February 1965, she arranged to have dinner with him at his hotel restaurant. When the subject of Malcolm X came up in conversation, the woman said, "he is going to be killed, you know," and predicted that the assassination would take place within the next two months. She further indicated that the Muslims would not be responsible, and that she had an inside knowledge of the plot to kill Malcolm X. "There is another gang after [Malcolm X] that is far more dangerous than the Muslims. They are going to get him, and it is going to be blamed on the Muslims," the woman allegedly told Farmer. When Farmer pressed her for further details, the woman became "almost hysterical," and refused to elaborate. A number of years later, while conducting research for his autobiography, Farmer tracked down the woman in New York City, where she was pursuing a career in the theater. Again she refused to give details of her apparent knowledge of the assassination, and when Farmer attempted to contact her later, he discovered that she had gotten an unlisted telephone number.[9] This episode convinced Farmer that the woman actually did have inside knowledge of the assassination and was covering up the information to protect herself.

Farmer's conversation with a Quaker friend also convinced him that the police were on the wrong track when they began to prosecute three members of the Nation of Islam for the assassination. This man had attended Malcolm X's meeting at the Audubon on that particular Sunday, grabbing a front-row seat so that he would be sure and see the action. Instead of hearing a rousing speech, he instead saw three men open fire on the speaker, and he was certain that the two men arrested later by the police were not the two men who had shot Malcolm X. He even told the police this when Johnson and Butler were placed in a lineup, but the police did not listen. "Leaving the police station [the Quaker] saw on the bulletin board an 'important notice' that said simply, 'Narcotics arrests needed.' "[10]

Farmer's theory that Harlem drug lords were behind the assassination has not received the publicity that other explanations—such as the government conspiracy theory—have gotten. One major reason is that there simply is little objective evidence to support Farmer's claims beyond his own personal recollections of a small number of conversations, none of which implicated specific drug dealers in the murder. Even Farmer admitted in an interview that he had no further evidence to support his theory. It was quite true that Malcolm X had always taken a vocal anti-drug position, backed up by his own knowledge of the insidious nature of drugs that he gained when he sold them and took them himself on the streets of Harlem. But there is no evidence available that his public lectures and private exhortations that his followers give up drugs made any difference whatsoever in the Harlem drug trade. Indeed, public consumption of drugs skyrocketed during the 1960s, and Malcolm X's nay-saying certainly had little effect on the overall scope of the drug trade. Farmer presents an interesting hypothesis, but his allegations must be dismissed in the face of far more plausible explanations of why Malcolm X was murdered.

Eric Norden's work is quite similar to a number of other conspiracy theorists, most prominently George Breitman, whose book, *The Assassination of Malcolm X*, is the only full-scale work, other than Goldman's, that is written about the assassination. Both Norden and Breitman approach the assassination from a Marxist perspective, arguing that it was Malcolm X's shift from capitalist to socialist, as well as his attempts to bring the United States before the United Nations, that drew the anger of the CIA and provoked its subsequent attempts to kill him.[11] These theories rely mostly on circumstantial evidence, much of which can be used to argue any number of different theories. But, placed together, this list of circumstantial evidence has established itself as a competing theory to the standard model which dictated that the Nation of Islam was ultimately responsible. This theory is at times compelling, sometimes far more so than the version of events that was presented by the district attorney's office at the trial of the men convicted of killing Malcolm X.

One of the key questions raised by these conspiracy theorists is the issue of the "Second Man." On February 22, 1965, the morning after Malcolm X's assassination, the first editions of the New York daily newspapers, the *Herald Tribune* and *The New York Times*, reported that two men had been arrested leaving the Audubon Ballroom and were being held for the murder. Both newspapers wrote in their headlines that two men were arrested, but neither reported in their article exactly who these two men were. One of them, clearly, was Talmadge Hayer, who was found with a bullet in his leg after being attacked by the crowd. But who was the other man? Ironically, the second editions of both newspapers omitted any mention of the second suspect whatsoever. Although the headline in the early edition of the *Herald Tribune* reported that "Police Rescue Two Suspects," this was changed in the later edition to "Police Rescue One Suspect." The same is true for *The New York Times*.

Breitman, Norden, and others have jumped on this issue as a key to their theories that the government was directly involved in the assassination. According to Norden, "another of the murderers [other than Hayer] was caught by the mob, but this time police authorities got to him in time, covered up his traces and spirited him away to safety. . . . Here, clearly, is a man whom both Patrolman Hoy [the officer who arrested Hayer and supposedly arrested the Second Man] and the crowd had good reason to believe was involved in the assassination. And yet, from that moment on, no more is heard of him."[12]

Norden's point raises a number of interesting issues. If there was a "Second Man," his disappearance would be crucial evidence of police complicity. If he was "spirited away," as Norden claims, then the NYPD clearly had something to hide, and did it in this manner, hoping that no one would catch on to their conspiracy. Breitman, in particular, was critical of the New York Police Department for not being more forthcoming with information on the "Second Man." In his typical style of asking rhetorical questions, Breitman asks:

> Who was he? Why did the press lose interest in him so suddenly, at a time when it was filling its pages with all kinds of material about the murder, including the silliest trivialities and wildest rumors? Was it because the police "advised" them to? . . . If [the police] decided he was innocent, why didn't they say so publicly? That is the usual practice. Why didn't they at least announce his name? That is usually done. What did the "second" man know about the murder plot and the identity of the killers?[13]

Although conspiracy theorists immediately jump to the conclusion that this constitutes proof that the NYPD was complicitous in Malcolm X's murder, there actually is no proof that the mysterious "Second Man" ever existed. After all, the only evidence that there was a second suspect is a headline in the daily papers. But newspapers are not usually the most accurate sources of information, especially in the heat of a major assassination. *The New York Times*, for example, had a number of inaccuracies in its various articles the next day, although none of the magnitude of the second suspect. This is one of the unfortunate truisms of journalism. Facts get garbled, incidents are taken out of context, and wrong impressions are accidentally given to the readers.

Furthermore, far more plausible explanations of the "Second Man" can be found than the elaborate tale of how the police, having accidentally allowed their agent to be arrested, took him to safety and convinced the press that it was all a mistake. First, there was actually a second person who was arrested that day. Reuben Francis, Malcolm X's bodyguard, was arrested after having shot Talmadge Hayer and was charged with felonious assault. Although he was not arrested as a suspect in the murder, it would be easy to believe that the impression was mistakenly given to the press that he was arrested for murdering Malcolm X. Considering the hectic pace that day for both the police and the press, such an error would be understandable. Once the newspapers realized their mistake the next morning, they quickly corrected it for their later editions.

Another more plausible explanation was forwarded by Peter Goldman after exhaustive interviews with the police who had been involved in the arrests that day. Patrolman Thomas Hoy was the first policeman on the scene, since he happened to be passing by at the time that the shooting began. Hoy pulled Hayer from the murderous crowd and gave him to Sergeant Alvin Aronoff and Patrolman Louis Angelos, who got the credit for the collar. These two officers barely succeeded in pushing Hayer into their squad car and managed to get him to the station house without further injuries. According to Goldman,

Hoy and Aronoff were debriefed separately at the time, Hoy at the scene and Aronoff at the stationhouse, and the earlier editions of the next day's papers reported that there had been two arrests. The two policemen, as it developed, were talking about the same man, but the confusion lasted long enough to create a whole folklore around the "arrest" of a mysterious Second Suspect—a mythology that endures to this day.[14]

The Mystery of the Second Man, Goldman contends, is much ado about nothing. The press was told separately about two suspects, without realizing that different officers were talking about the same man. The explanation seems credible enough, particularly in light of the "facts" that Breitman discusses in his book. He credits Hoy with arresting the Second Man and putting him into a squad car to be taken down to the precinct. He also credits another officer with arresting Hayer. But it is already known that Hoy was the one who arrested Hayer, not another policeman. And Hayer was placed in a squad car and taken to the precinct, just as was presumed to happen to the Second Man. It is clear from this evidence that the Second Man does not—and never did—exist and the fuss made about him by conspiracy theorists is misdirected.

Another main tenet of conspiracy theorists is that the government actually did try to kill Malcolm X on at least two different occasions prior to his death on February 21, 1965. The questions raised here are perhaps the most disturbing issues that have yet to be resolved, and it is understandable that from the available evidence, some observers would jump to the conclusion that the government was complicitous in Malcolm X's death. But since each case is unsolved, and in one case it is unknown whether or not it was even an assassination attempt, these instances do not represent proof—or even strong evidence—that the government played any role.

The first instance came while Malcolm X was in Cairo, Egypt, attending a meeting of the Organization of African

Unity, upon which he based his own Organization for Afro-American Unity. Malcolm X attended a dinner at the Cairo's Hilton Hotel on the day before he was prepared to give a major speech to the OAU. According to Milton Henry, an attorney friend of Malcolm X's,

> While we were in Cairo during the second week in August, someone tried to poison Malcolm X. He was lucky he didn't die then. Poison was put into some food he ate at a party or gathering of people. He awoke in the middle of the night with horrible stomach pains. He began screaming and was taken to a hospital. There the poison was pumped from his stomach and his life was saved.[15]

According to Malcolm X's half-sister, Ella Collins, her brother "told me that he felt that the CIA was definitely responsible for it."[16] Actually, the incident occurred on July 23, 1964—not in August, as Henry reported—and the rest of the facts that he related are far more vague than he would have the reader believe. It is still not really known whether Malcolm X was poisoned. He did fall sick after eating at the restaurant and was forced to have his stomach pumped at a local hospital. But the most reasonable explanation for this was simple food poisoning, and not an attempt to kill him. The notion that this was an assassination attempt did not surface until after his death, when Henry's article was published in the *New York Amsterdam News* in March 1965. Furthermore, even if this were an attempted assassination, which is by no means established, does this necessarily mean that the CIA was ultimately responsible? While in Africa, Malcolm X had been followed by American government agents (whether they were members of the CIA is unknown), but there is no evidence that they were involved in anything but surveillance, despite the claims by Henry, Norden, and others. It is also likely that if the CIA, with its extensive resources and experience with assassinations, had wanted Malcolm X dead, he would have been. A further blow to the hypothesis that the American government tried to kill Malcolm X in Cairo is that the State Department hadn't even really started to think about Malcolm X until August 1964, when Malcolm X sent a memorandum to several African heads of state. This was, of course, well after the alleged assassination attempt. "Washington in fact was slow responding to his trip even as a policy problem, much less as grounds for assassination."[17]

Furthermore, more than ten years after Malcolm X was killed, the CIA wrote an internal memorandum that revealed that the Agency played no part in influencing Malcolm X's organization. In response to continuing allegations that the CIA was involved in infiltrating the Organization for Afro-American Unity and eventually murdering Malcolm X, the Agency conducted an internal review of its files to determine whether such actions had been taken. According to a document dated January 30, 1976, the Agency concluded that "the records of the Office of Security do not reflect that the Agency penetrated the organization of Malcolm X for any reason." This inner-office document should be viewed as substantially accurate, since the CIA would have no reason to lie to itself eleven years after the fact. The incident of the alleged poisoning in Cairo is indeed suspicious, but conspiracy theorists have jumped to outrageous conclusions without solid evidence to substantiate their claims.

The second time that the government allegedly attempted to kill Malcolm X, according to conspiracy theorists, came only a week before he was finally killed in the Audubon Ballroom. The incident was the fire at Malcolm X's residence, which had been the source of an ongoing ownership dispute between the Nation of Islam and their former minister. Malcolm X had been ordered by the court to vacate the house, which had only been loaned to Malcolm X while he was a Muslim minister. Once he broke with the Nation, Elijah Muhammad demanded the return of the house and any materials that belonged to the Muslims. The fight over the house had been in the courts for almost a year, in large part because Malcolm X had been out of the country for long periods of time, and he finally vacated the house only after it had been gutted.

The fire began early on the morning of February 14, 1965, as a number of Molotov cocktails were thrown through the downstairs windows. One of them bounced off the house and set fire to a bush outside. A neighbor saw it and called the fire department. Luckily, Malcolm X and his wife were able to rouse their sleeping children, and together they brought their four daughters to safety. The questions raised by conspiracy theorists about the firebombing of Malcolm X's residence are compelling. The automatic assumption is that Malcolm X would not have bombed his own house, particularly with his wife and daughters at risk, despite arguments that Malcolm X had torched his own house as a "publicity stunt." The Muslims also would not have benefited from bombing the house, since they were on the verge of reclaiming it from their greatest enemy and claiming a symbolic victory over their former ally.

If the bombing was not perpetrated by the Nation of Islam or by Malcolm X, then who did it? A further complication in the picture is the discovery of an undisturbed can of gasoline standing on the dresser in one of Malcolm X's daughter's rooms. Upon the discovery of this "evidence," the fire and police departments issued a statement that the owner of the house had burned it down himself, accidentally leaving behind the gasoline as a clue that he was responsible.

But this version of events simply seems impossible. First, the can of gasoline was not found until after a number of people, both firefighters and friends of Malcolm X's family, looked through the house. The next-door neighbors had even gone into that room and taken clothes out for the youngest child, but they never saw the gasoline. "If anybody can find where I bombed my own house they can put a bullet through my head," Malcolm X angrily declared.[18] Also, if the police and fire department had evidence that Malcolm X set fire to his own house and put the lives of his family members at risk, then why didn't they arrest him? It is possible that political considerations intervened, but it also seems likely that the police were mainly trying to discredit the Muslim leader. Norden's conclusion, for which he has a great deal of support, is that "policemen on the scene of the fire apparently went so far [in their attempts to convince the press that the fire was set by Malcolm X] as to plant a tin of gasoline on the dresser."[19] According to Malcolm X's widow, Dr. Betty Shabazz, in an interview with Norden, "only someone in the uniform of a fireman or policeman could have planted the bottle of gasoline on my baby's dresser. It was to make it appear as if we had bombed our own home."[20]

According to Norden, Malcolm X had even received confirmation that the fire department had planted the gasoline in the house. In Rochester, New York, the fire marshal "met [Malcolm X] at the airport later and said that yes, it had been planted there."[21] There has been no other realistic counterhypothesis for how the gasoline came to be on that dresser. Bruce Perry, one of Malcolm X's biographers, has suggested that Malcolm X actually did torch his own house and endanger his own children, just as his father had done in a similar situation many years before, when Malcolm was young. But this pseudo-Freudian analysis does not fit well with Malcolm X's obvious shock that the Muslims, whom he believed started the fire, would actually be so maniacal as to try to kill his entire family, whom he loved dearly. A more reasonable alternative explanation is that individual members of the Nation of Islam had started the fire, without regard to the fact that the house belonged to the Nation. The goal of killing Malcolm X was certainly greater than the goal of reclaiming the house, and killing him in his own house would also have had an appeal to renegade Muslims who sought hero status within the Nation. Norden's argument that Muslims would not have tried to kill Malcolm X when it also endangered innocent bystanders can be discounted when it is noted that the assassination took place in front of 400 innocent bystanders, all of whose lives were at risk that day. Two non-combatants were actually shot in the melee, one in the stomach and one in the foot.

The basic argument of these conspiracy theorists is that the government—whether it be the NYPD, the New York fire department, the FBI or the CIA—had tried to kill Malcolm X by bombing his house. Having failed, and believing that the Black Muslims would not have tried to kill Malcolm X in this manner, they planted a bottle of gasoline in an attempt to frame the intended target. This theory does seem to be the most compelling explanation for the presence of the gasoline, but the incident still remains a mystery. The fire was immediately ruled to be arson, but no suspects were caught, and the case stalled in the police department.

But even if Norden's argument that the police started the fire and then framed Malcolm X proves to be fallacious, there are still a number of issues that must be resolved in terms of the role of the police. First, there was no serious attempt to find the arsonists responsible and solve the crime. Part of this was certainly due to a lack of clues, but an apparent unwillingness to get involved in the partisan dispute cannot be ignored. Although a crime was committed, the police did nothing to step in and try to reduce tension. Malcolm X's life was clearly in danger, and the New York Police Department was fully aware of it. Attempts had been made on his life in a number of cities across America, the latest being right in New York City, but the police did nothing to protect Malcolm X from his certain death. Despite repeated warnings that Malcolm X was in imminent danger, the NYPD sat on its hands and did nothing, thereby opening the door for Malcolm X's killers.

The basic argument of conspiracy theorists such as Norden or Breitman is that Malcolm X represented a direct threat to the national security interests of the United States. First, they argue, increasingly, during the final year of his life, he began drifting toward Marxism as the appropriate social and economic system for emerging African nations and also for the United States. Malcolm X's tacit support of presidential candidate Clifton DeBerry of the Socialist Workers Party and Malcolm X's speeches before the Militant Labor Forum are seen as proof that he was moving toward socialism. "Malcolm leaned more and more to socialism as an alternative to the American economic system, which he believed fostered and institutionalized racism," Norden wrote.[22] In a response to a question about his political leanings, Malcolm X responded, "I don't know. But I'm flexible. . . . All of the countries that are emerging today from under the shackles of colonialism are turning towards socialism. I don't think it's an accident."[23] Although such statements do not necessarily indicate his political views, American socialists highlighted them as a clear indication that Malcolm X's position "was being radicalized, and he was swinging left."[24] According to Norden and others, his drift leftward excited the paranoia of a capitalist government and created the mentality that Malcolm X was a threat that needed to be eliminated.

But if Malcolm X's leftward leanings were the background to the government's motive for killing him, then it was his attempts to bring the United States before the United Nations to face charges of racism that provided the impetus for the murder. Throughout his trips to Africa during 1964, Malcolm X intended to link the African-American struggle in the United States to the need to rid the African continent of European colonialism. He lobbied and cajoled leaders of numerous African countries in an attempt to gain their support in a move to make American racialism a global issue, as it was in South Africa. He met with some of the most important leaders on the continent, including Egyptian President Gamal Abdel Nasser and President Kwame Nkrumah of Ghana, and convinced many of them to support his efforts. According to John Lewis, the chair of the Student Nonviolent Coordinating Committee who met Malcolm X in Kenya, "Malcolm's impact was just fantastic. In every country he was known, and served as the main criteria for categorizing other Afro-Americans and their political views."[25] In July 1964, he attended the meeting of the Organization of African Unity with the specific purpose of passing a bill that would condemn America for its continuing racial problems.

Malcolm X inevitably attracted the attention of the American government. His efforts to turn Africa against the United States could have serious repercussions if he were to be successful. Africa was in the midst of dramatic change, as it quickly moved from under the chains of colonialism to the freedom of independent nationhood. Countries around the world, including the United States, sought to win the favor of the emerging nation-states in order to secure continued access to Africa's abundance of natural resources. Carl Rowan, who at the time served as the director of the United States Information Agency, tried his best to take the sting out of Malcolm X's attacks, pointing to the 1964 Civil Rights Act as a positive step in the struggle for equality in America. The problem, Rowan insisted to the various African leaders, was being overblown by Malcolm X, and he should not be believed. Meanwhile, the Justice Department began an investigation into Malcolm X's finances to see whether he was receiving funding from overseas. If so, he would have to register under the Foreign Agents Registration Act, which he had not yet done, and his failure to do so would be punishable by the United States government. The attorney general even sent Burke Marshall, the head of the Justice Department's Civil Rights Division, to interview Alex Haley, Malcolm X's collaborator on his autobiography, to determine whether he had gotten money from overseas. The FBI also investigated rumors that Nasser had funneled money to the OAAU, but nothing of this nature was discovered.

Malcolm X's efforts to condemn the United States in a global arena clearly irked the federal government, and a *New York Times* article from 1964 indicated that the State Department was eager to gain more information on the former Black Muslim. On August 13, 1964, *The New York Times* reported that "the State Department and the Justice

Department have begun to take an interest in Malcolm's campaign to convince African states to raise the question of persecution of American Negroes at the United Nations. . . . Officials said that if Malcolm succeeded in convincing just one African government to bring up the charge at the United Nations, the United States government could be faced with a touchy problem."[26] Certainly the specter of becoming an international pariah like South Africa did not please American leaders, conspiracy theorists have reasoned, and only by eliminating Malcolm X could they assure that the United States would not be censured.

But Malcolm X's threat to the United States in the world community has been greatly exaggerated by those who argue that he alone could have turned the continent of Africa against America. Despite his relentless efforts, Malcolm X never did persuade a single country or a single leader to take the issue to the United Nations. The recently independent countries had enough problems of their own without delving into the difficulties of another nation, particularly when that nation was as powerful and influential as the United States. It was one thing for the African nations to take on racism in South Africa, a regional power, but no nation would have dared to confront the wealth and power of the United States. The truth is that Malcolm X never represented anything more than an annoyance to the American government. His master plan of bringing the United States before the International Court of Justice never got off the ground; as much as he bragged of his connections in African governments, Malcolm X could not compete with the omnipresent influence of the United States.

The summit meeting of the Organization of African Unity is a good example. Malcolm X spent much of his time during his second 1964 trip to Africa lobbying various governments to support his condemnation of American racism. Although he was given free rein to circulate with various African diplomats as an observer, and even given access to the yacht *Isis*, which served as the entertainment area for the delegates, Malcolm X was forbidden to address the conference. While he was clearly an annoyance to the official representatives of the American government, he was not even allowed to deliver his plea to the meeting. Instead, he resorted to sending the various delegations a memorandum in which he outlined the racial situation as he saw it in America. But the conference did not go as Malcolm X had hoped, as Egyptian President Nasser, whom Malcolm X considered an ally, praised the improvements in the plight of African-Americans, citing Rowan's example of the 1964 Civil Rights Act as proof that things were changing. Malcolm X did, however, walk away with a single jewel in his crown: a resolution from the conference that politely asked the United States government to devote more resources to combat racism. Although it represented a step in the right direction, it was still a far smaller step than he had wanted.

Despite his persistence, Malcolm X was never able to secure the support of a single African leader in his quest to condemn the United States, and the American government was keenly aware of his failure. Norden declared in his article that "Malcolm had become, within a period of 9 months, Washington's black Public Enemy Number One."[27] But although he constantly reminded the African delegates at the OAU conference that "our problem is your problem," he was unable to overcome the "American dollarism" that replaced the old form of colonialism in Africa. His only success was a "moderately phrased, balanced declaration" of concern for the plight of African-Americans that was no more radical than the similar bill that had been adopted the year before at the OAU conference. Malcolm X, however, played up the success as much as he could, telling American journalists that the conference was an unqualified success story that gave the American government a black eye. But Malcolm X was never the threat to American security that he claimed to be, and despite the promises of friendship from various African leaders, that friendship clearly did not include political support.

Malcolm X presented a fearsome growl, but his actual

threat to the United States never matched his rhetoric, and this was blatantly clear to the American government. The CIA was never given real reason to be afraid of Malcolm X's activities overseas; although his actions were certainly worthy of being monitored, they never could have possibly forced the CIA to contemplate his murder. Certainly Malcolm X was an aggravation as he continually showed up the official American ambassadors through his audiences with African leaders, but he was never a genuine threat to the federal government. Conspiracy theorists who believe that the CIA was involved in planning the assassination are misdirected.

The claim from conspiracy theorists that the FBI was complicitous in the murder of Malcolm X must also be analyzed in terms of the threat, both perceived and actual, that he posed against the internal security of the United States. The FBI clearly had an interest in Malcolm X, far more so than the CIA had. The FBI began tracking him in 1953, ironically not for his racial activism but because he claimed in a letter from his prison cell, "I have always been a Communist."[28] The claim was clearly outrageous; he had never shown any proclivity so far in his life toward anything political, and had never had any contact with any members of the Communist Party. But this was enough for the FBI to begin keeping track of him as a possible security threat. Over the years, the FBI accumulated tens of thousands of documents reporting exactly what he had done and said, with whom he had associated, and how it was possible to counter the threat that he represented. They tapped his telephones, attended his meetings and press conferences, followed him from place to place, and even interviewed him on a couple occasions in order to gain more information. This relationship between Malcolm X and the FBI must be analyzed in order to determine whether the FBI had any involvement in Malcolm X's murder.

The FBI clearly held the African-American freedom struggle in utter contempt, largely because of the personal feelings of FBI Director J. Edgar Hoover, whose animosity set the tone for the entire organization. Hoover had been at the Bureau almost since its inception in 1908, and he had been shaped in the mentality of an organization that had no friendship with African-Americans. According to a 1910 document that outlined the FBI's refusal to involve itself in a series of vicious lynchings of blacks, the FBI claimed "no authority ... to protect citizens of African descent in the enjoyment of civil rights generally."[29] The organization's attitude had changed little until the 1960s, when it found itself in the middle of a heated battle between Southern racial activists and the entrenched white power structure. According to Hoover, the civil rights movement was a battle between federal interventionists and states-righters, and he firmly placed himself in the latter category, always preferring not to step on the toes of Southern lawmakers regardless of their crimes against blacks. Rather than taking an active role in protecting blacks from Southern racists, Hoover's FBI repeatedly adopted its increasingly hypocritical stance that "civil rights enforcement should remain the responsibility of local police officers." This approach was generally supplemented by the excuse, even as FBI agents witnessed numerous beatings that they could have prevented, that "we don't guard anybody. We are fact finders."[30]

The main focus of the FBI during the civil rights movement was the Southern Christian Leadership Conference under Dr. Martin Luther King, Jr. This organization was the symbolic leader of the entire movement, and Dr. King was able to galvanize mass movements in major cities across the South. At first, the FBI was content to sit back and observe King's actions, taking careful note of everything he did and said through their illegal surveillance. It was Hoover's firm belief, despite all available evidence, that SCLC and the movement for black equality were directed not from Atlanta but from Moscow, with scores of Communists infiltrating the organizations. According to Hoover, the Communists sought to infiltrate "the legitimate Negro organizations for the purpose of stepping up racial prejudice and hatred."[31] But despite the FBI's intensive search, they were unable to find any genuine Communist influence, beyond two advisors to King who was formerly in the American Communist Party. But rather than diminishing Hoover's concern, "the dearth of communists encouraged FBI officials to look harder."[32]

The FBI did not limit its tactics to simple investigation. Having failed to turn up any evidence of Communist infiltration, the FBI turned its attention to King's personal life, trying to turn up information on infidelity or any other "moral shortcomings." In this arena, the FBI was more successful, taping Dr. King's rendezvous with a number of women. Hoover forwarded much of this information directly to the White House, the Justice Department, and other government agencies that dealt with civil rights in an effort to turn them against King. He called King "the most notorious liar" in America, and began an anonymous letter-writing campaign in an attempt to discredit him once and for all. One of the anonymous letters in 1964 was accompanied by a tape of some of the "highlights" of the FBI's microphone surveillance, including one of King's romantic escapades that the FBI had overheard.[33] Hoover also offered information on King's personal life, as well as transcripts and tapes of personal conversations, to the media, which generally ignored the FBI's offers. The FBI, in short, declared war on an American citizen by following, harassing, and pulling dirty tricks on him in a manner that would later be formalized into the Counter-Intelligence Program (COINTELPRO).

But the degree of contempt that the FBI demonstrated toward Martin Luther King, Jr., was not applied uniformly to other civil rights leaders, at least initially. To the Bureau, King was "Washington's black Public Enemy Number One," the title that Eric Norden used for Malcolm X. "We regard Martin Luther King to be the most dangerous and effective Negro leader in the country," said an FBI official who testified before a Congressional committee.[34] King far surpassed Malcolm X in terms of his apparent "threat" to the nation. He had a larger following, he could gain more mass support, he was more of an activist than Malcolm X was, and he caused more trouble to the Southern white communities than Malcolm X caused in the North. Where the FBI viewed King as the paramount domestic danger to the security of the United States, it largely viewed Malcolm X as a man to be studied rather than combated. Although the FBI did wage a large surveillance campaign, it knew that it had little to worry about from Malcolm X and the Nation of Islam. Ministers in the Nation talked of armed self-defense and of hatred of the "white devils," but their actions showed that the Nation was a peaceful organization in its relations with whites. Despite their rhetoric, Muslims were generally respectful, law-abiding citizens who would be more likely to stop a riot than to start one, at least until Elijah Muhammad told his followers otherwise.[35]

Malcolm X had never led mass marches through the streets of major cities, inciting the wrath of entire white communities. Malcolm X had never brought a quarter of a million people to Washington D.C. to lobby for the passage of a civil rights bill; in fact, Malcolm X had fought against the March on Washington, which surely pleased the FBI. Malcolm X did not realistically threaten to profoundly change the country, pushing whites out of power and substituting blacks in their places. Malcolm X did not seek confrontation with racist whites the way that Martin Luther King, Jr., did in the South, creating potentially dangerous situations as law and order were sacrificed for the goals of achieving freedom and equality. Malcolm X did not represent the challenge to the power structure that King did, and as such he did not excite as much attention from the FBI as King. In the eyes of the FBI, Malcolm X was a peaceful, law-abiding citizen whose views were dangerous but whose actions were docile; on the other hand, King was a reckless lawbreaker whose actions were as dangerous and destabilizing as his rhetoric. If the FBI had really wanted to kill a civil rights leader in 1965, as conspiracy theorists have claimed, the Bureau would have murdered King, not Malcolm X.

Conspiracy theorists have generally pointed to two documents to prove that the FBI was integrally involved in plots to undermine Malcolm X and, by implication, to kill him. Both of the documents were written well after Malcolm X's death. The first document is one that was written on January 22, 1969, by an agent in the Chicago Bureau office to the FBI director. The memo discusses the Bureau's policy of trying to discredit the Nation of Islam by publicizing information about the group that would be embarrassing to the Muslim leadership. "Over the years considerable thought has been given, and action taken with Bureau approval, relating to methods through which the NOI could be discredited in the eyes of the general black populace or through which factionalism among the leadership can be created. . . . Factional disputes have been developed—the most notable being Malcolm X Little." Ward Churchill and Jim Vanderwall published a copy of this document in their book, *The COINTELPRO Papers*, and included a caption under the document that states; "Memo taking credit for the assassination of Malcolm X, killed in an FBI-provoked factional dispute on February 14, 1965."[36]

Even if the authors had gotten the date of the assassination correct, this is a blatant misreading of the document in an attempt to show FBI complicity in an event in which its role is disputed. The document makes no mention of the assassination; in fact, the only mention of Malcolm X is in the sentence previously cited. The operative phrase—that disputes such as that between Malcolm X and Elijah Muhammad "have been developed"—does imply that the FBI had a role in the rise in animosity between the two Muslim leaders. However, the extent of its involvement is unclear. It is almost certain that the split would have happened naturally, whether or not the FBI had been involved, given the various factors that were pushing Malcolm X away from his beloved leader. Perhaps the Bureau did have some role in spreading the rumors of Muhammad's adultery

and forced Malcolm X to finally recognize them and d
with them in the open. If the FBI played a part in the spl
in the Muslims—and there is no evidence beyond the content of this document that it did play such a role—then its
part in the conflict was certainly minor. It would not be unusual for the FBI to exaggerate the success of its own actions, trying to take credit for an event in which it had not
actually participated.

Furthermore, since the letter is written from the Chicago
Bureau chief to J. Edgar Hoover, his fanatical boss in
Washington whose demand for results was legendary, it is
even more likely that the Bureau would have exaggerated
the results of its actions. In their book, which focuses on
the FBI and not on Malcolm X, Churchill and Vanderwall
assert that the split between Malcolm X and Elijah
Muhammad had been created "by deliberate Bureau
actions—through infiltration and the 'sparking of acrimoni-
ous debates within the organization,' rumormongering, and
other tactics designed to foster internal disputes." Clearly,
from the available evidence, this claim is unsubstantiated
and probably as exaggerated as the original FBI document
that the authors use to prove their case.

The second document that conspiracy theorists use to
prove the FBI's complicity in Malcolm X's death is the famous March 4, 1968, document that outlines the goals and
targets of the Counterintelligence Program against "Black
Nationalist Hate Groups," which was the official title for
black liberation movements. The goals of the program, as
outlined in this document, include to "prevent the *coalition*
of militant black nationalist groups," to "prevent *violence*
on the part of black nationalist groups," and to "prevent
militant black nationalist groups and their leaders from
gaining *respectability*, by discrediting them." The most
cited part of the document is the goal that the FBI should
work to

prevent the *rise of a "messiah"* who could unify, and
electrify, the militant black nationalist movement. Mal-

colm X might have been such a "messiah"; he is the martyr of the movement today. Martin Luther King, [SNCC chair] Stokely Carmichael and Elijah Muhammad all aspire to this position.

This document is generally used as proof that the FBI was frightened of Malcolm X's potential, perhaps even frightened enough so that its agents would assassinate him. But this interpretation of the document is also incomplete and faulty. The quotation does indicate that when the document was written, the FBI would have tried to prevent Malcolm X from becoming a "messiah" for the movement. But Malcolm X had been dead for over three years when this document was written, and the nation had undergone some traumatic changes in his absence. Strong opposition had begun to develop against the Vietnam War, particularly in early 1968 just as this document was being written. Black nationalism and the Black Power slogan had taken the place of Dr. King's nonviolent approach to racial issues. The Black Panther Party had replaced King's SCLC as the most visible and "dangerous" organization of the civil rights movement, and the shotgun had apparently replaced the protest march as the main means of liberation. In short, the nation had radicalized and polarized, and the FBI switched tactics in its war against the American left. The formal initiation of COINTELPRO was a step in that direction, although some of the tactics mentioned in this document had been used before this time. But just because the FBI in 1968 branded Malcolm X as a potential "messiah" of the movement does not indicate, as many conspiracy theorists argue, that this was its attitude in 1965, when he was assassinated. Furthermore, it is another stretch of the imagination to believe that given the evidence of these two documents, the FBI was complicitous in the assassination of Malcolm X.

In fact, the FBI in its surveillance of Malcolm X, never indicated that it had a plan of action to combat the growing influence of the Muslim leader. Nor was there even a mention that such action was necessary or should be contemplated. Malcolm X's FBI files are simply a recitation of the facts as the Bureau perceived them, giving the reader a list of exactly where Malcolm X was on a given date and what he said. In fact, the only genuine order for action that can be found in Malcolm X's FBI files is that the Bureau should seek to do nothing to give him extra publicity. In a memo dated February 4, 1963, an agent following Malcolm X witnessed a television program on which the Muslim leader appeared. "The program did not put Malcolm X or the 'Black Muslims' in bad light. . . . While it was intended to have an adverse effect, it created interest in the organization which was out of proportion to its importance." The document ended with the innocuous conclusion that "it is recommended that we continue to follow the approved policy of taking no steps which would give [the Nation of Islam] additional publicity."[37]

But this policy was not always the operative direction for the Bureau. As it began to take more than a passing interest in the Nation of Islam in the early 1960s, it soon discovered the various secrets that the Nation of Islam had been hiding from public view. One of these secrets was a 1960 meeting between Muslim ministers and members of the Ku Klux Klan. Malcolm X was one of the ministers who attended the Atlanta meeting, although he always made it quite clear that he attended only under the orders of Elijah Muhammad and had some personal qualms about initiating a dialogue with a violent racist organization such as the Klan. The Bureau found out about the meeting through some of its sources within the Klan, and acquired this ammunition that could be used against Elijah Muhammad if the Messenger began to pose more of a threat to the white establishment. Another major secret to which the FBI was privy, thanks to its microphone surveillance, was the issue of Muhammad's sordid extramarital affairs, resulting in at least ten children by seven different women in addition to the children that he and his wife had produced. The Bureau learned about this secret early on and began accumulating a detailed summary of Muhammad's extramarital activities.

The Bureau also decided in 1962 to try to exploit its knowledge of Muhammad's weaknesses in an attempt to reduce his following by discrediting him in the eyes of the black masses. An FBI document from the Chicago office dated April 26, 1962, noted that the "Bureau continues to receive information . . . that Elijah Muhammad is engaging in extramarital activities with at least five female members of the National of Islam." The document goes on to discuss the rigid disciplining required of members of the Nation, pointing out that Muhammad had failed to live up to these requirements. "These paradoxes in the character of Elijah Muhammad make him extremely vulnerable to criticism by his followers. He wields absolute power in the hegemony of the NOI and any successful attack on his character or reputation might be disastrous to the NOI." The document concludes that the Bureau offices in Chicago and Phoenix "should make recommendations concerning the use of information thus obtained to discredit Elijah Muhammad with his followers. This could be handled through the use of carefully selected informants planting the seeds of dissension through anonymous letters and/or telephone calls. . . . Any such plans, of course, must be approved by the Bureau in advance before any action is taken."[38]

Another document from later that year indicates that the Chicago office had devised a plan to disseminate the information. According to the July 14, 1962 document, the Chicago office proposed to inform the Chicago Police Department's Security Unit of Mr. Muhammad's extramarital affairs. This action would enable the Chicago police to "conduct an independent investigation directed toward bringing the [adultery] to public attention and causing a bastardy charge to be filed against Muhammad. . . . Chicago assures this can be done without embarrassment to the Bureau." It is not known whether these plans were ever enacted by the Bureau, but two paternity suits were finally initiated against Muhammad in 1964.

The only available evidence that the FBI actually did initiate a misinformation plan against the Nation of Islam came from a 1978 article in *The New York Times*. According to the article, "Federal District Judge James B. Parsons, the first black ever named to the Federal bench, was 'utilized' by the Federal Bureau of Investigation in a counterintelligence program to discredit the Black Muslims in the 1960s, bureau documents show." The article goes on to say that Bureau memoranda indicated that Judge Parsons had repeatedly criticized the Muslims at the request of the Bureau. He reportedly called them a racist and violent organization. But Parsons denied that he had been requested by the FBI to do their bidding, while admitting that he had been critical of the Nation. "It is true that I sought information about the Muslims from the FBI," Parsons told the *Times*, "and there were occasions quite early in the 60s when I was critical of the Muslim movement, but under no circumstances did the FBI ever ask me to speak."[39] Again, it is possible that the FBI documents attempted to exaggerate the influence of the Bureau in sparking criticism of the Muslims. But whatever the case, there is no evidence that the Bureau went beyond its stated mission of spreading embarrassing information about the Nation. While this does overstep the intended boundaries of FBI conduct, it does not indicate that the FBI would take as extreme an act as conspiring to kill Malcolm X.

In fact, the document cited earlier that claimed that splits in the movement "have been developed" is actually an argument that the FBI should refrain from publicizing negative aspects of the Nation of Islam. "The media of the press has played down the NOI," the document states. "This appears to be the most effective tool as individuals such as Muhammad assuredly seek any and all publicity be it good or bad. . . . It is the opinion of this office that such exposure is ineffective, possibly creates interest and maybe envy among the lesser educated black man causing them out of curiosity to attend meetings and maybe join" the Nation of Islam. This 1969 document is essentially a recommendation for a repeal of the previous Bureau policy that as much negative publicity should be given to the Nation as possible. It is a continuation of the debate of whether the best Bureau policy was to ignore the Nation of Islam or to publicize its shortcomings. Clearly, even the discussion of such a policy is a violation of the essential investigatorial—as opposed to prosecutorial—function of the FBI. The Bureau had always been viewed as a body that would investigate federal crimes, but the discussion of such a policy toward the Nation of Islam directly contradicts that concept, instead creating the image of a policy organization that would directly engage in partisan disputes.

There is no evidence available that the FBI at any point went beyond its stated objectives of trying to discredit the Nation of Islam during the time that Malcolm X was alive.[40] Furthermore, a continuous debate raged between FBI Director Hoover and his supposed superiors in the Justice Department as to whether this engagement in the internal affairs of the Muslims was indeed necessary. One document from the Justice Department indicates that it disagreed with the FBI's classification of the Nation as subversive. "The First Amendment would require something more than language of prophecy and prediction and implied threats against the Government to establish the existence of a clear and present danger to the nation and its citizens," the document states. Scribbled onto the paper by an FBI official was the reaction, "Just Stalling!"[41]

The most visible case of FBI interference with the OAAU came when the black nationalist organization began to create ties with the Socialist Workers Party. The Bureau believed this alliance would endanger the national security. The FBI began a concerted program to create tensions between the groups that would result in their parting of ways. A May 25, 1965 letter from J. Edgar Hoover to the New York Bureau office demonstrated the director's attitude toward the FBI's role in the emerging alliance. "It would appear that the apparent attempt by the SWP to exploit the followers of the late Malcolm X for its own benefit offered some potential for the institution of disruptive tactics." Another document, written two months later by the head of the New York office, responded, "SWP influence on the followers of Malcolm X would be disrupted by emphasizing the atheism of the SWP as opposed to the basic religious orientation of the" Muslim Mosque, Inc., Malcolm X's orthodox Islamic temple. As the ties between the two organizations began to rupture later that year, the Bureau immediately took credit for the break. "It is believed probable that the disintegrating relations between the SWP and the [OAAU] can be attributed to the disruptive tactic authorized . . . and will result in a continued loss of influence by the SWP among this group of Negroes."[42]

This incident is often cited as further evidence that the Bureau was hostile enough toward Malcolm X to plan his assassination, but two crucial facts must be recognized that would alter this conclusion. First, the planning for this disruption happened after Malcolm X was dead, and there is no indication that such a plan would have been contemplated before Malcolm X's assassination, let alone a far more radical and illegal plan that would have involved them in his death. Second, the target in this disruption plan was primarily the Socialist Worker's Party, not the OAAU, since the SWP was an openly leftist organization with supposed communist ties. Such a group was J. Edgar Hoover's primary fear, and black nationalist organizations such as the OAAU did not initially elicit the intense paranoia from the Bureau that socialist and communist groups received. In fact, much of the attention that civil rights organizations received from Hoover was specifically because they were supposedly infiltrated and directed by Communists. By the language of the documents, it is clear that the Bureau's primary goal was to stymie the SWP, not Malcolm X's group, and the efforts of conspiracy theorists to use this episode to prove the FBI's hatred of Malcolm X are seriously misplaced.

The attitude that the conspiracy theorists attribute to the FBI against Malcolm X simply did not exist. The FBI was certainly hostile to the Nation of Islam and to Malcolm X's new organizations, but its desire and willingness to actually murder Malcolm X cannot be demonstrated. In fact, a careful study of the FBI's relationship with different civil rights organizations shows that the Bureau had far more contempt for groups and leaders other than the Nation of Islam. Dr. King and his SCLC always remained the primary target of the Bureau until King's death in 1968, at which time organizations such as the Black Panther Party took over as the main Bureau obsession. The assertion that Malcolm X was "Washington's black Public Enemy Number One" is simply false, and conspiracy theorists have been unable to piece together any substantial evidence that the FBI conspired in Malcolm X's assassination. This is not to say that the FBI mourned the death of the Muslim leader; instead, its members certainly must have felt a certain smug satisfaction that another civil rights leader had been eliminated by his own kind.

Far less is known about the New York Police Department's role in the assassination. The NYPD still has not released its records of their surveillance of the Muslim leader, although over twenty-five years have passed since his death. Conspiracy theorists have continually argued that the NYPD had an active role in the assassination, and others have held a more moderate position that the police were not directly involved, but did not do their utmost to ensure Malcolm X's safety. The latter argument seems fairly plausible, particularly considering that the police had confirmed evidence that Malcolm X would soon be killed by members of the Nation of Islam. Only two weeks before the assassination, police officials received an intelligence report that said that Malcolm X was about to be killed. His house had been bombed only a week before, and several attempts had been made on his life in recent trips to Los Angeles and Chicago, all of which was known by the police department. They "offered him round-the-clock protection, knowing he could never accept."[43]

The behavior of the police on the day of the assassination is indeed suspicious. Although early arrivals to the Audubon that day reported that a number of police officers were present, all of them seemed to have disappeared by the time the action began. NYPD officials reported that a special "detail" of police had been assigned to the event, but were stationed across the street in the Columbia Presbyterian Medical Center, ready to rush to the Audubon in case of trouble. Also, apparently, a couple of police officers were stationed in different rooms of the Audubon complex, but not close enough to make a difference in the assassination. This plan of action makes some sense when it is understood that police officers were the target of intense scorn at meetings of the Nation of Islam and the OAAU. But the police department easily could have beefed up security without inciting the wrath of the black nationalists present. After all, they were there to protect Malcolm X.

It is doubtful that the police had any specific, detailed knowledge of the imminent assassination and doubtful that they had a direct role in the killing. The sheer fact that Gene Roberts, an undercover officer who served as one of Malcolm X's bodyguards, gave mouth-to-mouth resuscitation to the dying black nationalist indicates that at least he was unaware of any police effort to kill Malcolm X. Roberts put his life on the line as he tried to stop Talmadge Hayer, one of the assassins, as he ran from the ballroom. Hayer shot at Roberts, but missed; Roberts then picked up a chair and floored Hayer before he was shot in the leg by Reuben Francis, another bodyguard. "My job was to keep [Malcolm X] alive," Roberts said in a recent interview. "Dead, Malcolm was useless to us [the police]. With him alive, we could keep tabs on him and his organization. I don't think the police had anything to do with his death. I believe it was orchestrated by the Black Muslims."[44]

But even if the New York police were innocent of direct responsibility for the crime, then they must certainly deserve some of the blame for allowing the crime to take place. They knew Malcolm X's life was about to end, yet they did almost nothing to stop it. Their disregard for his life—and their botched investigation after the fact—testify to their inadequate concern for Malcolm X's security. Although a detail of police was stationed across the street, it was a police officer who just happened to be passing by the ballroom, Thomas Hoy, who arrested Hayer. And Officers Aronoff and Angelos also happened to be driving by when they took the suspect from Hoy and brought him to the precinct. None of the officers who were supposedly assigned to protect Malcolm X were able to lift a finger in his defense, and also were unable to catch any of the assassins. The police in charge of the Audubon that day were clearly negligent in their duties, and their inability to protect Malcolm X opened the door for his assassins to do their job.

But the argument of conspiracy theorists that the NYPD, as well as the FBI and the CIA, were directly involved in the murder of Malcolm X is misdirected. All three government agencies have a number of questions to answer in terms of their relationships to Malcolm X, but they are of a far less serious nature than whether or not they murdered a major figure in the African-American struggle for equality. The CIA must answer to charges that it spied on him overseas. The FBI must explain its surveillance of the Muslim leader and whether it played a role in exacerbating the split between him and Elijah Muhammad. And the New York Police Department must open its files and provide more information on why it was unable to protect Malcolm X despite the obvious threats to his life.

Perhaps one explanation of this treatment of government agencies toward a major African-American figure of his time is that, as Malcolm X said repeatedly, blacks were only second-class citizens, if they were actually citizens at all. "The founding fathers—the ones who said 'liberty or death' and all those pretty-sounding speeches—were slave owners themselves," Malcolm X often shouted as he tried to incite his audiences to support his calls for a separate nation within the United States for African-Americans. "When they said 'liberty,' they didn't mean the black man, they meant the white people. When Lincoln said 'of the people, by the people and for the people,' Lincoln meant 'of white people, by white people and for white people.' "[45] "You sure don't catch hell because you're an American," he told his devoted followers, "because if you were an American you wouldn't catch no hell. You catch hell because you are a black man."[46] And as he said in his press conference when he first split from the Black Muslims, "If the government thinks I am wrong for [advocating armed self-defense], then let the government start doing its job."[47]

CHAPTER FIVE

The Confession

"I had to do something. I didn't know what to do, but I
had to do something. I had to try to exonerate the brothers."

—Talmadge Hayer

The end of the 1966 trial brought with it the final closing
of history's chapter on the assassination of Malcolm X, or
so everyone assumed at the time. The three defendants quietly began to serve their time in prison, and each gradually
faded from the public eye. While in prison, all three men
adopted formal Muslim names to replace their missing sur-
names. Talmadge Hayer became Mujahid Abdul Halim,
Johnson became Khalil Islam, and Butler changed his name
to Muhammad Abdul-Aziz. Once out of the public spotlight, Hayer resumed the outward practice of worshiping
Allah that he had denied during his trial.

All three men settled in at Sing Sing Penitentiary, then
were transferred to solitary confinement at a prison upstate.
The three men, soon separated from each other, did not
waste their time during their stints in prison. They began
taking college courses in hopes of getting their bachelor's
degrees. Their relationship with the outside world was generally tense. All three of them began having severe marital
problems, and Butler and Hayer were forced to watch their
wives leave them without being able to say much about it.

Johnson pleaded with his wife to divorce him so that she could salvage her life, but "to his sad wonderment, she has hung on."[1] Meanwhile, on the outside, Malcolm X became almost sanctified as a fallen martyr who had died trying to save his people, and Elijah Muhammad passed away silently in early 1975, leaving control of his fractured Nation of Islam to his son Wallace.

The three convicted assassins spent fourteen years in jail, most of that time apart from each other, before the case of Malcolm X's murder was revived. Sabbatino's prediction that history would regret the judgment on these three men finally began to come true, but not in the way that the defense lawyer had envisioned. Three years after the death of Muhammad, the Messenger of Allah, Hayer finally brought himself to reveal the secret that he had kept bottled up for so long. Caught up in the guilty emotions that resulted from the long imprisonment of his two innocent co-defendants, and freed from the responsibility of protecting others, Hayer finally recanted the confession that he gave at the trial and offered a new one. He, along with four fellow members of the Nation of Islam's Newark Mosque Number 25, had killed Malcolm X in 1965. Elijah Muhammad was now dead, and the need to protect the Messenger and his Nation of Islam had now evaporated over the years. At first Hayer revealed only the first names of the other assassins, then bowed to pressure and gave their full names and addresses, to the best of his knowledge. As before, he insisted that Johnson and Butler were innocent, but this time he had the names of the real assassins with which to bargain.

Hayer finally told how he had lied at his trial, not once but twice. The first set of lies was his original denial of culpability in the assassination of Malcolm X. Unaware of the futility of his case, he had pleaded innocent and claimed ignorance of how the physical evidence against him had come to be. The second set of lies came with his confession. He was indeed guilty, and the murder did happen in much the same way as he admitted it did during his trial. But his denial that the Muslims were responsible—and his continued denial that he himself was a Muslim—were lies designed to protect Elijah Muhammad and the Nation of Islam. In 1977 Hayer replaced his earlier confession with the true story of how he had been recruited into the cabal by Ben and Leon, both Muslim brothers in the Newark mosque.

Hayer wrote an affidavit in late 1977 and gave it to Nurriden Faiz, the prison's Muslim cleric. The affidavit, which consisted of three pages in Hayer's own handwriting, laid out the basic facts of the assassination: "I am writing this affidavit in the hope that it will clear my co-defendants of the charges brought against them in this case," Hayer wrote as his explanation for why he finally came forward after so many years. His recitation of the facts was brief, as he gave the first names of his fellow assassins and the basic outline of the sequence of events leading to the murder of Malcolm X. He told the court in writing how he was recruited during the summer of 1964 into the cabal by "a Brother named Lee and another Bro. named Ben."[2] From there the men recruited two others and began the planning for the assassination of the Nation of Islam's "chief hypocrite."

The affidavit does not lay out the motive for the crime, instead giving a brief introduction about Malcolm X defying the Honorable Elijah Muhammad and being declared a hypocrite for his actions. The rest of the motive, Hayer probably presumed, could be extrapolated. The language is clear and to the point, betraying little emotion or regret. The only statement that demonstrated his conviction was his explanation of why he felt that the assassination was necessary. "I thought it was very bad for anyone to go against the teachings of the Hon. Elijah, then known as the last Messenger of God. I was told that Muslims should more or less be willing to fight against hypocrites and I agreed w/ that. There was no money payed to me for my part in this. I thought I was fighting for truth and right." Hayer concludes the affidavit with a final plea for the freedom of his co-defendants, in the same style that he used throughout the legal document. "This affidavit is factural to the best of my knowledge. Thomas 15 Johnson and Norman 3X Butler had no thing to do with this crime whatsoever."

The overview of the crime as told by Hayer in his first affidavit was supplemented by a second signed statement that he wrote on February 25, 1978. The document begins:

I, Thomas Hagan, being duly sworn, disposes and says:
That this affidavit is an addition to my first affidavit. And that the statements made herein are more in detail and hopefully will clear up any doubt as to what took place in the killing of Malcolm X and the innocents of Norman Butler and Thomas Johnson

As promised, Hayer went into greater detail of the assassination in the second document. He detailed specifically how he was recruited into the plot by the two Muslim brothers. "Both of these men knew that I had a great love, respect and admiration for the Hon. Elijah Muhammad." Hayer went much further than he did in his original affidavit and released the full names and addresses of the assassins as he remembered them. His five-page handwritten document gave the details of how they planned the assassination, who held which gun, whose car they used to get to New York, and even the fact that "we parked a few blocks from the Ball Room on a street heading for the George Was. Bridge." He admitted that it was he who secured the weapons from a "man who had nothing to do with the crime" and that he had also made the smoke bomb that was used to create a disturbance. His conclusion was similar to that in his last statement. But in the new affidavit, he tagged a final sentence on the end: "And I am willing to state what took place in the matter before any court of law."

Hayer's revelation filled in many of the gaps that had been puzzling historians for years. Contrary to the prosecution's version, Hayer said he had been up front with the .45 automatic, and Leon was next to him with another pistol.

This story better fit the physical evidence than the prosecution's version of events, which held that Hayer had been in back starting the disturbance that allowed Johnson and Butler to open fire on the defenseless Muslim minister. After all, Hayer was seen up in front of the auditorium pumping pistol rounds in Malcolm X's prone body immediately after the initial shots erupted and felled him. According to Hayer, Willie carried the shotgun while Ben and Wilbur created the disturbance and set off the smoke bomb. The story correlated better with the actual evidence and presented a far more believable story than the prosecution had been able to construct thirteen years earlier. The notion that members of the Nation of Islam were behind the killing also fit the evidence well. The idea of a mysterious conspiracy in which Hayer was a hired gun made little sense, and it was easy to dismiss Hayer's first confession as a simple attempt to get Butler and Johnson off the hook.

The main gap in the historical record, however, that Hayer was unable to fill, was perhaps the most crucial question of the entire episode. Who gave the orders for the assassination of Malcolm X? Did Elijah Muhammad or the Muslim officials in Chicago have any foreknowledge of the crime? Did they order it? Or were they as surprised to hear of Malcolm X's death as was the rest of the world? Hayer's answer to these questions was that he simply didn't know. He was recruited by two Muslims who were older and more experienced than he was. He was not, however, privy to the information that they possessed on whether their superiors at the Newark mosque and in Chicago had known of or initiated the plot. One of the assassins, according to Hayer, was an official in the Newark mosque, but his position did not necessarily indicate that other Muslim officials in either Newark or Chicago were involved in the planning. While Hayer's testimony, if believed, solves many of the riddles of the assassination, it does not solve perhaps the most crucial question: who was ultimately responsible for the death of Malcolm X?

Wallace Muhammad,[3] the son of the Messenger, was able

to shed some light on the issue of whether his father had anything to do with the planning of the assassination. The elder Muhammad loved Malcolm X as if he were one of his own sons, and he treated Minister Malcolm with more affection and respect than any of the sons had ever received. The Messenger was even reportedly forced to tears when the break between himself and Malcolm X finally came in March 1964. According to Wallace Muhammad, the love between the men gradually became worn down as his father's retainers became jealous of Malcolm X, and the "eroding kind of suggestions and accusations had a toll on the Honorable Elijah Muhammad, and he actually began to believe that Malcolm was a threat."[4] When Malcolm X broke from the movement, "I saw [the Messenger] upset. *Very* upset."[5] And although the Messenger believed that Malcolm X deserved retribution for his actions against the Nation of Islam, he always believed that it would come in the form of divine retribution.

But other Muslims did not see it this way. In much the same way as Malcolm X thought the Muslims should take to the streets when a Muslim from Los Angeles was killed by the LAPD in a bloody rout, many Muslims similarly did not agree that the Muslims should wait for Allah to strike down Malcolm X. While Muhammad waited for a decree from Allah, other Muslims like Malcolm X took to the streets and sought their own form of justice. So did Hayer and his accomplices, as they sought vengeance against the man whom the Messenger labeled as the "chief hypocrite" of the Muslim movement. Perhaps Muhammad did not realize that his calls for divine retribution against Malcolm X would be inevitably translated into a call for his physical murder by members of the Nation of Islam. But, regardless of Muhammad's intentions, Malcolm X was brutally murdered as a direct result of his rhetoric.

In interviews with the author Peter Goldman, Hayer admitted that he had lied about the nameless conspiracy during his trial, all in the name of protecting Elijah Muhammad and the Nation of Islam.[6] But the death of

Muhammad and the restructuring of the Nation under Wallace Muhammad had eliminated the need for keeping the secret any longer. Besides, two innocent men were still languishing in prison, the result of a faulty police investigation and a flawed trial. Hayer experienced "a growing feeling of spiritual horror about what was going on with those two men."[7] Hayer at first told his story to Nurriden Faiz, the prison's Muslim cleric, who in turn passed the information to the radical attorney William Kunstler, who was known half-jokingly as the lawyer to the entire civil rights movement, from the Southern Christian Leadership Conference to the American Indian Movement. Kunstler had taken the lead from there, filing an affidavit with the court in an attempt to reopen the trial. The motion failed, as Judge Harold J. Rothwax of the New York Supreme Court denied the bid to set aside the convictions of Johnson and Butler. This forced Kunstler to approach the Congressional Black Caucus, where Harlem Democrat Charles Rangel agreed to lead the fight. But this motion similarly failed.

Benjamin Goodman, who gave the introductory speech for Malcolm X on the day he was killed, also signed an affidavit to the court, swearing that Butler and Johnson could not have been in the Audubon Ballroom that day. Goodman, who today goes by the name Benjamin Karim, told the court that none of the security officers present at the Audubon had come to him with the information that two well-known members of the Fruit of Islam, Butler and Johnson, were in the ballroom. Since security personnel were looking specifically for such FOI members, the ability of Butler and Johnson to slip through the security and assassinate Malcolm X would have been almost superhuman. In addition, Goodman scanned the audience for FOI members during his warm-up speech, as a standard precaution that he took to protect Malcolm X's life. Butler and Johnson were clearly not there. But Goodman's affidavit was similarly ignored by the court. Goodman had earlier testified to the grand jury investigating the assassination case, and although he had not been called to testify during the trial, the court did not consider his affidavit to be "new evidence".[8]

The only official reaction to Hayer's revelation was a letter from Congressman William J. Hughes to the FBI, dated May 29, 1980, asking the Bureau to reopen the investigation of the assassination of Malcolm X because of the new affidavits. Hughes' letter was in response to a petition that he received that asked Congress to look into the matter. "It is high time that a thorough investigation of [Malcolm X's] death took place so that two innocent men, who have already spent more than fourteen (14) years in jail, can win their freedom."[9] Hughes received a reply from an FBI bureaucrat, who assured him that the complaint had been forwarded to the Justice Department's Civil Rights Division. "A review of the records of the FBI . . . fails to reveal any information that the FBI has investigated, or been requested to investigate, the assassination of Al-Hajji Malik Shabazz (Malcolm X)."[10]

The consequences of the faulty trial were severe. The historical record of what actually happened on February 21, 1965, at the Audubon Ballroom has been unalterably subverted to the false version of a state prosecutor who was blindly trying to convict the three defendants rather than trying to find the truth. Even today, more than twenty-five years after the assassination and trial, the facts of the assassination are still disputed. But the effects of the trial on the historical record pale when compared to the deleterious effects on the two innocent men who were convicted of the crime. Both Johnson and Butler have been forced to endure a life behind bars because they unfortunately happened to resemble the men who actually committed the crime. Both were young men when they entered prison and were returned to the street as middle-aged men whose lives could never fully return to normalcy.

Thomas Johnson was first sent to Sing Sing Prison after his conviction, then moved to Attica in 1967. After that, he made the rounds among different New York prisons—Auburn, back to Attica, Wallkill, and Comstock. He was blamed for an incident in Wallkill where an inmate was injured, even though he said he was in his room asleep at the time. He was accused of the incident by what he called a "happy-go-lucky deputy warden" who "jumped the gun," and as a result he was transferred from Wallkill. "That's the story of my life," he reflected. "Always being accused of something I didn't do." The move from Wallkill was particularly difficult for Johnson. Since Wallkill was closer to his home in New York, he was able to see his wife and children "every couple of months," he said. "I was able to deal with my children, get their minds back together. They had someone to lean on, someone that cares about them."

Johnson tried to make the best of his life while he languished in the New York prison system. "I'm trying to make the best out of it," he said. "I'm going to college and trying to keep myself stable, and elevate and develop."[11] He retained his Muslim faith and took an Islamic name to reflect his belief in Allah. But, despite his efforts, his family life while he was in prison deteriorated dramatically, forcing his wife and children to endure the same pain that had afflicted him. "I tried to divorce her, y'know, and she won't," he explained. "I don't think it's fair to her. . . . I can't help but think of my family. They're choked down. I don't know how they're making it. [Hayer's and Butler's] wives left them, the children grow like weeds—I don't know. I have an extra-exceptional wife or something."

Johnson's wife, however, had been forced to deal with harassment from those angered by her husband's supposed involvement in the Malcolm X assassination. "When I call home, it upsets me," Johnson said.

Because when she tells me what she's been confronted with, y'know. These people—for the last two years they've been sabotaging her car. They finally destroyed it, from what I understand. Demolished it completely— would cost too much to have the engine fixed. And every week they would slash her tires and things like that. . . . What can I do? I feel helpless. I'm a very proud person.

So I stopped calling for long periods of time. Wouldn't call. And any time I do call, I get all tensed up because I know what I'm going to hear. So I figure that anybody that wants to—she's smart, she's had a couple of good jobs, she'd meet somebody and she'd be able to work things out.

Johnson also reported that some people inside the prison treated him differently because of his alleged involvement in the assassination of Malcolm X, although he did not receive the harassment that his wife endured. "No one ever approached me, but they would let me know," he explained. "I would get the drift that they didn't particularly care for me. At first it was very hostile. Very hostile. But I always had a lot of friends. Like I said, I come from let's say more or less the underworld, so I always had a lot. So it didn't really matter much. Nothing ever materialized from that, y'know. They would tell somebody that they didn't like me, or I should be dead, or something, but that was the end of that."

Norman Butler, who now uses the name Aziz, also tried to make the most of his years in prison. Like Johnson, his life was far from easy, as he went through the family crises and adjustment problems that are typical of prison inmates. His wife finally divorced him in 1971, six years after he was jailed for murder. Another subsequent long-term relationship that lasted a number of years while he was still in prison also failed. But as of 1979, Butler refused to focus on the negative aspects of his prison sentence when interviewed by Peter Goldman. "I think I gained something by being in here," Butler said. "I mean, I lost a lot. From a family perspective, there's no doubt about that. But I think that I gained something. Spiritually. Intellectually. I think that I've proven . . . the kind of development that can come in a place like this when a person is positively motivated. So I think that there are benefits from having done this or gone through it. Whether they outweigh the bad things that have happened remains to be seen."[12]

Butler retained the discipline that he had developed in the Nation of Islam, using it to combat the boredom that was a regular part of prison. During his stretches in solitary confinement, which he said he was given because they assumed that, as a Muslim, he deserved them, Butler continually read and exercised, working his mind and body. He began taking college courses while locked up in Attica Prison, slowly working his way toward a bachelor's degree. "I'm taking twelve more credits over here [in Sing Sing Penitentiary] now," he said. "I want to take business. Not that I want business, but that's the only thing that will make money." As he became increasingly enveloped by Islam, Butler also developed spiritually. During his years in prison, he constantly sought to bring the love of Allah to his fellow inmates and convert them to Islam. He credits the discipline of Islam for the absence of many problems with the Muslims for the prison authorities. "I've saved them an awful lot of problems," Butler remarked. "Not because I was trying to save them problems. I don't mean it that way. But just being me. Just doing the work that Islam assigns for a person to do, so to speak, saved them a lot of problems."

Butler spent much of his time serving as a Muslim counselor to the inmates. As a Muslim minister, he attempted to control the violent tendencies of some of his fellow inmates. He spent time in Attica shortly before the bloody 1971 uprising there. Butler was "working to control the furies when the authorities, nervous over his influence, abruptly transferred him out thirty-three days before the insurrection." According to Butler, "I had the influence to keep that riot from happening."[13] Butler is clearly proud of the effect that he has had on the inmates at the prisons where he has also served. By bringing them Islam, he also brought many of them the discipline that was necessary in the rough prison environment. Initially, the reputation of the Muslims caused prison guards to treat the Muslim inmates harshly, sometimes assigning them to solitary confinement, as they did to Butler. But his accomplishments did not go unnoticed after the fear of the Muslims had died down, and by 1979, Butler was seen as an influential inmate. At Sing Sing, he was even given a two-desk office from which he could conduct his work. His attitude, after many years of unnecessary confinement, was remarkably accepting and forgiving. At one point, he even insisted that he would remain in jail if pardoned by the New York Governor. "At this point I think I probably would [stay in prison]. I wouldn't get any money. I want to get out so my children can hold their heads up better or that those who have had faith in me over the years can get their faith rewarded—y'know what I'm saying? I mean, if I stayed in jail all this time, what's five more years?"

During his stay in prison, Hayer also went through some difficult times. He continually struggled with the knowledge that his silence about his role in the assassination of Malcolm X was keeping Butler and Johnson locked up in the New York State prison system. Like Butler, his wife finally divorced him in 1970 and went to college to get a bachelor's degree. "She went on to make the best out of her life that she possibly could," Hayer said. "She was pretty successful." In 1971 Hayer was transferred to Attica prison, where Butler had just finished his stay before he was moved to Green Haven prison. Shortly after Hayer arrived, the prison erupted in rioting. As Attica's Muslim minister, Hayer was in a position of authority and protected the kidnapped prison guards during the episode. "We took the position to keep the officers alive," Hayer said. " 'Cause a lot of guys was treated pretty bad, and they would try to get to them. We felt that it was important to protect the hostages." But despite his role in aiding the guards, Hayer was brought up on charges for his actions. "They indicted me. They said that I had kidnapped some officers. I didn't kidnap anybody. Only thing I did at Attica—if anything—was just keep the officers from getting their heads chopped off. That's all I did." The kidnapping charges were later dropped.

Hayer underwent profound religious changes when Elijah Muhammad died and Wallace D. Muhammad took his father's place as the head of the Nation of Islam. The younger Muhammad moved the Nation toward orthodox Islam and, in the process, admitted that his father had fathered the children that Malcolm X accused him of having. "I was like a ball of clay that was rolled up all over again. Had to be put back together again, man. Just broke down my whole concept of things." As a result of these revelations, Hayer also began to move away from the teachings of Elijah Muhammad toward orthodox Islam. "I began to understand why all this was happening," Hayer said. "I guess it was really just a test for myself. And believe me, I have never felt, man, that I was wrong. I never felt that I was wrong. I felt that I was right. And even now I can't say that I was wrong, because according to the way that I was thinking, I was just—I was doing what I would feel was right."

Hayer also moderated his views toward Malcolm X, the man he had slain over a decade before. Once he realized the human failings of Elijah Muhammad, Hayer soon also began to see the plight of Malcolm X during his final year. When Wallace Muhammad renamed the New York Muslim temple in Malcolm X's honor, it really struck Hayer. "I remember some of the ministers used to say—Malcolm used to say himself—that time reveals all things. Time will tell. Time will tell. And for the longest time, I always thought that time would tell that [Malcolm X] was wrong. That that man—that what he was saying wasn't true. Time *has* told. Time has told that a lot of the things he said was true. Even though the way that he said them and the wisdom that he used can be questioned. I'm quite sure that no mosque would have been named after Malcolm if he was truly the type of hypocrite that he was cast to be back then. I doubt it very seriously. You don't just name mosques after people like that. Not in Islam."

But despite the efforts of Hayer, Butler, and Johnson to make the most of their prison stays, all three of them remained bitter about the trial that sent them there in the first place. Hayer was not wrongly convicted, as were his co-defendants, but his guilt at covering up the Muslim conspiracy to kill Malcolm X, and the subsequent jailing of two innocent brothers after a faulty trial, took its toll over the years. His guilt finally overwhelmed him and forced him to confess the names of his fellow conspirators. He had suffered greatly because of his own need to protect Elijah Muhammad and because of the failure of the trial to illuminate the issues behind the assassination. Even a decade and a half after the trial, Hayer still seemed incredulous that Butler and Johnson were convicted, despite the evidence in their favor.

Hayer clearly misjudged the situation when he took the stand in the 1966 assassination trial and confessed his guilt in order to demonstrate the innocence of his co-defendants. "I didn't know what to do, but I had to do something," Hayer said. "I had to try to exonerate the brothers." Hayer did not foresee that his confession would contribute to the conviction of two innocent men. "Couldn't find no justice in that courtroom," Hayer stated. "Far as the state is concerned, justice is getting rid of a situation. . . . They knew I was gonna get my behind kicked in that courtroom. But at one time I thought they was gonna cut the other brothers [Johnson and Butler] loose. I was looking for them to go home, man. And then wow—these witnesses started saying they was there [in the Audubon], man." According to Hayer, going into a courtroom is like going to Hollywood.

> You know, people in Hollywood can make you cry, they can make you laugh, they can make you fall in love. And this courtroom is good at creating situations the same way. That the Nation of Islam and the FOI was like a very spooky type of thing—guys trained in karate, kicked doors down, stealing like this here. And they convinced people of this, man, with the revenge, the fear, the hate. Justice was a long way off in that courtroom, man.

Johnson and Butler were also understandably resentful over their treatment during the 1966 trial and their subsequent imprisonment. Butler showed his anger toward the defense lawyers who allowed him to be convicted. "I think they got paid to see us go down the drain," he said. "I mean not necessarily got paid money, but got paid in favors or some other kind of benefits. . . . They just wanted to get this case closed. They wanted to get somebody in prison so they could say the police had done their job."

Thomas Johnson knew early on in the trial that he and Butler would be convicted of the crime. "We were going to get life and we would have to do maybe ten, fifteen years of that, and I doubt if we'd be able to prove our innocence. Because of the way that that entrapment—that was a beautiful job that [the district attorney] did. That was a good frame-up. Best I've seen and I've seen a lot of them."

Even fifteen years later, Butler maintained that their participation in the assassination would have been impossible. First, the argument that he and Johnson could never have entered the Audubon Ballroom without being recognized was still valid. "All of these people [in the Audubon] knew me. They knew so much about me. How come they didn't recognize me walking in the door?" Also, Butler maintained that his leg injuries, sustained from the pistol whipping by the police who arrested him for the Benjamin Brown shooting, prevented him from taking part in the killing. "I wasn't in any condition to do anything. I couldn't even walk. My leg got infected. The day of the assassination I was in the hospital—the morning." Butler's legs had still not completely healed when Hayer gave his 1978 confession, with broken veins and numerous scars reminding him of his run-in with the police. "I was hurt. New York's finest made sure I didn't kill Malcolm. If I'm still carrying scars like this almost fifteen years later, think about it." According to Butler, "I would be for the death penalty myself if the power of the state was used not only to prove me guilty but to prove me innocent."

All three men have since been paroled from prison, the first being Muhammad Abdul-Aziz, formerly Norman 3X Butler, who was released in June 1985. After twenty years in prison, the 46-year-old man left the Arthur Kill Correctional Facility, having maintained his innocence since he was incarcerated in 1965. His parole was nearly blocked by a three-man panel charged with reviewing the decision to parole him. Then, after one of the panel members was charged with racism for complaining that Aziz had been treated too favorably while in prison, a new hearing was established and parole was granted. Aziz's co-defendants, Halim and Islam (Hayer and Johnson) were originally denied parole in 1984, but then finally granted freedom. They have assumed private lives, all of them trying to stay out of the public eye and forget the long years of incarceration.

Hayer's double confession, the apparent innocence of two of the men convicted of the crime, and the failure of the trial to illuminate many of the central issues of the assassination, have provided fertile breeding ground for conspiracy theorists who have attempted through the years to blame the murder on interests as diverse as the international drug cartel to the United States government. Civil rights leaders and Malcolm X's friends and enemies have all engaged in speculation as to whether the Nation of Islam actually did commit the crime, and the inability of the courts to settle the issue has only increased the barrage of conspiracy theories. Although none of the theorists has been able to provide enough evidence to adequately explain the crime, they have succeeded in raising crucial issues that must be examined in relation to Malcolm X's death. The role of the federal government in Malcolm X's life and death, and the failure of the criminal justice system to find and prosecute the assassins are but two of the issues that conspiracy theorists have added to the list of mysteries that surround Malcolm X. The hostility of the government toward Malcolm X was evident throughout his entire life, from his days as a petty criminal to those as a black nationalist leader. The government failed to prevent his impending murder, and then failed to provide a just retribution against his killers.

CHAPTER SIX

The Assassins

"I had a lot of love and admiration for the Honorable Elijah Muhammad, and I just felt like this is something that I have to stand up for. . . . I was just the type of person that if I had to stand up for what I believe, I would do it, man."

—Talmadge Hayer

The assassins were among the first to arrive at the Audubon Ballroom that afternoon of February 21, 1965. They got there early to ensure that they got the seats that they wanted, in perfect position to get a clear shot at the main speaker of the afternoon. The five assassins first met in Paterson, New Jersey, that morning, then drove to New York City. One of them told his wife that he was going across town to work on his father's car, but instead traveled to New York with his fellow co-conspirators. They parked their blue 1962 Cadillac on a street near the George Washington Bridge, several blocks from the ballroom, then got out and slowly made their way to the Audubon.

The five gunmen passed easily by the watchful eyes of Malcolm X's security staff. All wore long trench coats to cover the weapons that they carried with them. The security staff, told earlier by Malcolm X that the standard body searches of the guests were unnecessary, instead focused their attention on the impossible task of identifying those who looked as if they might want to kill Malcolm X. To this extent, they searched for members of the Fruit of Islam who might be trying to sneak into the ballroom. Most of the security personnel were former FOI members, all of whom would be able to easily identify their former colleagues. One Fruit of Islam member was identified in the ballroom that day; he had forgotten to take off his FOI pin before he entered the ballroom. He was questioned by George Whitney, one of Malcolm X's bodyguards, but after explaining that he was merely trying to hear what Malcolm X had to say, he was allowed to remain if he removed his pin.

But the actual assassins moved through the security unmolested. All of them, including young Talmadge Hayer, were members of the Newark mosque and had never been acquainted with the members of the New York FOI. The security staff, on the lookout for members of the New York FOI, let the assassins páss without a second thought. "There was a slight possibility" that they would be recognized, Hayer later admitted. "I was [from] out of town, for one thing. The other people that I was with, they was from out of town. Even though there was a few people now in Malcolm's organization that was also from Jersey. I don't know exactly how many. I don't recall seeing any of them."

Having gotten over the only possible hurdle in their way, the five assassins took their appointed places in the ballroom. Hayer and another Muslim brother named Leon made their way to the first row on the left side facing the stage, ready to fire away at the predetermined signal. Hayer carried a .45 automatic pistol beneath his topcoat; Brother Leon held a Luger.[1] Behind them in the second row sat William X, who concealed a sawed-off shotgun under his overcoat. The shotgun was the insurance weapon. As long as it was fired directly at Malcolm X, it was virtually guaranteed to kill him. The two pistols were meant merely to finish the job, if necessary.

The other two assassins made their way to different parts of the auditorium. Neither of them carried weapons. Their job was essentially to run interference for the assassination. Brother Wilbur was charged with the responsibility of creating an initial disturbance that would distract the guards and allow Talmadge, Leon, and Willie to get a clear shot at Malcolm X. He also held a smoke bomb that he would throw to magnify the confusion. Ben took a seat in the second row, apparently also with the responsibility of running interference. The five men sat and patiently waited for the rest of the visitors to find seats and for the program to begin. They sat silently, confident that Allah had willed the death of Malcolm X and that they were merely carrying out His orders. Doubtlessly they contemplated the murder that they were about to commit and the controversy that made Malcolm X's death a necessity.

The conspiracy to kill Malcolm X began in the summer of 1964, as tensions in New York flared between Malcolm X's supporters and those of Elijah Muhammad. Muhammad was scheduled to arrive in New York, Malcolm X's home territory, for a rally in late June, and the war of rhetoric had escalated. Malcolm X had recently begun an offensive against a series of extramarital affairs in which Elijah Muhammad had indulged, and the Nation of Islam had responded with a slew of scathing articles in *Muhammad Speaks* that attacked the former Black Muslim. Death threats were circulated against Elijah Muhammad, and the Muslims responded with similar threats against Malcolm X. "There was a lot of talk in the streets of Harlem," Hayer said. "A lot of tension, a lot of conflict. Rumors was being said that Muhammad better not come to Harlem—y'know, a lot of crazy stuff going on." According to Hayer, ministers in the mosques encouraged the growth of the hatred against Malcolm X and indirectly encouraged his assassination.

The talk them was real heavy coming from the ministers at that time, man. Because I'll tell you the truth, man, I felt that it was really putting the FOI to a test, y'know. And it was never in most cases said directly, but it was like a seed planting.

According to Hayer, it was Brother Benjamin from the Newark mosque who originally organized the conspiracy sometime in June 1964. As the tension between Malcolm X and his former leader intensified, the decision was made to hatch a plan to kill the New York Muslim and remove the threat that he represented to the Nation of Islam. The exact origin of the decision to launch the assassination plot is still undetermined, but Ben was the first to begin recruiting others into his plot. Ben was a lower-level official in the Muslim mosque—a secretary or assistant secretary—which gave him the impression of authority that allowed him to recruit in the name of his higher-ups in the Nation. Ben's first recruit into the cabal was Brother Leon X, who similarly felt that Malcolm X had to be silenced. They formed the core of the group into which they would now begin the process of recruiting others, the first of whom being Talmadge Hayer.

Talmadge Hayer led the life stereotypical of many black children of his time. He was shaped in a world of white domination, in which blacks largely accepted and internalized their lower status in American society. This acceptance of inferiority in turn reinforced it, as blacks fell far behind in education and job training, unable to overcome the rigid racial caste system. Their self-doubt preyed upon them, as they convinced themselves that their role in society was destined, as unchangeable as the color of their skin. Beset by their inner hatred, they often turned not to self-improvement but to self-destruction, as violence and drugs became standard features of black neighborhoods, where strength and "toughness" became the standard of success. Although many became mired in the battle against their internal conception of worthiness, still others, such as Talmadge Hayer, finally sought to fight back against the true source of their difficulties, America's racial hierarchy. By joining the Nation of Islam, or by joining the struggle for civil and human rights, some blacks attempted to turn

their self-denial into self-confidence by overturning an un-
just system.

But the fight for civil rights could take place only after
Talmadge Hayer and other blacks had resolved the battle
within themselves. The realization that poverty and community violence were not immutable characteristics of black
societies did not come easily. Like many other blacks,
Hayer had lived in poverty. He was born in Hackensack,
New Jersey, but soon moved to nearby Paterson, where he
spent his childhood. His father was a construction worker
and the supporter of eight children, of whom Talmadge was
the second-oldest boy. Their mother was far too busy raising the children and keeping up the apartment to have time
to bring in a second income; only after Hayer entered his
teen-age years could she leave the house to get a job. "My
mother's work was really just keeping the house together.
That was really heavy on her. I still remember my mother
doing a lot of heavy, heavy work. Just cleaning, man."[2] His
parents were originally from the South, somewhere around
the Carolinas, and migrated up north before their son
Talmadge was born. Both were religious and found a Baptist church to attend in New Jersey when they migrated
from the South. Hayer's mother was more religious than his
father, and it was she who often pressured her children to
go to church every Sunday. Talmadge went grudgingly, although he never gained the enthusiasm for Christianity that
his mother professed. "I used to go to church," he explained. "But then after a while it just wore off. We stopped
going. My mother used to encourage us to keep on going,
but it just kind of lost interest."

But religion did have an effect on young Talmadge. To
him, Christianity was a religion that promised bliss in the
afterlife, but condemned "Negroes" to remain in their oppressed status until then. When he finally found the Honorable Elijah Muhammad and the Nation of Islam in his later
teenage years, he finally discovered what he saw as a more
equitable religion in Islam. According to Hayer, Muhammad told blacks that "they should be able to have some-

thing in this life and not after they die." Hayer was also deeply affected by the stories of his parents' plight in the South, as they were forced to live under far greater oppression and an even more rigid social hierarchy. "My mother and father used to tell my brothers and sisters and me about the hard times in the South," he said.

> My mother and father always used to tell us about the lynching, y'know? The Ku Klux Klan. Hard work, hard labor—all of these type of things that was happening to black people at the time. I never could understand it, and I used to always ask. I used to always say, like, "How could you—if white people are doing all these things to you, why can't *you* get a gun? If they're shooting you, why can't you shoot back?".... And my mother used to say, "Well, you just don't understand." And she was right.

Too poor to afford a house, the Hayer family first found shelter in a railroad flat, until they were finally forced to move after it was condemned. The elder Hayer worked long hours, but his meager wages could barely feed his large family. Eventually, he was able to pool his money and buy a house for his family in the ghettos of Paterson. They lived in conditions that were far from ideal for raising children, but they had no other choice, forced by money and race to remain in the New Jersey slums.

It was in Paterson that Talmadge Hayer first went to school, in a nameless grammar school officially known as School Number Four. It was, according to Hayer, "a pretty notorious school," and fighting was the measure of a child's worth. Like the other children, the young Hayer developed a "tough-guy type of attitude" that hid his true self behind a blanket of fear. The neighborhood around School Number Four was rough, and the laws of the jungle were more appropriate than the laws of the land. "Trouble," Hayer described it. "Fighting. Bad situation, really, to grow up in." But when he moved from the railroad apartment, Hayer left behind much of the violence and entered a better school that more closely resembled education than day care. "It was like night and day to me," Hayer said.

> I had to adjust to the change. Teachers were different. Students' attitudes were different, and it really made *me* change. Matter of fact, my whole conduct was a lot better at that school than at the other school I was going to, y'know? I didn't have to have a tough-guy type of attitude at this school. Which is what most of the kids had at School Number Four. Pretty tough.

Talmadge soon graduated from grammar school and began attending high school. Increasingly, however, he lost his focus on schoolwork as he began to realize the apparent futility of his situation. Overcome by doubt over his self-worth, his goals faded into mere dreams. "I didn't have the right attitude when I went to high school," he said. "I guess I had a lot of doubts in myself." Like many black youths, before he ever got to high school, he began to revise his goals to fit his racial plight as he realized the station that was reserved for him in life by the hierarchical society.

> I remember even in grammar school, a teacher would ask, "What do you want to be, man? In life." And I remember I wanted to say something big. But I couldn't, y'know—I was afraid. So I said truck driver. My father was a truck driver. Man worked hard. . . . I don't know. I might have wanted to say doctor, lawyer. I don't know. I might have wanted deep down to say something like that. But I just, you know, didn't. I don't know.

Ironically, this childhood experience was quite similar to one of Malcolm X's memories, as he was forced to rethink his goals and his ambitions. Young Malcolm Little attended school in a mostly white classroom, where he was noticeably out of place and was often teased by his classmates because of his race. In the seventh grade, he was confronted by his white English reacher with a similar question about the future.

He told me, "Malcolm, you ought to be thinking about a 'career. Have you been giving it thought?" The truth is, I hadn't. I never have figured out why I told him, "Well, yes, sir, I've been thinking I'd like to be a lawyer". . . . Mr. Ostrowski looked surprised, I remember, and leaned back in his chair and clasped his hands behind his head. He kind of half-smiled and said, "Malcolm, one of life's first needs is for us to be realistic. Don't misunderstand me now. We all here like you, you know that. But you've got to be realistic about being a nigger. A lawyer—that's no realistic goal for a nigger. You need to think about something you *can* be. You're good with your hands—making things. Every body admires your carpentry shop work. Why don't you plan on carpentry. People like you as a person—you'd get all kinds of work."[3]

It was this event that in many ways shaped his future and was branded into Malcolm X's memory. The experience immediately became "the first major turning point of my life," Malcolm X later recalled.

For Talmadge Hayer, dropping out of high school seemed to be the natural alternative. "I realized that my mother and father couldn't get me the things that I wanted— y'know, as far as clothes and many other things. And I began to look for ways and means to make ends meet, so to speak. . . . I dropped out of high school and I went to work." He began taking random jobs, soon learning that he also could not provide the things that he wanted. He began by making $35 a week in Paterson's textile mills. Quickly he began getting jobs that paid slightly better— about $1.75 an hour—but he still made a meager wage that barely allowed him to make ends meet. "The realization really strikes home. You really learn things, and you realize that you still can't buy the things that you want." He worked in labor shops, learning how to operate the various machines and slowly creeping up the wage scale.

Hayer said he first heard about the Nation of Islam by reading the newspapers, which had reports about the progress of Islam in the nation's prisons. The budding influence of Islam in the penal system raised the concern of prison officials that the Muslim inmates would rise up against the "white devil" guards who maintained order in jail. This growing concern led to numerous struggles across the country as officials began refusing to allow Nation of Islam members to pray or otherwise express their religion. Although clearly unconstitutional, these measures served to restrict the Muslims momentarily, but it added pressure to the importance of the Muslim cause and indirectly encouraged greater inmate membership in the Nation. "I remember reading a couple of articles" on the prison struggles, Hayer said. "The fact that these people were stand-up people, y'know, I couldn't understand. What is it about this that the establishment seems to be afraid of?"

The Nation of Islam seemed to be the natural direction for Talmadge Hayer. Lacking a religion and a philosophy, he was attracted by the assertiveness of the Muslims. His knowledge of his parents' experience in the South, as well as his life of poverty in New Jersey, pushed him toward a greater militancy than his parents had ever considered. "When I first heard anything about the teachings of the Honorable Elijah Muhammad . . . it just struck a bell. It made sense to me because even though I didn't realize it then, it just made a connection with many of the things that my parents had been experiencing and telling me anyway." He was attracted to the Muslim philosophies of discipline and regimen. "So many of the brothers that I grew up with, coming out of prison as Muslims—I couldn't even believe the difference myself. Y'know, I knew some of these guys before they even went to prison, and you would never think, man, that even God could save them. But these guys were coming out of prison dignified young men, respectful. And I couldn't understand it."

So Talmadge Hayer finally decided to open himself up to the philosophies of the Nation of Islam. "One thing led to another, and I went to check this out," he said. "I attended, and it just made a lot of sense to me." Before long, Hayer rid himself of his "slave" name, and devoted himself fully to the program and the teachings of the Honorable Elijah Muhammad. The faith in Islam burned strongly within the new recruit. As with many of the recently converted Muslims, Hayer was willing to go to almost any lengths to prove his allegiance to Elijah Muhammad and his religion. "I wasn't really operating on what you might say a wisdom base, though. I guess you might say I was just a good brother." He was so fiercely devoted to the cause of the Black Muslims that he made the perfect assassin: willing to kill not for money, but for principle.

Hayer officially joined the Nation of Islam in late 1962, only a year before Malcolm X would be suspended by the Honorable Elijah Muhammad for his "chickens coming home to roost" comment. Hayer soon received his 'X,' which all Black Muslims adopted, after sending his requisite application letter to the Muslim officials in Chicago, and became a member of the Newark Temple Number 25. Hayer had trouble adapting to the world of the Muslims, not because he did not believe in the tenets of Islam as preached by the Messenger, but because of what he saw as the failure of others to believe as much as he did. His first sign of this came as a fellow Muslim was suspended from the Nation for getting himself into a shooting fight with some non-Muslims. To Hayer, battling non-Muslims was part of the point of being in the Nation of Islam. Why should a brother be punished for doing what he was taught he should do? Increasingly distraught by the episode, Hayer temporarily stopped attending the Muslim services.

Unwilling to go back to his fellow Muslims, Hayer sunk into a deep despair. As he lost the discipline that was required of the Muslims, he began moving toward crime. He hadn't spent much time on the street before he was arrested for possession of stolen guns. As he told Peter Goldman many years later, "my life started coming apart."⁴ But he could not stay away from the Nation of Islam for long. Convinced that rejoining the Muslims would put his life back on track, he again went to the Newark temple and resubscribed to the Nation's version of Islam. But after only a short time back in the temple, his burning faith in Islam again led to his loss of faith in his fellow Muslims. Eager to demonstrate his passion for Islam, he physically punished a fellow Muslim for violating the rigid rules of the Nation. Expecting commendations, he received censure from his higher-ups in the Newark temple. Again, he drifted away from the Nation, only to rejoin it when his love for Islam and Elijah Muhammad overcame his disappointment in the organization. When he came back the second time, he set himself in a direction where he would eventually commit an even greater sin, but one that was sanctioned by the Nation of Islam.

Ben and Leon first approached Talmadge not in the mosque, but on the street in downtown Paterson, New Jersey. The two conspirators drove up to Hayer in their car, then invited Hayer to get in and have a talk with them. The three of them drove around for a while, with Ben and Leon carefully probing Hayer's attitude toward Malcolm X. For security reasons, Ben and Leon had to know whether other Muslims would agree with a plan to kill Malcolm X before they revealed that they had actually created a plan to assassinate him. According to Hayer,

That first conversation was more or less around my feelings in regard to [the struggle between Malcolm X and Elijah Muhammad]. Nothing direct at first—just general conversation as to how did I feel about it. And then it was realized that my feelings was pretty much the same as theirs—you know, like the Messenger was being slandered, man. And this has to stop.

So Hayer became the third member of the secret plot to kill Malcolm X. "I had a lot of love and admiration for the

Honorable Elijah Muhammad, and I just felt that like this is something that I have to stand up for. This is what I believe," he said. "So that led to me getting involved to the extent that—you know, I would go all the way." Hayer was easily convinced that Malcolm X and his followers needed to be taught a lesson. After all, he had already followed his conscience once and ended up beating a brother in the mosque for going against the ways of Elijah Muhammad. There was no reason for Ben and Leon to believe that he would not do it again to someone whose sins were far greater. Malcolm X. "I was just the type of person that if I had to stand up for what I believe, I would do it, man, y'know?" Hayer said. "And maybe I was manipulated. Maybe I was a pawn. I don't know. I didn't see it that way at the time. I just believed, and that was my motivation."

Ben, Leon, and Talmadge then found two more Muslims fervent enough in their beliefs that they would kill Malcolm X to save the reputation of Elijah Muhammad. Willie X and Wilbur also readily joined the group, and the five of them began to plan the logistics of the assassination. At the time of the planning, tensions between Malcolm X and Elijah Muhammad were at an all-time high, with verbal assaults careening back and forth between New York and Chicago. Malcolm X and his former Muslim colleagues had recently confronted each other in a small New York City courtroom as the eviction proceedings against Malcolm X got underway. Although Malcolm X still lived in the brick house that the Muslims had provided for him for the duration of the time that he was minister of the New York mosque, he still tried to fight the losing battle of convincing a judge that the house was actually his even though it had the Nation of Islam's name on the deed.

With anger piqued, the five conspirators set about their business, enthusiastically discussing the optimum method and time for killing Malcolm X. Time was of the essence, since Malcolm X's sins against the Messenger were increasing by the day, and no one was certain exactly what inner secrets the Muslim held. He had already dipped into the secret of Muhammad's adultery with a number of secretaries, by whom he fathered more children than he had in his already large legitimate family. Although the charge of adultery apparently did little to turn the tide against the Messenger, Malcolm X also held a number of even juicier secrets that he learned while serving as Muhammad's chief aide. If he chose to expose these secrets, the damage could have been extensive, or so the Muslims reasoned. Besides, there was always the threat the Malcolm X would be able to destroy the Nation of Islam by out-recruiting them, stealing their potential converts and bringing them into his Organization for Afro-American Unity.

So the five men continued to discuss plans to remove the dagger that they saw pointing at the heart of the Nation of Islam. They met in various places, generally either at Ben's or Leon's house. At other times, they simply drove around Paterson, discussing their plans as they went. But almost as soon as they began laying down their strategy, Malcolm X left the country for Africa, and the controversy began to simmer down. He left New York in the early part of July and did not return for more than 18 weeks. In his absence, the controversy subsided somewhat, and the talk of his death similarly disappeared. "Around the time that he left the country, it seems to have been a cooling-off period, if I recall correctly," Hayer explained. "Nothing was happening. So I thought that maybe things were going to get better, man."

But despite Hayer's hopes, this was not the case. When Malcolm X returned to the United States on November 24, 1964, the controversy returned to its previous level. So, too, did the desire to see Malcolm X killed. Just before he flew back from Africa, Malcolm X once again became the target of scathing editorials in *Muhammad Speaks*, one of which was written by Boston Minister Louis X (later known as Louis Farrakhan). Brother Louis challenged his former mentor to return to New York and "face the music" and warned Malcolm X that he would meet his doom if he returned. "And then everything started hitting the fan again,"

Hayer recalled. "So we got together. Said, 'Alright, we're moving.'"

The first order of business for the assassins was determining how they would kill their prey. The first instinct was to try to get to him when he was in a vulnerable position in his own home. Not only would this accomplish their goal, it would also send a message about the power of the Muslims. They would kill Malcolm X in his own territory, in his own house, a clear message to future traitors to the Muslim movement. So the five men piled in the car and made their secret pilgrimage to Malcolm X's house. "We went out to wherever he lived at, y'know?" Hayer explained. "But he was very heavily guarded, and we came back." Malcolm X and his lieutenants had long anticipated that the Muslims would try to murder him in his home. To hinder such an attempt, armed guards kept an eye on the house, with others periodically driving by to make sure that all was well. Clearly, the Muslims would have to find another location for the assassination.

But most of the conspirators had little time for following Malcolm X around New York, charting his schedule and looking for the optimal assassination site. "We were all working, far as I know," Hayer said. "I know I was. I couldn't just run around New York and ride around, man, y'know. I got a wife and a family." So the five assassins got together and decided that there was only one place other than his home that they knew that Malcolm X would repeatedly visit: the Audubon Ballroom. It was here that Malcolm X held many of his meetings, where his rallies for his Organization for Afro-American Unity were generally held, where five unknown assassins would have a good chance of slipping into a crowd and getting close to the "chief hypocrite" of the Nation of Islam. So it was decided as simply as that. The Audubon Ballroom would serve as the backdrop for the assassination of a major figure in the African-American struggle for freedom.

The five men then went about the process of setting up the assassination. They first went to a meeting of the OAAU in the Audubon to check for security. None of them held any weapons, just in case the guests were being searched. After this first meeting, the site was finalized, and the five men decided that the Audubon would be perfect. The Audubon had two major advantages other than the lack of security precautions. First, the large crowd that was expected would allow for enough confusion so that the assassins would be able to slip into the background easily and escape undetected. They could simply pretend they were ordinary audience members after the killing and run out in fear with the rest of the mob. Second, the murder of Malcolm X in front of his supporters and security guards would send the same message that a murder in his house would send. The Audubon was his own territory, and the demonstration of his vulnerability would serve as the ultimate embarrassment in front of his supporters.

The next step was to line up the guns for the assassination. This job fell to Talmadge Hayer, who had some knowledge of the gun market on the streets of Paterson. "I could get my hands on something that was available," he said. He soon lined up three weapons—the Luger, the .45 automatic, and the shotgun—and distributed them to his fellow plotters. He got them from one of the gunrunners he knew on the street, and paid for the guns out of his own pocket. "Nobody gave me money. Any money that I laid off was really money that I was making off my job. If I had to spend it, I would spend it." Hayer also assembled the smoke bomb that was used to create a disturbance. Actually, the bomb consisted primarily of flammable film rolled up in a sock, but it served its purpose: it turned people's attention away from the center of the action and allowed four of the five conspirators to get away.

On Saturday night, February 20, 1965, as Malcolm X slept in his twelfth-floor room at the New York Hilton Hotel, his assassins again set out to the Audubon, where a dance was scheduled to take place. After the dance, they felt confident that the assassination would be successful. "At that point there, it was already out that there was going to be a meeting [of the OAAU at the Audubon] the next day," Hayer said. "So then it was only a matter of following then what we had planned to do." The five men all went to sleep after the dance in their respective homes, then reassembled the next morning at Ben's house, where the decision was made to go ahead that day with the killing. "We got a strategy together—decided what we were going to do," Hayer said. "Who was going to do what. And that's pretty much how we came to the decision of what would happen from that point on." The plan was finalized, the role of each man determined, and the five assassins set out for New York.

Like many of the others who were present at the assassination, Hayer also reported a lack of police officers present at the Audubon that cold winter day, given the immediate threat against Malcolm X's life. "I don't recall seeing any [police]," Hayer said. This also worked perfectly into the hands of the assassins. While there supposedly was an entire detail of police officers across the street at the Columbia Presbyterian Medical Center, at that distance they could not have interfered with the plans of the five Muslims. With a lack of police, another enormous hurdle had been avoided by the assassins. Now, sitting in their assigned places inside the Audubon Ballroom, all they had to do was wait for their victim.

With the .45 automatic pistol nestled inside his belt, Hayer sat quietly and thought about the crime that he was about to commit. "I didn't know what to expect [at the Audubon]," he admitted. "You know, I didn't come with any expectations about this, that or the other thing. I didn't know what to expect. This was it, man." Hayer had a certain amount of fear as he sat there and waited for the event that would define the rest of his life. But the fear was overcome with a sense that he was doing what he thought was right. He was striking a blow for justice and carrying out the will of Allah and His Messenger Elijah Muhammad. "I don't want to sound like any kind of hero," Hayer said, "because in my life—I've been through some changes with this whole thing, y'know? I don't know. You just do what you have to do, and that's all I can say, man. You know. And that's what I did. I won't say that I wasn't afraid. I don't talk in terms of that type of thing, or sound that way."

So the five men nervously waited. A sizable crowd of about 400 finally arrived and took their seats for the beginning of the program. Benjamin Goodman led off the show, giving a thirty-minute speech designed to prime the crowd for Malcolm X's entrance. For the assassins, everything went almost exactly as planned. Malcolm X strode to the podium, and was barely given the opportunity to begin when Wilbur X jumped up from his seat in the back of the auditorium, screaming, "Man, get your hands out of my pocket." Taking his cue, Willie X quickly stood up in the second row, unnoticed by the audience whose attention had been diverted by the disturbance in the back. As the guards moved from Malcolm X's side, and as Malcolm X stepped out from behind the plywood rostrum, Brother Willie opened his overcoat, produced his shotgun, aimed, and fired. Hayer and Brother Leon followed suit, pulling out their pistols and firing away at Malcolm X's lifeless body.

As Hayer's smoke bomb erupted in the back of the auditorium, the five men turned to flee. Wilbur and Ben, neither of whom took part in the shooting, easily slipped into the crowd and disappeared. Willie rid himself of the shotgun; then he and Leon also turned and fled. Only Talmadge Hayer, still holding his .45 automatic, failed to slip out the door unnoticed by the rest of the mob. "There was a lot of commotion and stuff. . . . I remember though—there was quite a few guns in that place being fired. I didn't even know I got shot in the left leg. Even to today I think I got shot in my right. Because there was this guy shooting at my right side. I didn't see how I got shot in my left side." As he ran, he tried desperately to clear the way for himself, but the more he tried, the more he pulled attention to himself. "I was just trying to make a commotion, man," he said. "I fired off a couple of shots."

Hayer said he didn't know if his friends got out of the

ballroom safely. "There was one person, he was running in front of me. I think it was Leon," he said. "He came out before I did. Because I was shot in my leg so I couldn't move fast. I was only trying to get outside. He was the only one I could say [that] went out before I did. Other people I couldn't see. They must have been after me.

There was one guy I think he said I shot in the foot or something like this here. For the most part, I was just trying to get out. And I was hit in the leg. I didn't see the guy that shot me, you know. So I just hopped, man. I was hopping with one leg, and I slid down the banister, fell on the ground and—I don't know. And don't ask me why and how—there was an officer out there. And it was fortunate, because my life was spared.

Hayer was immediately taken to the hospital, then to the police station for booking. In custody for the assassination of Malcolm X, Hayer was destined to spend more than twenty years in the New York prison system. In his mind, he had dutifully served his ultimate leader, Elijah Muhammad, but he could never reveal his inner motivations. To admit that he had assassinated Malcolm X to protect the Nation of Islam, he would have admitted the culpability of the Nation and its leader, the Messenger of Allah. To one whose entire life centered around the philosophy of the Muslims, this would be unforgivable. So he hid his knowledge of the assassination, at first claiming that he was merely an innocent bystander who was mistaken for the actual assassin. In so doing, he saved the Nation of Islam from blame and forced the world to wonder why Malcolm X had been killed.

CHAPTER SEVEN

The Prelude

"I was going downhill until [Muhammad] picked me up.
Come to think of it maybe we picked each other up."
—*Malcolm X*

The relationship between the Honorable Elijah Muhammad
and Malcolm X is a crucial link in the chain of events that
brought about Malcolm X's assassination. Muhammad was
everything to Malcolm, from mentor to surrogate father, but
the relationship between the two men contained the seeds
of conflict that finally erupted and caused a dangerous
schism between them. This irreparable rupture brought the
two Black Muslims into enemy camps and gave the
Muslims a far better motive for killing Malcolm X than any
other individual or group—including the government—
could claim, despite the arguments of conspiracy theorists
that this was not the case. In the eyes of Elijah Muhammad
and the Black Muslim leadership, Malcolm X had to be
killed. His knowledge of internal Nation of Islam affairs, as
well as Muhammad's personal life, was an enormous threat
to the well-being of the Nation, and his ability to form a
dedicated following transformed him from the Muslim's
chief spokesman to their chief rival. In order to fully com-
prehend the apparent need to kill Malcolm X, it becomes
necessary to analyze the growth and deterioration of the re-

lationship between him and his Muslim leader, and to determine how outside forces drove a permanent wedge between them that resulted in their animosity.

The relationship between Malcolm Little and the Honorable Elijah Muhammad began in 1949, sixteen years before their fractured alliance would eventually end in Malcolm X's death. Malcolm X was converted to the Nation of Islam midway through his prison term for robbery, as his brothers, Reginald, Wilfred, and Philbert, and his sister Hilda tried to teach him the "natural religion for the black man" while Malcolm languished in a Massachusetts jail. Malcolm, the bitter atheist, at first spurned his siblings' attempts at conversion, at one point writing a vicious reply to a letter from Philbert in which his brother said that "his 'holiness' church [the Nation of Islam] would pray for me."[1] Philbert received the same treatment when he sent Malcolm a second letter in which he told his brother that he should "pray to Allah for deliverance." But Malcolm's resistance to conversion to Islam almost disappeared when his younger brother Reginald visited from Detroit with the specific goal of turning his older brother toward Elijah Muhammad. As Reginald talked, Malcolm's arguments against religion vanished as he began to see the wisdom in his brother's words, particularly concerning the theory that whites are devils in disguise. He reviewed his life in his mind, trying desperately to find a white person who had not been cruel or had not discriminated against him. To his dismay, he could think of almost none. Shaken by his new realization, Malcolm slowly began to adapt his life to Islam: he quit using cigarettes and drugs, stopped eating pork, and finally, with great difficulty, brought himself to the point where he could prostrate himself before Allah and pray.

His first contact with the "Messenger of Allah" came in writing, as Malcolm took the advice of his brothers and penned a letter to his soon-to-be mentor. In his autobiography, he detailed the difficult time he had in doing something as simple as writing a letter:

At least twenty-five times I must have written that first one-page letter to him, over and over. I was trying to make it both legible and understandable. I practically couldn't read my handwriting myself; it shames me even to remember it. My spelling and my grammar were as bad, if not worse. Anyway, as well as I can express it, I said I had been told about him by my brothers and sisters, and I apologized for my poor letter.[2]

The Messenger responded personally to Malcolm's letter, as he did with much of his correspondence from such potential converts. He sent a typed response and offered Malcolm a five-dollar bill and a lesson about his being the victim of the white man's society. In the three years that he had remaining in prison before he was paroled in 1952, Malcolm worked feverishly, writing daily letters to Elijah Muhammad, improving his education by reading all the books that the prison library had to offer, and passing on the Nation of Islam's message to his fellow inmates and by letter to his friends in New York and Boston. And in an effort to broaden his vocabulary, he painstakingly copied a dictionary by hand into his writing tablet. In his extensive reading, he learned all he could about the "so-called Negro" people in America, the history of Africa, and the evils that the Europeans had inflicted on the "darker world."

On August 7, 1952, Malcolm Little was released from Norfolk Prison Colony under the sponsorship of his brother Wilfred, from Detroit. After buying a suitcase, a watch, and a better pair of eyeglasses, Malcolm traveled to Detroit to meet with his brother on the day after his release. Malcolm immediately began learning about the proper life of a Muslim as he observed his brother's family in their everyday activities. He began attending the Temple of Allah No. 1 in Detroit and applied for membership in the Nation of Islam. On August 31, 1952, the Sunday before Labor Day, he had his first opportunity to meet the "Prophet," Elijah Muhammad. That day the Messenger addressed about 10,000 people at the Chicago Temple No. 2, and about ten cars loaded with Detroit Muslims, including Malcolm, made the trip down to see their leader. "I was totally unprepared for the Messenger Elijah Muhammad's physical impact upon my emotions," Malcolm reported in his autobiography.[3] The Messenger gave his address to the cheering crowd, condemning the "blue-eyed devil white man" and exhorting the black man to uplift himself and his brothers and sisters. And then, Malcolm heard his name from the podium:

It was like an electric shock. Not looking at me directly, he asked me to stand. He told them that I was just out of prison. He said how "strong" I had been while in prison. "Every day," he said, "for years, Brother Malcolm has written a letter from prison to me. And I have written to him as often as I could.[4]

Elijah Muhammad used Malcolm's situation in a parable, comparing him to Job, who remained faithful to God even in the face of hardship. " 'We will see how [Malcolm] does,' Mr. Muhammad said, 'I believe that he is going remain faithful.' "[5] Malcolm got to meet the Messenger in person that night; he was invited to supper in Muhammad's spacious eighteen-room mansion in Hyde Park, Chicago.

During a conversational lull, I asked Mr. Muhammad how many Muslims were supposed to be in our Temple Number One in Detroit.

He said, "There are supposed to be in the thousands."

"Yes, sir," I said, "Sir, what is your opinion of the best way of getting thousands there?"

"Go after the young people," he said. "Once you get them, the older ones will follow through shame."

I made up my mind that we were going to follow that advice.[6]

Malcolm X's rise through the ranks of the Nation of Islam was as dramatic as was his original conversion from atheism to Islam. He got his first break when he was asked by the Detroit minister to address the congregation one Sunday; after an initial success, he was invited back. His relentless efforts in recruiting the "dead" of the Detroit ghetto eventually produced results as the membership in Muhammad's Temple No. 1 tripled, in large part because of Malcolm X's efforts. In the summer of 1953, Elijah Muhammad named Malcolm X assistant minister of the Detroit Temple. He began spending much of his time being personally trained by the Messenger and listening to the stories of Elijah's childhood from Muhammad's mother, Marie. Soon the 28-year-old Malcolm X quit his full-time job so that he could devote his time more fully to the Nation of Islam. His first major assignment came later that year, when he was sent to help organize a temple in Boston, where a small number of Muslims began meeting in their homes. The Boston temple was formalized by the end of 1953, and Malcolm X helped to find a permanent meeting place and rented some folding chairs on which to sit.

Elijah Muhammad, who early on recognized the potential of his young devotee, next moved Malcolm X to Philadelphia in mid-1954, where he was able to organize Muhammad's Temple Number 12 in only three months. In June 1954, Malcolm moved on to the assignment that he would retain for the next ten years: minister of New York's Temple Number Seven. Within two years, Malcolm X had moved from a new recruit straight out of the prison system in Massachusetts to minister of the largest Black Muslim temple in the country. His explosive rise came as a result of his enormous abilities and his personal relationship with Elijah Muhammad, which was often compared to that of father and son. Perhaps Malcolm X did look to Muhammad as the father he never really had. His real father had been a cruel tyrant, beating his wife and his children regularly, but his death when Malcolm was six years old left the young boy without a male role model when he was growing up. Elijah Muhammad took over that role when Malcolm X was growing up in the religious and political world of the Nation of Islam. The Messenger counseled him and molded him, preparing Malcolm X for the trials that he would face as a Muslim minister.

The two Muslim leaders had a relationship of love and mutual respect. Malcolm X looked up to the Messenger as "the most powerful Black man in America," a title that he often used in introducing Elijah Muhammad. Muhammad saw Malcolm X as a brilliant organizer and orator who moved the Nation of Islam from being a fringe group active in a few cities in the early 1950s to the nationwide voice for the black nationalist movement. While an accurate census of members of the Nation of Islam was never taken, it is clear that the fiery voice of Malcolm X expanded the membership dramatically, as he organized temples in Boston, Philadelphia, Washington D.C., and a number of other cities across the country. Malcolm X brought life to a movement that had seen little growth since its inception, twenty years before he became a Muslim minister and confidant to the Messenger. As Malcolm X's accomplishments grew, so, too, did his relationship with Elijah Muhammad.

Malcolm X took every opportunity to praise his mentor when he spoke to the press or to his congregation, continually prefacing his remarks with the phrase, "The Honorable Elijah Muhammad teaches us that . . ." Throughout most of his tenure with the Nation of Islam, he stood in awe of the Messenger, often telling the story of how Muhammad had picked him up out of prison and cleansed him of his evil ways. "Mr. Muhammad is everything and I am nothing," he said at a reception following one of his many debates. "When you hear Charlie McCarthy speak, you listen and marvel at what he says. What you forget is that Charlie is nothing but a dummy—he is a hunk of wood sitting on Edgar Bergen's lap. If Bergen quits talking, McCarthy is struck dumb; if Bergen turns loose, McCarthy will fall to the floor, a plank of sawdust fit for nothing but the fire. This is the way it is with the Messenger and me. It is my mouth working, but the voice is his."[7] In an interview with a Nigerian scholar, Malcolm X said, "I owe my present moral stature to Mr. Muhammad for whom I would give my life so that he may live. He has done so much for me."[8] It was this type of exaggerated admiration that blinded Malcolm X to the genuine nature of the Nation of Islam and the Messenger, and his gradual disillusionment led directly to his fall from grace within the Muslim movement.

The Honorable Elijah Muhammad heaped a good deal of praise on his young minister, as well. Muhammad referred to Malcolm X on several occasions as "my beloved Minister Malcolm." In a speech in Milwaukee, Muhammad took a moment to demonstrate his affection for his protégé. "Anywhere you will find me you will find him . . . He is one of the most faithful ministers I have. He will go everywhere—North, South, East or West, to China if I say go to China, he will go there. So I thank Allah for my Brother Minister Malcolm."[9] Often, Muhammad praised Malcolm X as "my hardest-working minister."[10] As a demonstration of his trust in Malcolm X, Muhammad generally saved the difficult duties for the New York minister, such as trying to prevent a guerilla war between the Los Angeles Muslims and the police after a Muslim was killed, or serving as his advance man before his trip to Africa and the Middle East. Under Muhammad's guidance, Malcolm X served as the "troubleshooter" for the Nation as he created new temples and handled problems in the established ones. When Muhammad named Malcolm X as the Nation's first National Minister in late 1963, he hailed the New York minister as "my most faithful, hardworking minister. He will follow me until he dies."[11]

But despite the public adoration that the two men professed for each other, fissures could be seen privately long before Malcolm X was suspended for his comments on President Kennedy's assassination. Although Elijah Muhammad praised his student in public, he nevertheless expressed misgivings about him to some of his confidants in private. Malcolm X later learned about several of these comments when he spoke to the Muhammad's former secretaries who filed paternity suits against their ex-employer. "I heard that Elijah Muhammad had told them I was the best, the greatest minister he ever had, but that someday I would leave him, turn against him—so I was 'dangerous.' I learned from these former secretaries of Mr. Muhammad that while he was praising me to my face, he was tearing me apart behind my back. That deeply hurt me."[12]

But the signs of a split between the two Muslim leaders did not come solely from Elijah Muhammad. Alex Haley, in the epilogue to Malcolm X's autobiography, revealed an instance in which Malcolm X showed some divergence from the official teachings of the Messenger.

From Malcolm X himself, I had seen, or heard, a few unusual things which had caused me some little private wonder and speculation, and then, with nothing to hang them onto, I had dismissed them. One day in his car, we had stopped for the red light at an intersection, another car with a white man driving had stopped alongside, and when the white man saw Malcolm X, he instantly called across to him, "I don't blame your people for turning to you. If I were a Negro, I'd follow you, too. Keep up the fight!" Malcolm X said to the man very sincerely, "I wish I could have a white chapter of the people I meet like you." The light changed, and as both cars drove on, Malcolm X quickly said to me, firmly, "Not only don't write that, never repeat it. Mr. Muhammad would have a fit." The significant thing was that it was the first time I had ever heard him speak of Elijah Muhammad with anything less than reverence.[13]

Public criticism from Malcolm X against the Messenger was unheard of, even immediately after the minister had broken from the ranks of the Black Muslims. One veiled criticism, however, found its way into Essien-Udom's 1962 book about the Nation of Islam, although the significance of the comment cannot be appreciated without an understanding of the context behind it. When asked about the membership of the Nation, Malcolm X responded, "That is difficult to say. I would add, however, that New York has the largest active membership in the Nation; Los Angeles has the highest record attendance. I am distressed about the small membership in Chicago."[14] On the surface, this comment seems fairly innocuous, even though it is a criticism of the ability of the Muhammad's Chicago headquarters to attract members. But this response must be coupled with an observation that he made in his autobiography. "By late 1962, I learned reliably that numerous Muslims were leaving Mosque Number Two in Chicago. The ugly rumor [of Elijah Muhammad's adultery] was spreading swiftly—even among non-Muslim Negroes."[15] It seems likely that this comment on Chicago's membership problems was actually a veiled criticism against Elijah Muhammad for his adultery, although Malcolm X had not yet come to terms with it and had not yet confronted Muhammad with the rumor.

Malcolm X attempted to put some context behind his break with the Nation of Islam in his autobiography, although his account is certainly only a small portion of the picture. First, Malcolm X identified one of his key criticisms of the Nation of Islam: the lack of concerted action on the part of the Muslims. "If I harbored any personal disappointment whatsoever, it was that I was convinced that our Nation of Islam could be an even greater force in the American black man's overall struggle—if we engaged in more action. By that, I mean I thought privately that we should have amended, or relaxed, our general non-engagement policy." Malcolm X's attitude was the result of the criticism that "those Muslims *talk* tough, but they never *do* anything."[16] One of the stipulations of membership in the Nation of Islam was that Muslims were not allowed to engage in any civil rights activity, nor were they allowed to participate in community groups that were not affiliated with the Nation. In fact, one Boston Muslim was verbally attacked by Boston Minister Louis X when he joined a community group that protested police brutality against African-Americans.

Much of Malcolm X's criticism against the Nation's noninvolvement policy stemmed from an April 27, 1962, incident in Los Angeles in which an unarmed Muslim was killed unnecessarily by the police. Two police officers stopped two Muslims whom they believed were selling stolen suits from their car. In fact, the suits in question were being delivered to one of the Muslims from a dry-cleaning establishment. A scuffle that involved the two policemen and the Muslims ensued, which Malcolm X blamed on the policemen's overreaction to the "submissiveness of the Muslims." Reinforcements from both sides poured into the area as a passing officer called for help and Muslims from the nearby mosque realized what was happening. The "blazing gunfight" that followed left at least two patrolmen and six Muslims wounded and one Muslim, Ronald Stokes, dead. Stokes was shot through the heart by patrolman Donald Weese, despite the officer's subsequent admission that he knew Stokes was unarmed. A coroner's jury later ruled that the killing had been "justifiable homicide under lawful performance of duty and in self-defense."[17]

The Nation of Islam immediately denounced the tactics of the Los Angeles Police Department, and many Muslims awaited the word from Chicago to initiate an attack against the police. Malcolm X called the killing "one of the most ferocious, inhuman atrocities ever inflicted in a so-called 'democratic' and 'civilized' society," a somewhat exaggerated statement but one that expressed the anger of the Muslims.[18] "Meanwhile, back at Temple Twenty-seven, hundreds of blacks gathered, eagerly awaiting word from the Messenger to begin the Battle of Armageddon that Elijah Muhammad promised would end the era of white supremacy."[19] But instead of receiving instructions to attack the white devils, the Los Angeles Muslims received a message from Chicago that instructed them to stick with nonviolence:

Hold fast to Islam. Hold fast to Islam. Allah has promised that no devil will ever get away with the death of a Muslim. We are going out into the streets now to begin war with the devil. Not the kind of war he expects. . . .

No, we are going to let the world know he is the devil: we are going to sell newspapers.[20]

Although the Muslims initially complied with the Messenger's orders, increasing numbers would take revenge by beating and killing drunken whites coming out of bars on Skid Row. In response to the muted insurrection, Elijah Muhammad decided to send Malcolm X to Los Angeles, not to incite a war but to prevent it. Malcolm X sought to persuade the Muslims that Allah would take care of the injustice. "You will begin to see more automobile crashes on your freeways and I also feel that you will see aeroplane crashes that cannot be explained," he told one white reporter.[21] "This will be the work of God." When an airplane did crash over France the following weekend, Malcolm X announced:

> I got a wire from God today. Well, somebody came and told me that He had answered our prayers, over in France. He dropped an aeroplane out of the sky with one hundred and twenty people on it. Because Muslims believe in an eye for an eye and a tooth for a tooth.[22]

But despite Malcolm X's attempts to mollify the Muslims and deliver them from the brink of disaster, the evidence is clear that what he really wanted was a showdown with the police and white society. He had prepared to go to Los Angeles with the intent of leading the charge in the search for revenge, but the officials in Chicago prevented him from engaging himself and the L.A. Muslims in what could only be a bloody and futile attempt at justice. Before Malcolm X left for Los Angeles from New York, he told Lewis Michaux, a bookstore owner and vocal black nationalist, that "I got to go out there now and do what I've been preaching all this time," by which he presumably meant to seek revenge in self-defense.[23] One L.A. Muslim quoted Malcolm X as saying, "If the devil should ever kill a Muslim, he'll pay dearly. Allah has said . . . 'If the devil takes the least of mine, I will make the devil pay at the rate of ten of his very best.' "[24] An interview conducted by Peter Goldman with a Muslim from Los Angeles confirms this notion that Malcolm X actually sought maximum physical retaliation. " 'He wanted to do what most Muslims wanted to do—seek revenge,' a former member told me. 'You mean take heads?' I asked. He looked at me and nodded slowly." Malcolm X apparently later regretted that he had not used the opportunity of Ronald Stokes' death to engage in direct action. According to a Los Angeles Muslim who escorted the former Black Muslim on his final trip to California in early 1965, Malcolm X blamed his failure to act on direct orders from Chicago. Malcolm X later explained:

> Brother Jamal, I was sick myself. You know that I knew Brother Ronald [Stokes] in Boston. I knew his family. I had my orders. I didn't understand them then, but I did as I was told. We all did. What we wanted to do, couldn't be done. We were told that Allah would take care of things. We believed. We obeyed. Yes, I was angry with myself. I had thought that we would have moved. That was the one thing for which I am truly sorry.[25]

Although Malcolm X was forbidden to engage in action against the police in response to the Ronald Stokes killing, he nevertheless attempted to go beyond the traditional reluctance of the Muslims to participate in protest activity. In February 1963, he led a rush-hour march of Black Muslims through Times Square in New York to protest police pressure against Muslims in New York, where two Muslims were arrested for selling the Nation's newspapers, and Rochester, where the police conducted a raid on the local temple.[26] According to one of Malcolm X's aides, Charles Kenyatta, the New York minister was "so angry and depressed he didn't care what happened."[27] The march was as uncharacteristic for the Muslims as violent retaliation would have been for Martin Luther King, Jr. The protest reflected not a change in the policy of the Nation, but a shift in Malcolm X's attitudes away from those of Elijah Muhammad. Malcolm X began demonstrating a greater willingness to engage in direct action, although his ability to change was stifled by Elijah Muhammad.

Malcolm X's desire for a movement that was more action oriented became evident in his press conference on March 12, 1964, that announced his break from the Nation of Islam and his intention to create the Muslim Mosque, Incorporated.

> I myself intend to be very active in every phase of the American Negro's struggle for human rights. . . . Separation back to Africa is still a long-range program, and while it is yet to materialize, 22 million of our people who are still here in America need better food, clothing, housing, education and jobs right now. Mr. Muhammad's program does point us back homeward, but it also contains within it what we could and should be doing to help solve many of our own problems while we are still here.[28]

Further evidence of his desire to engage in direct action was his attendance at the August 1963 March on Washington. The official policy of the Nation of Islam was that there was to be no cooperation on the part of Muslims in organizing the event, and even Muslim attendance was banned. This was an extension of the general nonengagement policy that prohibited Black Muslims from taking part in civil rights activities. Given the attention the upcoming march was receiving in the media, the Nation of Islam went out of its way to ensure that Muslims would not participate. According to Malcolm X's public pronouncements, the March on Washington was the "Farce on Washington," a "picnic" rather than a protest, and an Oscar-award-winning performance for white marchers for pretending that they actually liked black people. He even threatened Muslims whose unions required attendance at the march, telling them that they had better call in sick that day.

But despite his threats against the Muslims, Malcolm X broke his own rule and attended the march. It was not a wholesale reversal on his part; he went under the pretense of discrediting the march and presenting the media with a more militant viewpoint. He took no part in the festivities, instead hanging around the fringes of the march and talking to any part of the mass of marchers and reporters that would listen. Spending much of his time circulating around the march headquarters at a local hotel, Malcolm X castigated the march leaders for selling out to their white "masters" while organizing the event, and boldly predicted that by the end of the day, "this dream of King's is going to be a nightmare."[29]

Although he spent much of his time in Washington attacking the march and its leaders, Malcolm's attendance demonstrated his internal struggle between his realization that direct action was a necessary weapon in the fight for African-American dignity and the constraints placed upon him by Elijah Muhammad and the Nation of Islam. Malcolm X had spent the past year lobbying the Messenger, trying to persuade him of the importance of direct action, but Muhammad had not budged. In November 1963 Muhammad finally put his foot down and forbade his "most faithful" minister from participating in any civil rights demonstrations.[30] Although the disagreement between the two never became public, this was the clearest sign to insiders that a break between Malcolm X and the Nation of Islam was imminent.

While he did not fully understand the depth of it, Malcolm X had, of course, realized that a substantial amount of jealousy was present on the part of Muslim officials in Chicago, as well as members of Elijah Muhammad's family. He had been forewarned by the Messenger early in his career that such jealousy would erupt, and although he did not understand it at the time, the prophecy had since come true. Opposition to Malcolm X came in the form of Muslim officials such as Raymond Sharrieff, the Supreme Captain of the FOI; John Ali, Malcolm X's onetime protégé who became the NOI's National Secretary in charge of finances; and Captain Joseph, the head of the New York Fruit of Islam. Malcolm X reported that as early as 1961 the jealousy was coming to the forefront. He began hearing bitter comments about "Malcolm's ministers," the Muslims whom Malcolm X had sent to establish temples across the country.[31] And then, after *Muhammad Speaks* was taken from his control, he saw mentions of his name in the Nation's newspaper become increasingly rare, apparently as a result of an order from Elijah's son, Herbert, that Malcolm X's activities be ignored.[32] "There was more in the Muslim paper about integrationist Negro 'leaders' than there was about me," Brother Malcolm griped. "I could read more about myself in the European, Asian, and African press."[33]

The high-profile image of Malcolm X was one of the major contributors to the envy that was directed at him from other Muslim officials. In the eyes of some, Malcolm X was more important to the movement than the Messenger, and this upset the natural order of the Nation of Islam. While it is difficult to gauge his overall importance to the movement, it is clear that Malcolm X certainly received more press than did his leader. In fact, one statistic from 1964 showed that he was the second most sought-after speaker on college campuses, behind only presidential candidate Barry Goldwater. The press quoted him more than the Messenger, the FBI followed him more than the Messenger, and various authors wrote about him more than the Messenger. While Elijah Muhammad was holed up in his Arizona home in his low-profile role of running the Nation of Islam, Malcolm X was in the process of writing his autobiography with Alex Haley, being interviewed by nationwide television programs and major magazines such as *Playboy*, and serving as the highly visible mouthpiece of the Muslim movement. In terms of name recognition across

MALCOLM X:
THE ASSASSINATION

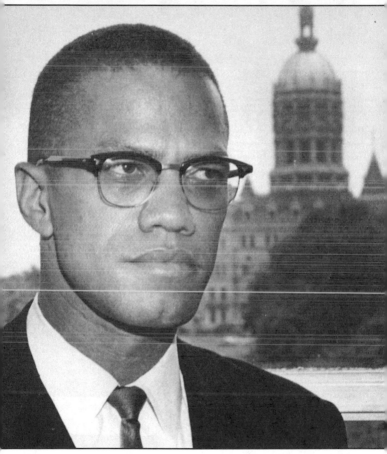

Malcolm X standing in front of the dome of the Connecticut
Capitol in Hartford during a visit in June 1963.
The Bettmann Archive

The Honorable Elijah Muhammad, the self-proclaimed "Messenger of Allah," during a Nation of Islam rally at Griffith Stadium in Washington, D.C.
UPI/Bettmann Newsphotos

Malcolm X talking with reporters during the trial of two members of the Nation of Islam in 1963. The two members were stopped by police for blocking a subway entrance in Times Square while selling *Muhammad Speaks*, the movement's newspaper.
UPI/Bettmann

Cassius Clay, the soon-to-be Muhammad Ali, delivering a crushing blow to heavyweight champion Sonny Liston. Clay went on to defeat Liston, declare his devotion to the Nation of Islam, and become a key trophy in the battle between Malcolm X and Elijah Muhammad.
UPI/Bettmann

Malcolm X getting out of his familiar blue Oldsmobile to inspect his firebombed house the week before he was assassinated.
UPI/Bettmann

Outside the Audubon Ballroom in Harlem, where Malcolm X was assassinated on February 21, 1965.
UPI/Bettmann

The bloody body of Malcolm X being carried across the street from the Audubon Ballroom to the Columbia Presbyterian Medical Center shortly after the fatal shooting. After unsuccessfully massaging his heart, doctors declared Malcolm X dead.
UPI/Bettmann

Betty Shabazz, Malcolm X's widow, leaving the city morgue after identifying her husband's body. At the time of the assassination, Mrs. Shabazz was pregnant with female twins, bringing the total to six daughters. At left is Percy Sutton, Malcolm X's attorney.
UPI/Bettmann

Talmadge Hayer, Malcolm X's assassin, being taken away to the Jewish Memorial Hospital on a stretcher after he was wounded in the leg at the scene of the killing.
UPI/Bettmann

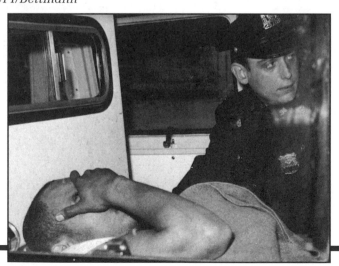

Norman 3X Butler after his February 26, 1965, arrest for Malcolm X's assassination. Butler is wearing the tweed coat that several witnesses reported seeing on one of the assassins.
UPI/Bettmann

Thomas 15X Johnson (center) being booked for first-degree murder in Malcolm X's assassination. Johnson was arrested after police interviewed Malcolm X's bodyguard Gary Thomas, who identified all three suspected assassins.
UPI/Bettmann

Actor Ossie Davis delivering the eulogy before Malcolm X's coffin and 1,000 followers at Faith Temple Church of God in Christ on February 27, 1965. "Harlem has come to bid farewell to one of its brightest hopes—extinguished now, and gone from us forever," Davis intoned.
UPI/Bettmann Newsphotos

the country, Malcolm X eclipsed his leader and mentor, and it was this fame that inspired the envy of Elijah Muhammad's retainers. This issue finally came out in a bitter conversation between Malcolm X and Elijah Muhammad in January 1964, after the New York minister had been silenced. According to the FBI, "Elijah mentioned an article from Los Angeles . . . which stated that Malcolm ruled the fence and had power over Elijah's family and Elijah did not like such stories."[34]

A second major factor in the onset of Muslim jealousy was the deterioration in the health of Elijah Muhammad. In 1961 the 64-year-old Muslim leader could barely even keep his public engagements because of the continual coughing and wheezing that plagued him. On the advice of his doctors, the Messenger moved to a drier climate and purchased a large house in Arizona, compliments of the Nation of Islam. Despite his status as a prophet of Allah, Muhammad had never made any claims of immortality, and because of his poor health, speculation abounded as to who would succeed him as the head of the Nation. The elder Muhammad had made it clear for a number of years before that his son Wallace was his choice as a successor. But the clarity in succession became markedly less pronounced as Malcolm X became a major focus of the movement. While the New York minister made no claims to the leadership of the movement in the Messenger's absence, speculation abounded that he had the power to take over the movement and would do so if given the opportunity. A further worry for the Muhammad clan was that Malcolm X's family would begin a dynasty in which Malcolm X and his brothers, Detroit minister Wilfred and Lansing minister Philbert, would overtake the Muhammad clan in its importance to the Muslim movement.

It is difficult to ascertain whether Malcolm X actually harbored such ambitions. He could certainly envision himself as the leader, changing a number of the more objectionable guidelines of the movement, such as the nonengagement policy. And even the FBI believed that he would try to take over the movement, stating in one report that one of their sources had reported that Malcolm X "desires to take over the NOI on death of Elijah Muhammad."[35] But the FBI also believed that Malcolm X would run for the Harlem Congressional seat held by Adam Clayton Powell, and this seems inconceivable, given Malcolm X's political orientation. Whereas Powell was a black liberal who fought from inside the system, Malcolm X was a black revolutionary who battled outside the system, and his conversion from Black Muslim to Congressional representative would probably never have happened. But whether or not Malcolm X actually sought to position himself as the next leader of the Muslims is not the point. What is significant is that Muslim officials believed that he was trying to do so, and the subsequent jealousy and resentment proved to be his undoing.

The FBI reports on Elijah Muhammad include a number of examples of Muslim officials attacking Malcolm X when talking to the Messenger. The FBI had an ideal opportunity to measure the sentiment against Malcolm X in Chicago, since it had a number of surveillance devices in Elijah Muhammad's home and office on South Woodlawn Avenue in Chicago. In one overheard telephone conversation that took place on March 25, 1963, the FBI reported that a Muslim official talking to the Messenger had attacked Malcolm X, telling Muhammad that "too much power had gone to his head."[36]

The first public sign of the tension that existed between Malcolm X and the Muslim officials in Chicago was their joint appearance onstage during the national convention and graduation ceremony for the University of Islam on February 26, 1963. Exactly what happened has not been definitively established.[37] Malcolm X monopolized the proceedings when Elijah Muhammad was forced to pull out of the program because of his health, and it was clear that Muhammad's family resented him for not allowing them to speak. According to the FBI informants who attended the graduation, Malcolm X's "speech was interrupted several times by an apparent request to allow Elijah's son Wallace Muhammad to speak. Subject refused to heed this request and stated that due to the late start it would not be possible for Wallace to speak."[38]

The FBI further stated in its report that "the family was especially resentful of subject's attempts to advise and tell the family what to do and of statements he was allegedly making against Elijah and his family."[39] Malcolm X apparently further aggravated the family when he remained in Chicago long after the convention was over, consulting with Elijah Muhammad and conducting his normal hectic schedule of appearances with the media. Finally, according to the FBI, Muhammad asked Malcolm X to return to New York, which he quickly did after canceling the remainder of his scheduled public appearances in Chicago.

According to Malcolm X, however, the graduation ceremony only demonstrated that many Muslims were aware of the Messenger's infidelity, as they showed a remarkable animosity toward his family. The Muslims did not demand to hear Wallace Muhammad speak instead of Malcolm X; in fact, they demonstrated their disdain for the Muhammad family, Malcolm X believed. "In February, 1963, I officiated at the University of Islam graduation exercises; when I introduced various members of the Muhammad family, I could feel the cold chill toward them from the Muslims in the audience."[40] It is likely that neither version of the event was really incorrect, but that they represented different interpretations of what happened. Malcolm X, who was by this time painfully aware of Mr. Muhammad's extramarital affairs, knew that many Chicago Muslims also knew of his adulteries and interpreted the incident as a condemnation of the Muhammad family. The resentment toward Malcolm X at this time was also well developed, and Muhammad's relatives may have interpreted some coolness from the audience as an anti-Malcolm sentiment. What the incident did show, however, was that the mutual animosity had now become public, and that the antagonism was feeding upon itself, causing different interpretations of the same event.

The relations between Malcolm X and Muhammad were dealt another setback in April 1963, when an article in *The New York Times* gave more credit to Malcolm X for the rise in black nationalism across the country than to Elijah Muhammad. The article, written by M. S. Handler, contained one statement that particularly galled Muhammad and his family. "Malcolm X, who is of impressive bearing and is endowed with a shrewd mind, today overshadows Elijah Muhammad." The article proceeded to outline a portion of Malcolm X's philosophy, and the reactions of more moderate civil rights leaders to Malcolm X, with hardly a mention of his supposed boss, Mr. Muhammad. Also included with the article was a prominent mug shot of Malcolm X with the caption, "BLACK MUSLIM HEAD: Malcolm X, leader of extremist group in New York," which implied that he was the leader of the Black Muslims.

A further blow to amiable relations came with the publication of Louis Loma's book, *When the Word Is Given*, which detailed some of the inner workings of the movement. Lomax printed a number of Malcolm X's speeches and seemed to portray him—rather than Elijah Muhammad—as the most important Muslim in the Nation of Islam. The FBI noticed the changes in relations and included a report in Malcolm X's file that detailed the rising resentment toward the New York Muslim representative. "On several dates during March, April and May, 1963 [Bureau deletion] advised that there continues to be a feeling of hostility and resentment between [Malcolm X] and members of Elijah Muhammad's family."[41]

If the jealousy of Muslim officials and the differences in doctrine between Malcolm X and Elijah Muhammad were the problems that set the stage for a split in the movement, then it was the specific issue of the paternity suits against Elijah Muhammad that finally brought down the curtain on the reverent relationship that had lasted for almost fifteen years. Malcolm X said he had first heard rumors of the adultery back in 1955, only three years after he received his

"X" from Chicago, but he was not able to confirm the rumors and confront the Messenger with them for another eight years.[42] The Nation had been plagued for a number of years by these rumors that centered around a string of the Messenger's unmarried secretaries who had suddenly become pregnant. These women were then brought up on charges of having premarital affairs and banished from the Nation of Islam. It was, of course, never confirmed who the father of these children was while the women were on trial, although it was obvious to those within Muhammad's inner circle that the resemblance that the children bore to the Messenger was no mere coincidence. Malcolm X's confirmation that Elijah Muhammad had fathered the children destroyed his faith in Muhammad as divine prophet and set the wheels in motion for his exile from the Nation.

Malcolm X's realization that the rumors were true undermined everything in which he had believed for the past fifteen years. The confirmation of the rumors did not come easily. He had heard the whisperings for years, and only slowly began putting the pieces together. As he began to catch on to the truth, he was forced to accept that the moral system that he had adopted was created by someone whom he began to see as an immoral hypocrite. His inner turmoil remained inside of him, as he was unable to reconcile his professed obedience to the Messenger with his newfound knowledge. One incident that Betty Shabazz discussed in a recent article for *Essence* magazine brought the truth home to her husband, as he was finally forced to accept that Mr. Muhammad was not the moral model that he appeared to be.

Malcolm always dismissed the rumors—he believed people were just talking. What happened is that he had gone to Detroit to Elijah Muhammad's house and met three young women and their children standing on the front porch.[43] All the children looked like they had a common father. The women wanted their children to go to school, and they needed Elijah Muhammad's signature or needed to use his name. Muhammad would not give his name—he wouldn't even let the women in the house. Malcolm called me that night. "The foundation of my life seems to be coming apart," he told me.[44]

According to his autobiography, when Malcolm X confirmed his suspicions with Wallace Muhammad, he began to preach less and less about the subject of morality, choosing to focus more on racial relations or the hypocrisy of white society. His entire moral system had been undermined to the point that he was unsure of the basis of his beliefs. "And the reason for this was that my faith had been shaken in a way that I can never fully describe. For I had discovered Muslims had been betrayed by Elijah Muhammad himself."[45] The FBI quoted him as saying on a radio program in June 1964 that "as long as he [Malcolm X] believed the Muslims stood for moral reformation, he was able to represent Muhammad, but he could not do so once Muhammad shattered it."[46]

But his final realization of Muhammad's adultery did nothing to ease the storm that had been brewing inside of him. Rather, the knowledge made him essentially impotent as a leader while he battled with himself over what to do. His acceptance of the "fulfillment of prophecy" explanation for Muhammad's behavior could last only so long, and when this acceptance faded, he was confronted with a dramatic choice. He certainly could have left the movement, but Elijah Muhammad was his reformer, his mentor, his lifeblood. Leaving would have meant abandoning his power base and turning a swarm of angry and faithful Muslims against him. By the same token, his continuation in the movement would have turned him into a hypocrite because he would have to teach a moral framework whose creator violated it. The decision, however, was finally made at the end of 1963 not by Malcolm X, but by Muhammad himself, as Minister Malcolm was suspended and effectively banished from the Nation of Islam.

It was the mutual mistrust between Malcolm X and the

Muslim officials that finally forced the paternity issue to become a major factor in the New York minister's exile from the Nation of Islam. As with his conduct at the graduation ceremony a few months before, Malcolm X's actions surrounding his discovery of Muhammad's adultery were carefully scrutinized—and misinterpreted—by the Muslim officials in Chicago. His moves were perfectly reasonable given his position and the need for him to know the full extent of the crisis, but his actions also could easily be perceived by his enemies as an attempt to escalate the crisis rather than to avoid it. Malcolm X's first confirmation of the rumor came from Elijah Muhammad's son Wallace, who had known for some time of his father's deception. In one interview with a Massachusetts radio station on June 12, 1964, Malcolm X stated that it was Wallace who first told him the secret of the Messenger's adultery, but actually Wallace merely confirmed what Malcolm X already knew.[47] Several members of Muhammad's family were surprised that Malcolm X knew so little about the affairs. Betty Shabazz reported that when he returned from Chicago once in 1963, her husband "told me that some of Elijah Muhammad's relatives had said to him, 'We thought you knew. We thought you *knew*.' "[48] According to his autobiography,

There was no one I could turn to with this problem, except Mr. Muhammad himself. Ultimately that had to be the case. But first I went to Chicago to see Mr. Muhammad's second son, Wallace Muhammad. . . . And Wallace knew, when he saw me, why I had come to see him. "I know," he said. I said I thought we should rally to help his father. Wallace said he didn't feel that his father would welcome any efforts to help him. I told myself that Wallace must be crazy.[49]

Malcolm X's next move was to confirm the story with three of the secretaries who allegedly had given birth to Muhammad's children. The need to verify the rumor was crucial before he confronted Elijah Muhammad, because to accuse the Messenger of such a sin without corroboration would have meant the end of Malcolm X's tenure in the movement if the rumor were not true. But approaching the secretaries was a risky move for Malcolm X. The Muslim code stipulated that once Muslims had been excommunicated, as happened to the secretaries when they became pregnant out of wedlock, no other Muslim in good standing could have any contact with them. Malcolm X took this rule seriously and was not likely to flaunt it without reasonable cause. Years earlier, when his younger brother was exiled from the ranks of the Muslims, Malcolm X had refused to talk to him despite their shared blood. When he finally did confront the secretaries, they confirmed his worst fear, telling the story of his leader's duplicity.

Malcolm X's justification for these actions and for confronting Muhammad with his knowledge seemed to be a necessary first step in crisis management. "As long as I did nothing, I felt it was the same as being disloyal. I felt that as long as I sat down, I was not helping Mr. Muhammad—when somebody needed to be standing up," he wrote.[50] Malcolm X was not the type of person who could simply wait to see how events unfolded; he had to be an active participant, in this case making sure that the Messenger's adultery did not cripple the movement. But his attempts to investigate the paternity charges came back to haunt him as Muslim officials discovered his actions and sought to capitalize upon his curiosity. They billed his actions as traitorous and accused him of trying to depose the Messenger and take over the Nation of Islam by spreading false rumors about their leader. Just as the FBI sought to discredit Elijah Muhammad, these Muslim officials sought to spread misinformation about Malcolm X, thus removing him from the chain of command and ensuring that he would never succeed Muhammad as the leader of the Nation of Islam.

Malcolm X was finally able to confront Muhammad with the rumors in April 1963. After writing Muhammad a letter that outlined the "poison" that was being said about him,

Malcolm X got a phone call from the Messenger, who told him that they would talk about it when they next saw each other. Meanwhile, Malcolm X and Wallace Muhammad began researching the Bible and the Koran for examples of respected leaders with personal weaknesses, so that these parts of the scriptures could be taught as prophecy. In the next few weeks, Malcolm X began priming the Muslims in New York with lessons that individual weaknesses in a person's character were less important than his overall accomplishments, although he was careful never to explain why he had changed his preachings. When he finally did see Muhammad at his house in Arizona, Malcolm X finally bluntly stated what he had heard and what he had done in the past weeks to try to anticipate further revelations.

Muhammad's response to the allegations left Malcolm X reeling. He made no apologies for his actions, instead choosing to adopt the same false front that Malcolm X and Wallace had constructed with their research on the Scriptures. He accepted no fault for his activities, instead giving the impression that it was something that was not under his control.

> "I'm David," he said. "When you read about how David took another man's wife, I'm that David. You read about Noah, who got drunk—that's me. You read about Lot, who went and laid up with his own daughters. I have to fulfill all of those things."[51]

Malcolm X's next move was a critical mistake, one that allowed his enemies in the movement to prove to the Messenger that Malcolm X was conspiring against him. When he returned to New York from Phoenix, Malcolm X assembled some of the leaders of various East Coast mosques to prepare them for the upcoming crisis. Although he soon realized that the rumor had not spread far outside Chicago, he was surprised to find that a number of the assembled ministers had already encountered the rumors and had been trying to figure out how to react to the news. Louis X, the minister of the Boston mosque, had known even before Malcolm X had confirmed the rumor. The purpose of the meeting, according to Malcolm X, was to reveal the research that he and Wallace had done on the Scriptures, in order to organize the opposition to the rumor and to prepare the official line of the Muslims in case Muhammad's adultery was revealed. But Malcolm X made the mistake of not anticipating how the jealousy of other Muslim officials would interfere with his attempts to manage the crisis.

> I never dreamed that the Chicago Muslim officials were going to make it appear that I was throwing gasoline on the fire instead of water. I never dreamed that they were going to try to make it appear that instead of innoculating against an epidemic, I had started it.[52]

Even though he was aware that others were conspiring against him, Malcolm X still did not realize that he was in no position to take the lead in this crisis, particularly when it dealt with something as sensitive as Muhammad's adultery. While he could still serve as the official mouthpiece of the movement, the Messenger's personal life was off-limits to him. The fear of Muslim officials surrounding Muhammad that Malcolm X would try to use his new information in an attempt to discredit the Messenger and take power for himself translated into a vengeful attempt to turn the tables. Instead of discussing the actions of Muhammad, the Muslim officials succeeded in making a larger issue out of Malcolm X's actions. With their proximity to their leader, these officials were able to convince Muhammad that his New York minister did not have his best interests in mind. In an organization such as the Nation of Islam, where respect for authority was preeminent, such independence from the Messenger's best interests could be a fatal affliction.

CHAPTER EIGHT

The Split

"I only [suspended Malcolm X] because I knew that he was not going to accept it. And I said, 'Just keep quiet for 90 days.' And he would not do it, and I knew he would not do it because he felt that he would be losing his prestige."

—*Elijah Muhammad*

The rift that had been developing between Elijah Muhammad and his chief minister finally erupted publicly on December 4, 1963, as the nation mourned the death of its president, John F. Kennedy. The president's November 22 assassination in Dallas set in motion the events that would finally result in the assassination of one of Kennedy's harshest and most uncompromising critics, Malcolm X. Malcolm X continually castigated the president as another one of the white devils who displayed a sympathetic facade toward the civil rights movement that hid his inner racism. John F. Kennedy was the sly fox who courted the African-American vote in the 1960 election, only to betray blacks in the end, while the wolf Richard M. Nixon was honest and openly demonstrated his disdain for civil rights. It was an analogy that Malcolm X loved to use, and he applied it again in 1964 when the fox Lyndon B. Johnson ran against the wolf Barry Goldwater. Like most Muslims, Malcolm X had no love for the slain president, and it was his refusal to do an about-face with the rest of the Muslim leadership and mourn the fallen president that finally drove the permanent wedge between himself and his Prophet.

The battle within the Nation of Islam was clearly not over the attitude toward the slain president. Everyone inside and outside the Black Muslims knew that there was no love lost over the death of another "devil." Rather, the controversy represented the war between Malcolm X and Elijah Muhammad, as well as his retainers. The suspension was only the first shot in the conflict. Over the next year, the conflict went through a number of distinct phases, as Malcolm X attempted to come to terms with what had happened, and belatedly decided to set out on his own. The rhetoric against Malcolm X was violent and served as a call to individual Muslims to murder their former minister. Even if there was not a direct order for Talmadge Hayer and his co-conspirators to act as they did, they did receive an indirect order from the vicious words of Muhammad and his Muslim ministers. Those threats set the stage for Malcolm X's death, portraying him as the "chief hypocrite" who was "worthy of death." The responsibility for the death of Malcolm X must be shared not only by the gunmen, but by the Muslim leadership who made his death inevitable. The assassination of Malcolm X cannot be divorced from the context of this struggle within the Black Muslim world, and an understanding of the events of Malcolm X's final year is necessary for a complete understanding of his death. It was the forces acting within this struggle that defined his final year, as he was forced to act and react in accordance with the struggle, and it was this conflict that finally brought him to his death.

The stage for the controversy was the Manhattan Center in New York City, where Elijah Muhammad was scheduled to speak before 700 Muslims and members of the press on December 1, 1963, only nine days after the president's assassination. As often happened in those days, Muhammad abruptly canceled the engagement, and Malcolm X stepped in, so as not to forfeit the money already spent to rent the auditorium. The Muslim minister seemed particularly agi-

tated about the content of his speech for that day; for the
first time in the memory of his associates, he typed out the
speech ahead of time and read from note cards instead of
speaking off the cuff as he always did. The sensitivity necessary for the topic that he proposed to address was the
most likely reason for his unusual preparation. The subject
of his speech was "God's Judgment on White America," in
which he attacked white liberals, including the dead president, for being disingenuous with the "Negro" populations
that were often the deciding votes in close elections, as in
1960. As he constructed his speech, Malcolm X must have
kept in mind the two directives sent by Elijah Muhammad
in the wake of the assassination that the Nation of Islam's
official stance on the president and his murder would be silence. According to Malcolm X, during his speech:

> It is easy to understand why the presidential candidates
> of both political parties put on such a false show with the
> Civil Rights Bill and with false promises of integration.
> They must impress the 3 million voting Negroes who are
> the actual "integration seekers" . . . The white liberals
> control the Negro and the Negro vote by controlling the
> Negro civil rights leaders. As long as they control the Ne-
> gro civil rights leaders, they can also control and contain
> the Negro struggle, as they can control the Negro's so-
> called "revolt." The Negro revolution is controlled by foxy
> white liberals, by the Government itself. But the Black
> Revolution is controlled only by God.[1]

Despite the criticism of the president and his policies, it
was not Malcolm X's formal speech that invoked the ire of
Elijah Muhammad and the rest of America. The question-
and-answer period began with the "inevitable" question of
Malcolm X's opinion on the Kennedy assassination. According to the autobiography, "without a second thought, I
said what I honestly felt—that it was, as I saw it, a case of
'the chickens coming home to roost.' "[2] He then went on to
condemn the president for "twiddling his thumbs" as the

president of South Vietnam, Ngo Dinh Diem, and his brother, Ngo Dinh Nhu, were murdered with the complicity of the American government. He also cited the assassinations of Congo leader Patrice Lumumba and Mississippi NAACP leader Medgar Evers as evidence of the rising tide of violence of whites against blacks. It was, in fact, a prophetic statement on the increasing violence that was then sweeping America, originating with the violence of white against black and culminating with the assassination of the president of the United States. Had he restricted his remarks to such political commentary, he most likely would not have generated the storm of criticism that he eventually received. But instead he elaborated on his early "chickens coming home to roost" comment that gave the impression that he was gloating about the death of the president. Amid laughter and applause, he added, "being an old farm boy myself, chickens coming home to roost never did make me sad; they've always made me glad."[3]

Malcolm X later protested that the media took this comment out of context in which he placed it. The comment, he argued, should be viewed in relation to his comments concerning the escalation of violence in America. The media reports of his speech "took all the salt out of the bread and presented only the salt."[4] But regardless of the context, Malcolm X had shown apparent pleasure at the death of an American hero, a killing that wrenched the American psyche and caused the greatest outpouring of shock and raw grief since the 1941 bombing of Pearl Harbor by Japan. His comments would have been acceptable and insightful to much of America if he had not added his own personal opinion of John F. Kennedy. But Malcolm X cannot be blamed for presenting his own viewpoint, as painful as it was for Americans to hear. Kennedy was no friend of the Muslims. He represented the leader of the devils, an enemy with overwhelming influence and power. His death was not an event to mourn, but one to celebrate. According to the Muslims, the death of every devil was a positive step for the black world, and the death of one of the most powerful

devils in the world was certainly not a cause to mourn. All
Malcolm X did was articulate these feelings, as he did with
many of the unpopular beliefs that the Muslims held.

Malcolm X's crime was not that he offended mainstream
society, for the goal of the Nation of Islam was certainly not
to cater to whites and conservative blacks. The reason for his
downfall was that he directly defied Elijah Muhammad, his
superior. Muhammad had specifically stated to his ministers
on two occasions that no mention was to be made of the late
president or of his assassination. To say what the Muslims
really felt would have been to evoke the outrage of a dolor-
ous nation, but actively mourning the president's death with
the rest of the country would have violated everything in
which the Muslims believed. Silence was the most reasonable policy, but it was never one of Malcolm X's strongest
points. Some observers have contended that Malcolm X purposely made provocative statements in order to challenge
Muhammad's directives and Muhammad himself, but it
seems more likely that he had simply voiced his sentiments
without regard to the consequences.

The consequences were severe for the high-ranking
Muslim. Three days after the speech, on December 4, 1963,
Malcolm X flew to Chicago on a routine trip to see Elijah
Muhammad. According to Malcolm X's recollection,
Muhammad told his most devoted follower that "that was
a very bad statement. The whole country loved this man.
The whole country is in mourning. That was very ill-timed.
A statement like that can make it hard on Muslims in gen-
eral." The next words out of Muhammad's mouth caught
Malcolm X entirely by surprise:

And then, as if Mr. Muhammad's voice came from
afar, I heard his words: "I'll have to silence you for the
next ninety days—so that the Muslims everywhere can
be disassociated from the blunder." I was numb. But I
was a follower of Mr. Muhammad. Many times I had
said to my own assistants that anyone in a position to
discipline others must be able to take disciplining him-

self. I told Mr. Muhammad, "Sir, I agree with you, and I submit, one hundred percent."[5]

The aftermath of Malcolm X's suspension was rife with some of the same misunderstandings that had been first seen publicly at the 1963 annual convention, and they served to widen the rift between the two former allies and lessen the possibility of any type of reconciliation. The first misunderstanding came on the part of Malcolm X, as he flew back to New York from Phoenix, believing that his suspension would be a routine disciplining of a top aide. When he returned, he discovered the extent of the planning that had taken place before his suspension. As he prepared to brief his assistants on his silencing, he realized that they had already been notified by officials in Chicago, an unusual step in a routine silencing. But soon he discovered an even greater slap in the face from his Chicago rivals; not only had his assistants been notified, but the media as well, in a telegram that read:

Have suspended for the present time Minister Malcolm Shabazz of New York because of statements made Sunday, Dec. 1 at Manhattan Center. Minister Malcolm did not speak for Muhammad, the Nation of Islam or any of Mr. Muhammad's followers. The correct statement on the death of the President is: "We with the world are very shocked at the assassination of President Kennedy."[6]

A further unexpected insult to Malcolm X was the extension of his silencing to include not only public appearances, but also his lectures to the Muslim faithful within the New York mosque. Originally, Malcolm X saw the silencing as an opportunity to concentrate his efforts on his own congregation. "I am the minister of the mosque and I shall be carrying out my responsibilities for the mosque whatever they may entail," he told *The New York Times*. "I will just exclude public speaking engagements."[7] But he did not share this view with Elijah Muhammad, who quickly made it known that Malcolm X's silencing included speaking before the New York Muslims. Strategically, this order removed Malcolm X's power base and alienated him from the New York Muslims who had been his source of inspiration. Rumors began circulating within days of the suspension that Elijah Muhammad intended to replace Malcolm X permanently as the minister of the New York Mosque Number 7. A December 6 article in *The New York Times* cited "sources . . . in close contact with many key members of the mosque" that Muhammad had a list of possible successors for Malcolm X that included his son Akbar Muhammad, Lonnie X of the Washington mosque, and Jeremiah X of the Birmingham mosque. "I know of no such rumors," Malcolm X responded. The suspended Muslim was criticized by these sources as having "emerged as a 'personality' rather than as a spokesman for the movement."[8]

The media immediately grabbed the story and barraged Malcolm X with questions of whether this decree indicated a split between himself and Muhammad. With as much composure as he could muster, he calmly told them that he was still the Honorable Elijah Muhammad's most devoted follower and that he submitted completely to the Messenger's wisdom. "I shouldn't have said what I did," Malcolm X admitted. "Anything that Mr. Muhammad does is alright with me; I believe absolutely in his wisdom and his authority."[9] And to *Newsweek* magazine: "I'm in complete submission to any judgment Mr. Muhammad makes. I should have kept my big mouth shut."[10] The *New York Amsterdam News* was told, "Yes, I'm wrong. I disobeyed Muhammad's order. He was justified 100 percent. I agree I need to withdraw from public appearance."[11] But an unusual statement came next from Chicago, announcing to the press that Malcolm X would be reinstated to the Nation after 90 days *if he submitted* to the Messenger, despite the fact that Malcolm X made clear to his leader and to the press that he already had submitted in no uncertain terms. Later, in an interview with *The New York Times*, Elijah Muhammad hedged on whether Malcolm X would be reinstated after his term of silencing was over. "I would not say [when he would be reinstated]. I will decide," he declared.[12]

"This made me suspicious—for the first time," Malcolm X wrote in his autobiography. "I had completely submitted. But, deliberately, Muslims were being given the impression that I had rebelled. I hadn't hustled in the streets for years for nothing. I knew when I was being set up."[13] Malcolm X was slowly beginning to realize that his suspension was not a routine disciplinary action against a Muslim who made a mistake. Rather, the action was a premeditated attempt to cut off his power base in case he had ambitions to succeed Elijah Muhammad as the leader of the Muslims. It is doubtful that Mr. Muhammad intended to remove Malcolm X permanently, particularly in the light of Muhammad's emotionalism when his former protégé announced that he was breaking from the Nation of Islam. Rather, Muhammad most likely sought simply to send Malcolm X the message that he was still supreme; despite his higher profile across the country, Malcolm X was still subordinate to the Messenger. But the message had a different effect. Instead of seeing it as a simple reminder of the hierarchy of the Nation, Malcolm X viewed it as proof of the conspiracy of Chicago officials against him. He blamed not Mr. Muhammad for the disgrace of his suspension, but instead the officials who surrounded the Messenger for implanting the idea in the leader's head that Malcolm X needed discipline.

Malcolm X and Elijah Muhammad were able to discuss many of their differences in a face-to-face meeting in Chicago on the day after New Year's Day, 1964. Malcolm X apparently expected to meet with the Messenger by himself, but throughout the meeting Muhammad was flanked by two of Malcolm X's greatest enemies in the movement: Raymond Sharrieff and John Ali.[14] Instead of clearing the air between Muhammad and his New York minister, the meeting was a battleground, with the Messenger throwing verbal assaults and Malcolm X trying desperately to defend himself. Malcolm X was clearly overmatched throughout the discussion; although he continually professed his loyalty to Muhammad, he could scarcely counter the contention that he was meddling in the Messenger's private life. The FBI secretly recorded the conversation and included a summary in one of its reports on Elijah Muhammad. Although it is often difficult to understand the summary, it remains as the only record of the conversation.

Elijah Muhammad began the conversation with a series of parables and pronouncements that "he has followed everything Allah has told him." After reminding Malcolm X of how Muhammad had gotten him started in New York, the "Messenger of Allah" told him that "he had been hearing about Malcolm this and Malcolm that and even Malcolm being called leader. Elijah said now this one and that one is getting jealous." In an attempt to explain his comments on Kennedy's assassination, Malcolm X "stated he had asked permission in a letter before he said anything and he understood it was all right. Elijah stated he certainly didn't say any such thing." The subject of Elijah Muhammad's extramarital affairs monopolized much of the discussion, with Muhammad demanding to know "why Malcolm had been checking into Elijah's personal affairs." Malcolm X responded that he had not been actively seeking information, but instead heard rumors from a number of different sources. He told his mentor that most people that he talked to already knew about the rumors and that he did nothing to spread them. But Muhammad refused to believe him. "He told Malcolm he could not walk through the woods with a fire and not start a fire. He said one must carry a bucket of water and not fire."

It was clear from the conversation that Elijah Muhammad had already made up his mind on many of the issues that surrounded Malcolm X's suspension, and cared little about hearing Malcolm X's side of the story. Indeed, in FBI eavesdropping reports prior to the meeting between the two combating Muslims, it is apparent that Muhammad took the view that Malcolm X was usurping power and sought to discredit him through spreading the rumors of his adultery.

In a conversation with a Muslim from Baltimore on New Year's Eve, 1963, Muhammad said that "the man on the East Coast [Minister Malcolm] had been telling . . . some rotten stuff. . . . [Muhammad] said Malcolm was only out for 'grandishment.' "[15] Muhammad went on to warn the Baltimore Muslim that "any laborer or minister that takes any of this poison [adultery rumors] shall be removed at once." And, in a final demonstration of his determination to ruin Malcolm X, Muhammad declared that "he would not let a man like that [Malcolm X] mess him up with 20 million people," referring to the African-American population of the United States.

"My head felt like it was bleeding inside. I felt like my brain was damaged" as a result of the suspension, Malcolm X reported.[16] Having been relieved of his duties as minister of the New York mosque, he took his doctor's advice and went on vacation. He spent his time in Florida, where he attended the training camp of Cassius Clay. Clay was scheduled to challenge Sonny Liston for the heavyweight championship of the world. On the day after his win over Liston, Clay shocked the world by announcing that he was a member of the Nation of Islam whose true name was Muhammad Ali. Malcolm X was billed as Clay's "spiritual advisor" and the man who brought Clay into the ranks of the Nation of Islam. To Malcolm X, the fight between Clay and Liston represented a battle between Islam and Christianity, in which Islam would inevitably prevail. Malcolm X reminded Clay that Allah had already willed that he would win the fight and that He would use this boxing match to bring instant worldwide recognition to the Nation of Islam and its leader, Elijah Muhammad. But Muhammad and his officials in Chicago failed to see it in this light. First, the Chicago Muslims criticized Malcolm X for his attendance at a sports event, which was strictly forbidden in the highly regulated Nation of Islam—or at least until Cassius Clay came along. Sports, according to the Messenger, "cause delinquency, murder, theft and other forms of wicked and immoral crimes."[17] Second, they attacked the besieged New

York minister behind his back as linking the Nation of Islam to a losing cause. Clay, an unheralded underdog, was about to fight the undisputed—and seemingly unbeatable—heavyweight champion of the world, and no respectable commentator saw much of a chance of Clay beating Liston.

A further worry for Muslim officials in Chicago was that Malcolm X might try to wean Muhammad Ali away from the Nation of Islam and use him as the basis of a new, rival organization. The combination of Malcolm X and Muhammad Ali would have enormous appeal not only to Muslims but to African-Americans across the country, and their potential unification was a direct threat to the well-being of the Nation of Islam. As it was, none of the various fears of the Muslim officials came to fruition, and in fact Malcolm X's attendance at the Clay-Liston bout proved to be an enormous boon to the Nation. The fight was almost canceled because of the negative publicity surrounding Malcolm X's presence, and the controversy was settled only when the Muslim minister promised to leave Clay's training camp for New York and return later for the fight. When Clay upset the champion with a knockout, his subsequent announcement that he was a Muslim brought instant publicity to the Nation of Islam and brought the organization a worldwide recognition that it had previously lacked. It also gave the Nation a high-profile personality to replace the one that it was about to lose when Malcolm X announced his break from the Nation on March 8, 1964.

Malcolm X's vacation in Florida served as the perfect opportunity to reflect upon his role in the Nation of Islam and the potential for starting a new religious group, one that would preach—and fight for—the goals of black nationalism. It was early in his suspension that he first began contemplating the possibility of becoming independent, although he kept his plans secret until it was clear that Elijah Muhammad would not invite him back into the Nation after his suspension was due to end. Peter Bailey, a friend of Malcolm X's who was in the audience during the assassination, later reported that Malcolm X had begun to think of forming his own black nationalist party even before he attended Clay's training camp. "In the latter part of December or early January, a friend of mine approached me and said, 'How would you like to be part of a new organization?' . . . It was all very secretive. She called me, told me where to meet and what time. . . . We sat around and talked for a while. And then in walks Brother Malcolm. . . . That's when I found out he was planning on forming an organization where people like myself, who were non-Muslim, could work with his program."[18]

Malcolm X's decision to leave the Nation was less the result of a personal conviction that he wanted to start out on his own than it was the result of being forced into the realization that he would be unable to rejoin and reform the Nation of Islam. To Malcolm X, the Nation of Islam was the most important organization in the reformation of the Afro-American, an indispensable tool on the road to recovery. But he soon realized that it was a tool that he was forbidden to wield ever again. While his instincts told him to continue fighting for change from within the Nation, the choice between staying and leaving was clearly not his. His ninety-day suspension was due to expire in early March, but as the day approached, it became increasingly clear to Malcolm X that the Messenger had little intention of returning the crucial Harlem mosque to a minister with ambiguous loyalties. When Malcolm X did not receive an invitation to the annual Nation of Islam convention in late February, the New York minister called the Messenger to request a clarification of his status. In reply, Muhammad sent a letter to New York that purposely failed to elucidate the situation. "At the Cassius Clay fight camp, I told the various sportswriters repeatedly what I gradually had come to know within myself was a lie—that I would be reinstated within ninety days. But I could not let myself psychologically face what I knew: that already the Nation of Islam and I were physically divorced."[19]

Before he left the organization formally, Malcolm X tried in vain to recruit some of the higher-profile Muslims who would be enormous assets to him in the creation of a rival black-nationalist group. His main target was Cassius Clay, who quickly made it known that he had no intention of leaving the Messenger of Allah for a disgraced Muslim minister. According to Jim Brown, the famed football player who attended the Clay-Liston fight and soon became friends with Muhammad Ali:

> Malcolm was planning to leave the Nation of Islam because of a falling-out with Elijah Muhammad, and wanted Ali to come with him. . . . [Ali] took me to a little black motel with Malcolm and the three or four other Muslim ministers. Malcolm said to me, "Well, Brown, don't you think it's time for this young man to stop spouting off and get serious?" And I agreed, but that night made it clear to me that Malcolm's swan song was coming as far as Ali was concerned. Ali took me into a back room. And he told me how Elijah Muhammad was such a little man physically but such a great man, and he was going to have to reject Malcolm and choose Elijah.[20]

The break between Malcolm and the Nation of Islam finally occurred on March 8, 1964, although the ultimate split was obvious to insiders weeks before it became public. Elijah Muhammad's failure to invite Malcolm X to attend the Muslims' annual convention, held on February 24, 1964 in Chicago, was the final straw. The ninety-day suspension ended officially on March 3, 1964, with no sign of the Messenger's willingness to budge from his position. The break came in the form of a press release that Malcolm X gave to the media, formally announcing that "I have reached the conclusion that I can best spread Mr. Muhammad's message by staying out of the Nation of Islam and continuing to work on my own among America's 22 million non-Muslim Negroes." He announced that he would work to form a "black nationalist party" and would "cooperate in local civil rights actions in the South and elsewhere."[21] He justified his break with the analogy that "it's hard to make a rooster stop crowing once the sun has risen."[22] He slighted the Nation of Islam by telling reporters that jealousy had been the reason for his leaving the Muslims, saying that "envy blinds men and makes it impossible for them to think clearly. This is what happened."[23] But in a major concession to Muhammad, he advised his Muslim brethren that they "stay in the Nation of Islam under the spiritual guidance of Elijah Muhammad."[24] At the press conference, Malcolm X also passed out to reporters a copy of a telegram that he had sent to the Messenger in which he praised his former leader as the teacher who gets "full credit for what I know and who I am."[25]

Four days later, Malcolm X scheduled another press conference to announce the formation of his Muslim Mosque, Inc., a new religious organization that would serve as his black-nationalist party. "Our political philosophy will be black nationalism," he declared. "Our economic and social philosophy will be black nationalism. Our cultural emphasis will be black nationalism." Speaking of his former organization, he announced that "internal differences within the Nation of Islam forced me out of it. I did not leave of my own free will. But now that it has happened, I intend to make the most of it. Now that I have independence of action, I intend to use a more flexible approach toward working with others to get a solution to this problem." As in his announcement of his break with the Nation of Islam, he pointedly professed his respect and adoration for the Messenger, clarifying that it was the Messenger's cronies and not the man himself who was at the root of the dispute. And again he indicated that he would continue teaching the lessons that had been taught to him by the Honorable Elijah Muhammad. "I am and always will be a Muslim. My religion is Islam. I still believe that Mr. Muhammad's analysis of the problem is the most realistic, and that his solution is the best one."[26]

But despite the conciliatory language, the all-out war between Malcolm X and the Muslim hierarchy had just begun. In an interview with the *Amsterdam News*, Malcolm X blasted members of Muhammad's inner circle, charging that "they forced me to take the stand I am taking because I had to find a way to circumvent the forces in the movement that opposed me and at the same time to expedite Mr. Muhammad's program as I understand it."[27]

Muhammad escalated the war of words in his weekly column in a number of sympathetic newspapers by declaring that Malcolm X had intentionally disobeyed his orders to be silenced. In a direct warning to those of his followers who were entertaining ideas of joining Malcolm X, Muhammad declared that "I am sorry for the poor fools who refuse to trust the god of the Honorable Elijah Muhammad, and follow Malcolm for self-victory."[28] Even Malcolm X's brother Philbert, also a Muslim minister, got into the fracas, saying that "now I see my brother pursue a dangerous course which parallels that of the precedents set by Judas, Brutus, Benedict Arnold and the others who betrayed the fiduciary relationship between them and their leaders." And, in an ominous warning, Philbert X wrote: "I see where the reckless efforts of my brother Malcolm will cause many of our unsuspecting people who listen and follow him unnecessary loss of blood and life."[29] This same issue of *Muhammad Speaks* displayed a cartoon portraying Malcolm X's severed head bouncing down a lane toward the heads of Judas and Brutus. As his head rolls down the lane, it says, "I split because no man wants to be Number 2 man in nothing! and the officials at headquarters fear my public image! and the Messenger's family was jealous of me! and even the Messenger . . . bla-bla-bla-bla." Increasingly, as the head rolls toward its ignominious destination, horns begin growing from his temples and the expression on his face becomes increasingly distorted into the scowl of a devil. Clearly this cartoon of a beheaded Malcolm X and the public warning from his brother added to the tensions of the time and brought individual members of the Nation of Islam closer to the point where they wanted to see Malcolm X killed.

The first attempt to kill Malcolm X by the Black Muslims came even before he had announced that he was formally leaving the Nation of Islam to start his own organization. But the attempt clearly backfired in that it only served to push Malcolm X farther from the ranks of the Black Muslims and virtually made it inevitable that he would break from the Nation and establish a rival organization. The only record of the assassination attempt comes in his own autobiography, but various sources, including the FBI and the New York Police Department, chose to view the incident as a publicity event, since Malcolm X told the news to the newspapers as well as the proper authorities. According to the autobiography:

> The first direct order for my death was issued through a Mosque Seven official who previously had been a close assistant. Another previously close assistant of mine was assigned to do the job. He was a brother with a knowledge of demolition; he was asked to wire my car to explode when I turned the ignition key. But this brother, it happened, had seen too much of my total loyalty to the Nation to carry out his order. Instead, he came to me. I thanked him for my life. I told him what was going on in Chicago. He was stunned almost beyond belief.[30]

Since Malcolm X provided almost no details of the incident, it is difficult to determine the seriousness of the attempt on his life. One of the crucial details that he left out was the identity of the Muslim official who ordered the assassination and the identity of the demolition expert. This is the only case among the various assassination attempts against Malcolm X that a clear chain of command emerges, in which a Muslim is directed to kill Malcolm X by a senior official within the mosque. Unfortunately, however, Malcolm X does not elucidate that chain of command and forces historians to guess at the identities of the men involved.[31] But regardless of the identities of the men, it is clear that the orders came from someone higher than a Muslim official in New York. "As any official in the Nation of Islam would instantly have known, any death-talk for me could have been approved of—if not initiated—by only one man," the Honorable Elijah Muhammad.[32]

This first attempt to assassinate Malcolm X on behalf of the Nation of Islam is highly significant in a number of ways. First, it inexorably set the wheels in motion that would eventually lead to Malcolm X's death. A death sentence is far easier to initiate than to stop, since such a proclamation brings along with it a series of hostile actions that are not forgotten easily. Even if Malcolm X's assassins were not armed with orders from their superiors to carry out the killing, they knew they were acting upon the desires of Muslim officials that were demonstrated in this first assassination attempt. Furthermore, the death sentence pushed Malcolm X into a different set of relations with his former colleagues. It is certainly possible that the relations between Malcolm X and the Black Muslims could have been amicable, as Malcolm X desired from the beginning. But this attempt to murder him inevitably destroyed any potential for a healthy relationship and instantly made Malcolm X an enemy in the eyes of the Muslims, and vice versa. Rather than eliminating an annoyance of the Nation of Islam, the death sentence instead created a monster that threatened the very survival of the Muslim movement. "This first direct death-order was how, finally, I began to arrive at my psychological divorce from the Nation of Islam," Malcolm X recalled later.[33] But the divorce need not have been so hostile, and eventually violent, if the Nation of Islam had not taken this approach so early in its split with Malcolm X.

Although Malcolm X's life was never truly in danger when the order for his assassination was circulated, this first attempt almost automatically led to further assassination tries, whether or not they were condoned by the Muslim leadership. An order, once given, is difficult to rescind, and there was no evidence that the leadership of the Nation of Islam even had any intention of halting the process of assassinating Malcolm X. Instead of attempting to deter an assassination, the leadership of the Nation of Islam

actively encouraged such violence, as they created a climate
in which it became certain that Malcolm X would be killed.
By castigating the former Black Muslim as an enemy of
Elijah Muhammad and declaring publicly that he was worthy of death, the leadership issued an open invitation for individual members of the Nation to murder their former
minister. Although the act was presumably committed by
five low-ranking Black Muslims, their superiors in Chicago
were also to blame. As Malcolm X said in his autobiography:

> I went few places without constant awareness that any
> number of my former brothers felt they would make he-
> roes of themselves if they killed me. I knew how Elijah
> Muhammad's followers thought; I had taught so many of
> them to think. I knew that no one would kill you quicker
> than a Muslim if he felt that's what Allah wanted him to
> do.[34]

As Malcolm X moved into a vastly different and less
rigid political arena, he immediately attempted to distance
himself from his earlier stances on a number of issues. The
evolution of his thought had slowly progressed in the year
before his break with the Nation; upon his withdrawal, the
limitations of the Nation's official teachings were removed,
and he used the opportunity to undergo a dramatic
transformation in thought. Although he did not yet know it,
the limitations of the Muslims' doctrines were soon to be
replaced by other political realities and limitations that also
thwarted his transformation from a black racist to a leader
for civil rights. At an April 7, 1964, meeting with the Inter-
denominational Ministers, a group of New York clergy,
Malcolm X was challenged for his views on Christianity,
which had been one of the evils that the Muslim minister
had preached against while he associated with the Nation of
Islam. "I don't care what I said last year," he said with a
smile. "That was last year. This is 1964."[35] And in his announcement of the formation of the Muslim Mosque, Inc.,

he sought to distance himself from many of his utterances that he made as a minister for the Nation of Islam:

> I'm not out to fight other Negro leaders or organizations. We must find a common approach, a common solution, to a common problem. As of this minute, I've forgotten everything bad that the other leaders have said about me, and I pray that they can also forget the many bad things I've said about them.[36]

But it was Malcolm X's journey to the Middle East and Africa that provided the best opportunity for him to revise his thinking, as well as an opportunity for the brewing dispute between him and Elijah Muhammad to settle down. He decided soon after his break with the Muslims that he would follow the orthodox Islamic teachings and join a pilgrimage to Mecca, which is required of all Muslims who are able to do so. "I'd had it in my mind for a long time—as a servant of Allah," he said.[37] After borrowing money from his half-sister to pay for the trip, Malcolm X left New York bound for Cairo on April 13, 1964. In the course of his six-week journey, Malcolm X visited over half a dozen different countries, all of them in his search for "spiritual strength" and a political context for the struggle between blacks and whites in America. In the process, he converted to orthodox Islam, surprised at himself for not knowing many of the basic Islamic prayers and rituals, even though he had always called himself a Muslim minister. He also began to redefine his entire approach to the struggle for civil rights as he came to the "realization" that blanket denunciations of whites were often inaccurate, and discovered that the African-American struggle was a global issue rather than a problem of national politics.

In a letter written in Mecca to several friends and members of the press, Malcolm X outlined some of his "new" revelations. "Never have I witnessed such sincere hospitality and the overwhelming spirit of true brotherhood as is practiced by people of all colors and races here in the ancient holy land," he began the letter. After outlining his experiences in the pilgrimage, he credited the Islamic religion with converting white people and "removing the 'white' from their minds." He wrote that the "whites as well as non-whites who accept Islam become a changed people. I have eaten from the same plate with people whose eyes were the bluest of blue, whose hair was the blondest of blonde, and whose skin was the whitest of white. . . . and I felt the same sincerity in the words of and deeds of these 'white' Muslims that I felt among the African Muslims of Nigeria, Sudan and Ghana."[38] He acknowledged that this transformation in beliefs would shock many of his followers, but defended himself as a "man who tries to face facts, and to accept the reality of life as new experiences and knowledge unfold it."[39]

Although the transformation was indeed shocking to many of Malcolm X's friends and enemies, it is now possible to detect a gradual evolution toward this position. Rather than suddenly coming to the conclusion that not all whites were bad (although the vast majority in America certainly were, in his mind), Malcolm X slowly began to drift away from the Nation of Islam's position that the white race was a race of genetically engineered devils. Although his initial conversion to Islam and his rise in the Nation of Islam had brought with it a spate of attacks against the "white devils," Malcolm X had quietly reduced his reliance on this phrase during his later years in the Nation of Islam. His retelling of the story of the evil scientist Yacub who, according to Nation of Islam doctrine, was responsible for creating the white race, had become increasingly rare in his later days.[40] Upon his exit from the Nation, he even indicated that he would allow the support of whites for his new black-nationalist party. "The Muslim Mosque, Inc., will remain wide open for ideas and financial aid from all quarters. Whites can help us, but they can't join us. There can be no black-white unity until there is first some black unity."[41] Although this policy was far more rigid than such civil rights organizations as the NAACP, it still represented an enormous step away from the doctrine of black superiority and self-reliance espoused by Elijah Muhammad.

As Malcolm X sought to remodel himself in the new nations of Africa, his name was continually being muddied back at home. *Muhammad Speaks,* the Nation of Islam's newspaper, seemed almost obsessed with condemning its former minister, devoting numerous articles and drawings to attacking Malcolm X and warning other Muslims that "Divine Messengers Must Be Obeyed," as one headline read. "We believe that Malcolm wants to be the No. 1 man [the Messenger of Allah]. He loves worldly praises; he likes to see his picture in the newspapers, over the radio and television."[42] Every issue contained new attacks against him, almost all of them calling him the "hypocrite" of the movement. Often, verses of the Koran were cited to demonstrate that even Allah was against Malcolm X. "And whosoever acts hostilely to the Messenger after guidance has become manifest to him and follows other than the way of the believers, we turn him to that which he himself turns and make him enter hell: And it is an evil resort."[43]

The newspaper *Muhammad Speaks* was a central institution in the Nation of Islam. It was one of the primary means of conveying information to the Muslim membership across the country and was often used to transmit official policy from Chicago. All Muslim men were required to sell a quota of the newspapers, thereby spreading the gospel outside the Muslim community as well as within it.

The importance of the newspaper in the Nation of Islam makes the threats against Malcolm X inside its pages that much more serious. The continual attacks against Malcolm X in the paper were spread to the Muslim faithful across the country and were accepted as official policy. Threats of retribution against Malcolm X in *Muhammad Speaks* were often given the weight of the words from the lips of the Messenger himself, and any talk of his death would have been seen by some as a divine call for an assassination. Many of the articles contained not so subtle warnings to Malcolm X and his followers that psychological and bodily harm would come to them if they did not mend their ways. Condemning them to hell was one such tactic, warning them that Allah would punish them for their evil doings.

Although initially there were no outright calls for the Muslim membership to assassinate Malcolm X, there were a number of references to the former Black Muslim's death. Often it came in the form of references to divine retribution. "Malcolm has not believed the Honorable Elijah Muhammad to be the Messenger of Allah. If he did, he would be afraid for his future."[44] And even Muhammad spread the threats, quoting the Koran in one of his editorials as saying, "O Prophet, strive hard against the disbelievers and the hypocrites and be firm against them. And their abode is hell and evil is the destination."[45] An even more suggestive warning came from Muhammad on April 10, 1964: "Your evils and false accusations of me and my followers are only to frighten already so-called Negroes from coming to Allah that they may inherit the earth. You frighten especially the proud so-called Negroes whom you have made like yourself. Allah is sufficient as a helper. You will not be able to help yourself pretty soon . . ."[46] This was spread as the official position of Elijah Muhammad and, to some Muslims, this was the equivalent of a direct order.

One of the Muslims who was the most vocal against Malcolm X was Minister Louis X of Boston,[47] who wrote a three-part series in *Muhammad Speaks*, attacking his former friend. Although Malcolm X was the minister who had recruited Louis X into the Muslim ranks, there was now no amity between them. Minister Louis condemned his fellow Muslim for his "almost unbelievable treachery and defection," arguing that Malcolm X had continuously lied about his reasons for leaving the Nation. Malcolm X's supposed jealousy of Elijah Muhammad "became obvious during his period of suspension, when, instead of maintaining a discreet silence, he began to fill the newspapers with stories to the effect that there was a 'split' in the ranks of the

Muslims, and that such information came from inside sources." According to Louis X, the New York minister's statements to the press were "filled with lies, slander and filth designed to cast aspersions upon Mr. Muhammad and his family."[48]

When Malcolm X returned from his trip abroad on May 21, 1964, the tensions that had been building before his departure had not subsided, but had only increased. Not only was he the subject of incessant public slanders from the Muslims, he also had to face eviction from his seven-room East Elmhurst home, which was the property of the Nation of Islam. As long as Malcolm X remained as the minister of the Harlem mosque, the house was his; when he left the Muslims, the two-story house, valued at a little over $16,000 at the time, became the most visible battle-ground in the fight between the Muslim factions. Malcolm X had actually rejected earlier appeals from the Messenger and from his family that he put the house in his name, and his refusal brought on the conflict over ownership of the house. Before he left for the Middle East, he was sent a letter that indicated that he should immediately return the house and "several items such as letters, Mosque film, Negro documents, etc., relative to the Muslims and their affairs." The letter also informed Malcolm X that he should discontinue using the Nation of Islam's name for his car insurance or else "the Mosque will have to take possession of the car." Malcolm X made no response to the letter, and the Nation of Islam filed eviction proceedings a month later on April 8, 1964. An initial hearing was set for April 17, but because of Malcolm X's trip abroad, it was postponed a number of times until June 15.[49]

The eviction proceedings were particularly galling to Malcolm X. After all, the house was his, even if his name was not on the deed. He had lived there ever since his marriage to Sister Betty, and although his expanding family was beginning to outgrow the seven-room residence, Malcolm X had no other place to live and no money to find another house. The decision to evict Malcolm X was a brilliant tactical move by the Nation of Islam, since it would inflict a tremendous blow to the former minister and allow the Nation to remain free of undue retribution; after all, it was only trying to retrieve property that legally belonged to it. But Malcolm X never did see it this way. He tried his hardest to remain in the house for the longest time possible. Although the proceedings were filed in civil court in April 1964, Malcolm X was not formally told to leave the house until the following February, shortly before his death. The Nation's tactic worked perfectly, however, as the eviction wore on Malcolm X's mind and hurt him and his family. "The elders in the Nation, being men of affairs, saw these actions as matters of simple equity. Malcolm, who had served and enriched the Nation over a dozen years and who owned nothing, read them as a declaration of war."[50]

The eviction hearing on June 15, 1964, was the tensest moment yet in the escalating war between Elijah Muhammad and Malcolm X. The New York newspapers had been receiving rumors that Malcolm X would be killed at the hearing if he showed up, and security was heavy for the main event. Malcolm X reportedly arrived with eight of his own bodyguards and thirty-two policemen to protect him from any renegade Muslims who might want to kill him. The followers of Malcolm X and those of Elijah Muhammad sat on opposite sides of the court, their anger seething just below the surface. The courtroom was deadly silent throughout the hearing, without even the standard murmurings of most other courtroom sessions. The hearing was essentially a formality, since Malcolm X and his lawyer, Percy Sutton, didn't really have a legal basis for their arguments. First, Sutton argued that the house really did belong to Malcolm X, even though the deed showed otherwise. It was a gift from Elijah Muhammad, he argued, although it was never certified by changing the deed. When this approach faltered, he tried another tack: Malcolm X had never really been fired as the minister of the Harlem mosque, and so therefore the house should still be his. Both arguments were flimsy from a legal standpoint, and the judge rejected them both.

During the hearing, Malcolm X did his best to inject the reasons for his departure from the Muslim ranks into his testimony, despite the fact that the New York Captain of the Fruit of Islam, Joseph X, sat in the courtroom along with a number of his muscle-bound underlings. He brought up the issue of Muhammad's adultery in response to questions that had nothing to do with the Messenger, and even his lawyer could not steer him clear of getting mired in the partisan dispute. Malcolm X had gone to the press a number of times in the previous week with the story of Muhammad's adultery, but the media did not bite; they were unwilling to print unsubstantiated allegations in such a tense dispute. The hearing, however, was the perfect platform for Malcolm X's story, since the press would be there in force. Although at first he seemed unwilling to discuss the matter, he soon delved into his extensive knowledge of the internal affairs of the Black Muslims. He said he was only willing to do so "because they have driven me to the point where I have to tell it in order to protect myself, but I have been trying to keep it quiet." Finally, Malcolm X nervously blurted out that the Honorable Elijah Muhammad had "taken on nine wives."[51]

The inevitable result of the hearing was an increase in tension between the followers of Malcolm X and those of Elijah Muhammad. Malcolm X went home to find that his phone had been disconnected; someone who called herself "Mrs. Small" apparently notified the phone company that the service should be ended. Six of Malcolm X's people got worried when there was no answer at his house and immediately rushed to Queens to see if he was alright. The station wagon that they drove was equipped with an M-1 semi-automatic carbine, a 6.75 Beretta rifle, walkie-talkies and binoculars; in case of a shoot-out with the Black Muslims, Malcolm X's people wanted to make sure that they didn't lose. They soon left after they realized that Malcolm X was fine, and they apparently went to buy a newspaper. They ended up, however, right in front of the Nation of Islam's restaurant on Lenox and 116th Streets, and the tensions between the two groups erupted as a Muslim punched one of Malcolm X's followers. Various weapons were immediately produced—everything from sticks to rifles. Luckily, the police arrived in time to head off further violence, and they arrested six of Malcolm X's people and confiscated two rifles that they had brandished. The six were charged with disorderly conduct, unlawful assembly, and carrying a loaded weapon in an automobile, which is illegal in New York.

June 1964 was a difficult month for Malcolm X. Tensions between him and his former colleagues were at a peak, with a number of important events demonstrating the deteriorating relations between the two sides. While the eviction hearing was the most visible confrontation, perhaps an even more important one was the visit of Elijah Muhammad to New York City in late June. The Nation of Islam publicized the rally as much as they could; a high turnout would prove to Malcolm X that Elijah Muhammad still had more followers. The event was Muhammad's first visit to New York in three years and was touted as "the largest gathering of black people ever assembled in America."[52] Tensions boiled as Muhammad prepared to invade Malcolm X's turf and show him up in his own backyard. But Malcolm X made a surprise move in order to ease the tensions between the two groups. On June 26, 1964, shortly before Muhammad's New York visit, Malcolm X called for a cease-fire in the escalating war. In an open letter to Muhammad, Malcolm X wrote:

> Instead of wasting all of this energy fighting each other, we should be working in unity and harmony with other leaders and organizations in an effort to solve the very serious problems facing all Afro-Americans. Historians would then credit us with intelligence and sincerity.[53]

In a speech the next night, Malcolm X continued his plea: "We should all band together and go to Mississippi," he told a crowd of 600 people. "This is my closing message to Elijah Muhammad: Lead us against our enemy. Don't lead us against each other."[54]

But Malcolm X's plea for peace was never heeded, and the rhetoric from each side continued unabated. Death threats were publicized in the newspapers against Muhammad, but that did not deter the Messenger of Allah from staging his meeting. Muhammad's rally continued as scheduled, but they were far from their goal of organizing a "mammoth rally." According to *The New York Times*, only about 6,500 people attended the event in the 369th Regiment Armory, far fewer than the number expected.[55] A good portion of the meeting was spent in attacking Malcolm X, if not by name then by implication. A Pakistani Muslim who was a supporter of the Nation of Islam, Abdul Basit Naceni, addressed the rally, castigating an unnamed individual "who once served as an important aide to the Honorable Elijah Muhammad." He urged the audience not to "pay heed to rumors or gossip or engage in idle talk. . . . Believing in false rumors can never do you any good, but it can do much [unnecessary] harm. You should particularly ignore the blasphemous remarks or insults of erratic individuals." Muhammad also attacked his former protégé, telling the audience that there is "some person who wants to be what I am, but that person is not able to be what I am." As the speeches droned on inside, hatred flared between the Black Muslims and a supposed follower of Malcolm X. Muslim guards set upon a 21-year-old man who they thought had broken from the Muslims. "Kill him, kill him now," the crowd shouted before the police were able to rescue the man.[56]

This period of time also saw two apparent assassination attempts against Malcolm X, although it is unsure exactly what the intention of his pursuers was. On June 12, Malcolm X and some of his men flew to Boston. That day, he was the subject of a radio interview called "Conversation for Peace" in which he told the story of Muhammad's adultery, which certainly inflamed the tempers of the Boston Muslims. Although he was scheduled to stay in Boston for a few days, he decided to leave early for some reason, telling his aide, Benjamin Goodman, to take over his scheduled appearances. After one such speech, Goodman and seven other men were driving in two vehicles through Boston when two cars full of Muslims began to follow them. One of the cars managed to cut off Goodman's cars in a Boston tunnel. The Muslims pounced out of the car, threatening Malcolm X's people with knives. "We're going to kill the so-and-so," they said, referring to Malcolm X, whom they thought was in one of the cars. "You're not going to get out of here alive."[57] But the Muslims immediately backed off when one of Malcolm X's people produced a shotgun and threatened to use it, and the cars went on their way.

The second apparent attempt came on July 3, 1964, as Malcolm X was returning to his home in Queens. As he was getting out of his car, he saw two black men running at him, carrying what he thought were knives. He immediately jumped back into his car and sped off. He soon returned to his house to get his rifle, but the men had vanished. In a conversation overheard by the FBI, Malcolm X told one of his people that the orders to kill him had come from Chicago. Malcolm X immediately notified the NYPD of the incident, and the police placed a guard at the house until the next day. Again, it is not known what the intention of the pursuers was, but it must be assumed that these were genuine attempts to kill Malcolm X. His life was clearly in danger.

It was perhaps for this reason that Malcolm X decided to leave the country again. The thought of putting himself out of reach of the Black Muslim assassins was certainly appealing, and he left for Cairo on July 9, 1964, less than a week after the third attempt was made on his life by the Nation of Islam. He spent more than eighteen weeks during this trip in a number of African nations; it was more than triple the time that he had originally intended to spend. He attended the annual meeting of the Organization of African Unity as an observer and spent his time lobbying the African heads of state that he met in his attempt to bring up charges against the United States in the World Court. Frustrated in these efforts, he nevertheless wrote home of his great "triumph" of persuading the Africans to pass a bill expressing concern about American racism, although the bill was no more critical than the one the OAU had passed the year before. While in Africa, he tried to further disassociate himself from Elijah Muhammad and define his new program for human rights in America. In August, Malcolm X wrote a letter from Egypt to M. S. Handler of *The New York Times*, in which he lamented his waste of long years and effort in the Nation of Islam. "For twelve long years, I lived within the narrow-minded confines of the 'straitjacket world' created by my strong belief that Elijah Muhammad was a messenger from God Himself and my faith in what I now see to be a pseudo-religious philosophy that he preaches. . . . I shall never rest until I have undone that harm I did to so many well-meaning, innocent Negroes who through my own evangelical zeal now believe in him even more fanatically and more blindly than I did."[58]

Malcolm X was equally unsuccessful at easing the tensions between himself and the Black Muslims while he was abroad. Although he was insulated from the rhetoric that was being thrown around recklessly at home, he still was destined to face the same problems when he returned. The Harlem riots had occurred that summer, and Malcolm X received his share of the blame for the violence even though he hadn't even been on the same continent at that time. The ruling also came down from the eviction hearing, as Civil Court Judge Maurice Wahl ruled in early September that Malcolm X would have to vacate his home and return it to the Nation of Islam by January 31 of the next year. And Malcolm X was still the target of scathing articles and editorials in *Muhammad Speaks*, which temporarily stopped its rhetoric but resumed it when Malcolm X's return date approached. The newspaper featured a series of Muslim ministers writing articles attacking Malcolm X, each trying to outdo each other in their viciousness. Clarence X Gill, the FOI captain of the Boston Mosque who was arrested more than once for assaults on Muslims who had left the Nation of Islam, wrote:

> My constant prayer to Allah is that I never turn on my heels and deviate, or because of weakness, turn hypocrite as others have done. May Allah burn them in hell.[59]

An article by John Shabazz began: "I would have referred to you as 'Uncle Tom,' Malcolm, except that it would have been an insult to all the Uncle Toms on earth to class you with them. The worst Uncle Toms you yourself ever criticized look ten feet tall beside you now." He said that Malcolm X was never a true Muslim because a true Muslim would not do the things that Malcolm X had done. "The Bible accurately describes you as 'a dog returning to his own vomit.' You've even gotten shaggy like a dog," Shabazz wrote, referring to Malcolm X's new beard that he grew while on his pilgrimage.[60] One minister accused that "no good Malcolm Little" of teaming up with "those two prostitutes who accuse the Messenger of getting babies."[61] A July 31, 1964, front-page article by Elijah Muhammad warned the Muslim faithful to "Beware of False Prophets," which of course referred to Malcolm X. "You can never trust hypocrites. They are liars. They are worse than disbelievers because a disbeliever has not lied, saying that he believed and then turned back. This makes hypocrites the most hated of all people."[62] One quotation from the Koran cited in the newspaper read: "Give news to the hypocrites that for them is a painful chastisement," followed by the warning: "Let the hypocrite read and weep."[63]

Malcolm X finally returned to New York on November 29, 1964, to a boisterous crowd in Kennedy airport cheering his return under a banner that read, "Welcome Home Malcolm."[64] He didn't even stay in New York for two days before he left again, this time bound for England, where he spoke at Oxford University in a debate sponsored by students there. When he returned again, he faced a severe warning from his former Muslim allies. In a telegram dated December 7, 1964, Raymond Sharrieff, the Supreme Captain of the paramilitary Fruit of Islam, warned Malcolm X that "the Nation of Islam shall no longer tolerate your scandalizing the name of our leader and teacher the Honorable Elijah Muhammad regardless of where such scandalizing has been."[65] His trip overseas had obviously done nothing to stem the seething conflict at home, and Malcolm X's life was in as much danger as it had ever been.

The December 4, 1964, issue of *Muhammad Speaks* contained the most vicious and suggestive attack that the newspaper had yet printed on Malcolm X. It came from a familiar mouthpiece: Minister Louis X of the Boston mosque. Minister Louis was born with the "slave" name Louis Eugene Walcott. His father was a West Indian servant in New York City who raised Louis as an Episcopalian. But religion was not as important to Louis as was his music, and the young singer and songwriter put his talents to use in various Harlem nightclubs, where he was known by the name "The Charmer." But in the late 1950s, his attention was diverted by the dynamic oratory of the leader of the New York Muslim temple, Malcolm X. Louis soon began attending the weekly meetings of the Nation of Islam in Harlem, and he joined the temple as Malcolm X burned the Muslim faith into him. He soon gave up his name, his drugs, and finally his musical career, a profession that was frowned upon by the austere Muslims. But Louis X did not completely forsake music and soon wrote what would become the unofficial anthem of the Nation of Islam: "White Man's Heaven is Black Man's Hell." He also called upon his theatrical talents and wrote *The Trial*, a play about the trial of the white race for its sins against the darker world. Louis X also had a talent for oratory, and after Malcolm X helped establish the Boston mosque, Louis became its minister. Ministers Malcolm and Louis remained friends until it was clear that Malcolm was on his way out of the Nation of Islam. Up to that time, Malcolm X, in a show of affection, sometimes referred to Louis X as "my little brother." But the relationship came to a bitter end as Elijah Muhammad persuaded Minister Louis to remain in the Nation of Islam and attack his former friend for betraying the Muslim movement.[66]

In December 1964, Minister Louis's call for the assassination of Malcolm X was clearer than it had ever been. The officials in Chicago had their wish granted only two months later, when five Black Muslims gunned him down at the Audubon Ballroom. "Is Malcolm bold enough to return and face the music—since he ordered the notes to be played—after bowing out and leaving the musician with untrained dancers?" the five-page article queried. "You are now the target of the dissatisfaction of both your own followers (which are very few) and the followers of Muhammad." The article continued by comparing Malcolm X to various hypocrites in Islamic history. "Malcolm lashed out with his venomous poison to wash Messenger Muhammad with mud and filth . . . but Malcolm X is no match for the wisdom of Muhammad." Instead, he is "the great liar and scandalizer of his master" who "went on the warpath without a complete army and without the wisdom."

Only those who wish to be led to hell, or to their doom, will follow Malcolm. The die is set, and Malcolm shall not escape, especially after such evil, foolish talk about his benefactor [Elijah Muhammad] in trying to rob him of the divine glory which Allah has bestowed upon him. Such a man as Malcolm is worthy of death, and would have met with death if it had not been for Muhammad's confidence in Allah for victory over the enemies.[67]

Another attempt was made on Malcolm X's life during his final trip to Los Angeles in late January 1965, only a

month after Minister Louis's call went out to Muslims
across the country. The trip was made in order for him to
meet with the two former Nation of Islam secretaries who
filed paternity suits against Elijah Muhammad. In preparation for his brief stop in California, Malcolm X telephoned
Hakim Jamal, a former member of the Los Angeles
Mosque who resigned from the Nation of Islam after the
April 27, 1962, shooting of NOI member Ronald Stokes by
the Los Angeles Police Department. As tensions soared
over the shooting in the Muslim community and the L.A.
Fruit of Islam prepared to battle the police, Elijah
Muhammad dispatched Malcolm X to control the hostile
members and prevent open warfare in the streets of Los
Angeles. Although Malcolm X succeeded in restoring calm
to the community, many NOI members, including Jamal,
resigned from the mosque because of what they saw as the
inability of the NOI to match its rhetoric with action.

Jamal, born Allen Donaldson, was initially attracted to the
Nation by the fiery words of Malcolm X, whose sermons in
Los Angeles convinced Jamal to quit his long-standing addic-
tion to drugs, and Jamal was eager to return the favor when
Malcolm X needed help in January 1965. According to
Jamal, in his 1971 book *From the Dead Level: Malcolm X
and Me*, he and the two secretaries agreed to use the code
name "David" in reference to Malcolm X when they discussed his upcoming visit to L.A. in order to ensure his security. Malcolm X arrived in Los Angeles on January 28,
1965 and was greeted at the airport by Jamal and his friend
Edward Bradley,[68] who later wrote an eyewitness account of
the Los Angeles incident with reporter Louis E. Lomax. Before Malcolm X's plane landed, Jamal and Bradley reported
noticing a black man whom Jamal suspected of being a
member of the Nation of Islam at the gate where Malcolm X was soon to arrive. (Jamal later realized that this
man was John Ali, the Nation of Islam's National Secretary.)
While they were waiting, airport security, whom Jamal notified of the possible danger to Malcolm X's life, quietly told

Jamal and Bradley that the gate had been changed and was now at the other end of the airport.

When they arrived at the new gate, Malcolm X arrived, "alone and apparently unconcerned."[69] After scanning the terminal for potential assassins, Malcolm X and his party strode confidently through the airport to claim his luggage and then to their waiting car. The trip to his hotel was uneventful, although Malcolm X became furious when they had to stop for gas. "Brother," he steamed, "never set out on any journey with less than three-quarters of a tank of gas. That is a very bad thing, to be chased and then find out that you are almost out of gas."[70] The three men finally got to the hotel, went up to Malcolm X's room and dropped off his bags, then returned downstairs to the main lobby before leaving the hotel. As they got off the elevator, Jamal turned to see John Shabazz, the minister of the Los Angeles Muslim mosque, and Edward Sherill, the captain of the local FOI, getting off a nearby escalator.

> They absolutely froze, mouths open. Then Edward frowned—his mouth turned up on the side, exposing his teeth, like a dog when it growls. I caught myself with my mouth open. I stopped walking. I was petrified. Now I believed. Those looks could not be counterfeited. There was hate. Face to face. They wanted to kill Malcolm X standing right there.[71]

According to Jamal, Malcolm X smiled calmly and continued to walk toward the entrance to the hotel, quietly imploring Jamal to keep moving and not to stop. But as Jamal looked across the lobby, he saw a group of Muslims whom he recognized as members of the Los Angeles Fruit of Islam who, after seeing Malcolm X, looked toward Sherill, presumably for orders. "They were zombies. They couldn't think for themselves. . . . Thanks be to either Malcolm X or his Allah—this gave us time."[72]

The two men walked outside the hotel to their waiting car, and Malcolm X took the precaution of rolling up the car's windows in case the FOI would try to douse them with acid. The car then raced off, leaving the Muslims standing outside the hotel staring at the speeding vehicle that held their worst enemy. Malcolm X visited the two women who had filed the paternity suits against Muhammad, bringing them and their children to their lawyer's office, where they could talk without fear of FOI followers. After returning the women to their homes and getting something to eat, Malcolm X was driven back to his hotel, where he bravely marched through the well-lit lobby, almost surrounded by the angry stares of the Fruit of Islam, and proceeded up to his room.

According to Edward Bradley, the driver of the car, he learned through some of his Muslim friends that the Fruit of Islam called an emergency meeting that night in order to discuss how to "get Malcolm, Jamal and me."[73] Bradley showed up at 9:30 the next morning to drive Malcolm X to his scheduled appointments, but the New York Muslim finally decided to cancel his meetings because of a series of death threats that he had received throughout the night, culminating with one in which the caller simply said, "You are dead. You are a dead nigger."[74] Before finally leaving the hotel for a 12:30 flight to Chicago, Malcolm X showed Bradley his single-shot gun, which was disguised as a fountain pen. "It only shoots one bullet, but at least I'll take one of them with me," he quipped. Bradley called the police and alerted them to be waiting at the TWA terminal of the airport in case of trouble, and the two men zipped through the hotel lobby and into Bradley's car, which was quickly followed by two carloads of Muslims that had been patrolling outside the hotel.

"By zigzagging and executing several U-turns, I was able to elude one of the cars but the second car followed us onto the freeway," Bradley later reported. As they cruised down the freeway at 70 miles an hour,

> the carload of Muslims was gaining on us. I took the far, left lane of the [freeway] and the Muslims inched

alongside to our right. . . . I expected any moment to see their car window lower and a volley of shots blaze toward us. . . . Then Malcolm acted. He reached on the floor of my car and picked up a walking cane I had been carrying since a back injury several months ago. Malcolm then lowered the back window of my car and lifted the cane as if it were a shotgun and aimed it at the Muslims who were then almost directly alongside us. The Muslim driver suddenly reduced his speed and fell into traffic behind us.[75]

Malcolm X was met at the airport by a detail of police and pushed through the airport by eight plainclothes policemen, who intercepted the Muslims whom Malcolm X and Bradley identified as they walked through the terminal. Two Muslims began walking directly toward Malcolm X and the policemen, who immediately rushed to meet them before they got within striking distance of their target. Malcolm X warned the police that these intercepted Muslims were only decoys who would provide an opening for the real killers. This, of course, is what happened several weeks later, when decoys in the Audubon Ballroom created a diversion as the real killers pumped Malcolm X's body full of shrapnel. Finally, Malcolm X was ushered through the underground passageway to the awaiting plane. "Malcolm and I had missed death by inches and we knew it," Bradley reported. As Malcolm X said his final goodbye to Bradley, he told him, "I am a marked man. I'm ready to die. I just don't want them to hurt my family."[76]

It is likely that this story of Malcolm X's final visit to Los Angeles was somewhat overdramatized, since the only real record of it came from Jamal and Bradley, who both published their stories. But the tale should be regarded as substantially accurate, even if some of the details—including quotes from Malcolm X—may be exaggerated. Although he emerged from California unscathed, his life was clearly in danger at the hands of the Muslims several weeks before he was killed. In the Los Angeles assassination attempt, the Muslims used some of the same tactics that were used by other Muslims in his death the next month. Luckily for Malcolm X, the L.A. Muslims either did not formulate a workable plan for killing him, or else they were never given the orders to seek his death, although Bradley's sources suggest that they were. Malcolm X lived with the constant fear that any minute might be his last. He realized that even though he lived through his experience in California, it was not likely that he could survive for very long, given the number of people who sought his death and their commitment to the cause.

Malcolm X's life was threatened throughout his final year, culminating in the firebombing of his house and his assassination a week later. Although there is still confusion over who was guilty of the arson, what is clear from Malcolm X's final year is that the conflict between the different Muslim factions set Malcolm X up for his ignominious death. He spent an entire year trying to outrun the guns of his former allies, but he could not escape them any longer. The five Muslims who killed Malcolm X had been primed for their duty by continual verbal assaults on their target over the past year. The rhetoric was violent and amounted to a direct call for the death of the "chief hypocrite," Malcolm X. This rhetoric prepared the future assassins for their job and gave the murder official sanction from the Nation's leaders, including Elijah Muhammad himself. It is virtually irrelevant whether Talmadge Hayer and the other gunmen had direct orders to kill Malcolm X. They knew that they had the blessing of the Muslim leadership, who had been calling for Malcolm X's death even before he formally broke with the Nation of Islam. Elijah Muhammad, Minister Louis X, and other members of the Muslim leadership were responsible for Malcolm X's death regardless of where they were on the day of February 21, 1965. They set the stage for the final killing. Then they watched the drama unfold from the comfort and safety of Chicago.

CHAPTER NINE

The Motive

"As we began to grow, jealousy arose in the ranks against Malcolm. . . . As Malcolm began to evolve and to grow, this jealousy would intensify."

—*Louis Farrakhan*

Despite the argument of conspiracy theorists that the federal government had the only developed motive for killing Malcolm X, it was actually the Nation of Islam, and not the government, whose driving desire to see the black nationalist silenced could have led to murder. For a variety of reasons, the government—and specifically the FBI, the CIA and the New York Police Department—had little desire to see Malcolm X killed. While they were certainly interested in tracking his movements and even inhibiting his growth as a revolutionary force, they had no interest in killing him. The Nation of Islam, however, had a complex web of reasons for wanting to see Malcolm X dead. Indeed, its motive was far more developed than in many cases in which its members used violence against their enemies.

Malcolm X represented the greatest threat to the Nation of Islam that it had faced since the inception of the movement in the 1930s. Its former minister had the potential to draw large numbers of the Islamic faithful into his organization. His failure to capitalize upon this talent represented the chaos of his final year, rather than his inability to lead large numbers of people. Although Malcolm X was eventually unable to live up to his potential in creating a movement that would rival the Nation of Islam, his threat remained real, making him a dagger in Elijah Muhammad's side that would be removed only when he was killed. But rivalry was not the only reason for his death. Equally important in Elijah Muhammad's need to silence his former protégé was the information that Malcolm X possessed that would be embarrassing to the movement. Malcolm X spent over ten years as a trusted advisor to the Messenger, privy to the innermost secrets of the Nation of Islam, many of which would shock the Black Muslim membership and induce mass withdrawal of membership if they were made public. In this context, Malcolm X's death would be not just a luxury but a necessity for Elijah Muhammad, who conceivably faced the end of his movement in a worst-case scenario.

But Malcolm X's ability to draw large numbers of the Nation's faithful into his own organization was his greatest initial threat to Elijah Muhammad. Malcolm X was not the only one in the movement who was dissatisfied. Many Muslims, such as those in Los Angeles who quit the Nation after the Ronald Stokes murder, agreed that the movement was far too complacent when it came to organizing for the revolution. Civil rights activity was an attractive proposition for many Muslims, and Malcolm X's militant alternative to Martin Luther King's nonviolent strategy seemed certain to gain a large following. While many Muslims were upset with Elijah Muhammad's nonengagement policy, so, too, were many non-Muslims upset with the rigid discipline mandated by the Nation of Islam, although they certainly admired the Nation's organizational abilities.

Although a smaller group than those who were dissatisfied with the nonengagement policy, some Muslims had forsaken Elijah Muhammad's teachings because they deviated from orthodox Islam. Even two of Muhammad's sons had realized that their father's form of Islam was in direct conflict with orthodox Islam. His teachings concerning the white race as devils particularly rankled orthodox Muslims in the United States and forced them to denounce his philosophy as contrary to the true Islam. The Messenger's son, Akbar, was a student of orthodox Islam at Cairo's Al-Azhar University, the center of the academic study of Islam. Upon his return to the United States, he began teaching Arabic at the Nation's University of Islam,[1] but soon broke from the movement because of his objections to his father's non-Muslim teachings and extramarital affairs. Wallace Muhammad, another of the Messenger's sons, broke with his father after discovering the corruption of the movement and the deviation of its philosophy from orthodox Islam. After his break with the movement, he told the FBI that his father had attacked him for believing in the "true Muhammedan religion" rather than the Nation's brand of Islam.[2] When Malcolm X was killed, Wallace immediately rejoined the movement and inherited it when his father died. Over serious objection and a number of splintering fractures within the movement, he quickly steered it toward orthodox Islam. Both of these sons, as well as others who objected to Elijah Muhammad's non-Muslim philosophies, represented potential converts to Malcolm X's Muslim Mosque, Inc., especially after he converted to orthodox Islam during his pilgrimage to Mecca.

For a variety of reasons, Malcolm X was unable to translate his extraordinary influence in the Nation of Islam and in militant non-Muslim circles into an effective organization to fight for black nationalism. Clearly, his forte was not in organizing but in orating, and his ability to create a viable civil rights group was severely hampered by a number of preoccupations that turned his attention away from organizing. In the year starting with his break from the Nation of Islam in March 1964, and ending with his death in February 1965, Malcolm X spent almost half of his time traveling through Africa and the Middle East. While his pilgrimage to Mecca and his subsequent travels further defined the difference between himself and Elijah Muhammad, his absence from the United States came at a critical time, leaving him with an organization lacking in membership and a staff lacking morale. His reeducation in Africa brought an international perspective to his own philosophy and to the civil rights movement as a whole, but it was at the expense of his followers, who often could not wait for his return to the United States.

Another difficulty that Malcolm X faced in his final year was the inherent ambiguity in his philosophy. He spent much of his time attempting to define his own philosophy, which underwent dramatic changes after his break with the Nation. Although there is a substantial body of evidence that suggests that Malcolm X had secretly made many of the philosophical changes even before 1964, he still had a tremendous difficulty in "turning the corner," as he often said. His transition from Black Muslim to black nationalist was a difficult one, as he lost many of his original followers he had brought with him out of the Nation of Islam. Many of the former Black Muslims were particularly incensed by his reversal on the evil nature of the white devils, a notion that he denounced during and after his pilgrimage. Even his closest associates, such as Charles Kenyatta and Benjamin Karim, expressed some ambivalence about Malcolm X's changes, and the flexibility of his philosophy cost him large numbers of supporters in the long run.

A further difficulty that Malcolm X faced after he left the Nation of Islam was the basic need to survive. He was, of course, well aware of the danger that he faced from his former colleagues and followers, and it took much of his energy to stay one step ahead of them. While he was trying to stave off death, he was simultaneously attempting to go on the offensive against his former boss. In June 1964, after repeated attacks from the Black Muslims, he began revealing his knowledge of Elijah Muhammad's adultery, as well as information in other areas that would be potentially embarrassing to the Muslims. This preoccupation with alternatively defending himself against attack and going on the offensive took up much of his time during his last months and prevented him from devoting himself fully to defining his ideology and organizing his following.

But Malcolm X's potential for diminishing the ranks of the Muslims by leading them into his own organization was not his only threat to the Nation of Islam. Malcolm X spent over ten years as the chief minister of the Nation of Islam. He represented the Messenger across the country, and in his travels he became privy to some of the innermost secrets of the movement. And although Muhammad tried to keep a number of more embarrassing secrets from him, Malcolm X inevitably learned many of the details that were hidden from him, albeit a little late. When he was finally transformed from the National Minister into the "chief hypocrite," Malcolm X was pushed to the point where he began revealing the insights that he had gained as a Muslim minister. While many of his revelations had little significance in his battle with Elijah Muhammad, some of the secrets that he publicized threatened to splinter the Black Muslim movement. At the very least, the Muslims' secrets would be highly embarrassing to Elijah Muhammad and the Nation of Islam. As such, Malcolm X represented an enormous threat to Elijah Muhammad that could be eliminated only by his death.

The most important issue that Malcolm X hoped to publicize upon his return from Africa was the Messenger's adultery with six of his secretaries. On June 8, 1964, Malcolm X was in contact with CBS News and promised to give them an exclusive interview that detailed his knowledge of the extramarital affairs, and later that day the beleaguered Muslim received an anonymous phone message telling him that "he's as good as dead."[3] Then, four days later, he spoke of the issue on a Boston radio program, but the response to his attacks was negligible. The difficulty that Malcolm X faced in his attempts to publicize Muhammad's immorality was that the media simply wasn't biting. Most of them were afraid to air Malcolm X's version of the story without some objective proof of his allegations. Publishing Malcolm X's assaults would have meant taking sides in a partisan dispute and opening themselves up to a libel lawsuit from the Nation of Islam. So, when he failed to get the media's attention, Malcolm X decided to make the charges public during his eviction trial, which the Muslims had brought against him for living in their house after he broke with them. The trial was slated for June 15, 1964, and although he was eventually evicted, just as he expected, he used the platform to denounce his former mentor. Still, the press didn't bite. Malcolm X complained to a reporter the next month that he wasn't receiving the attention that he deserved because his allegations were over an issue of morality that "can't be brought into public before it is brought into court."[4] Luckily for Malcolm X, the issue was about to reach the court. Two of the former secretaries filed paternity suits naming Elijah Muhammad as the father of their children.

Malcolm X was not the only one who knew about Elijah Muhammad's extramarital affairs. According to Elijah Muhammad's FBI files, the Bureau knew about the various women in the Messenger's life at least as early as Malcolm X did, and the FBI had far more details. Surveillance devices were installed at Muhammad's house in Chicago as early as 1956; the justification was that the FBI needed to be kept apprised of "not only data concerning the fanatical and violent nature of the [Nation of Islam], but also data regarding the current plans of the MCI (Muslim Cult of Islam, the FBI's name for the NOI) to expand its activities throughout the United States."[5] Additional devices were installed in an apartment that Muhammad kept in Chicago, as well as his home in Arizona which the Nation purchased in 1961. Most of the FBI information comes from these "surveillance devices," which recorded both conversations that Muhammad conducted within the safety of his house, as well as telephone conversations with other Muslims. Periodic reports were made by the FBI that give summaries of the surveillance, including many enlightening telephone conversations that he had with his various secretaries.

Many of the telephone calls were requests for child-support money from the Messenger, who often gave the women a significant amount of money to care for his children. He offered at one time to pay for the education of at least two of the women, since they were planning to return to school. In January 1964, he told one woman that "he had been very sick and he had decided he would do something for 'them' to give them a future after he is gone. . . . He told her not to tell anyone about this." But, on other occasions, he showed a casual disregard for the women with whom he had slept and the children he had fathered. In one conversation, on May 5, 1962, Muhammad received a call from one of the secretaries, whose name is withheld from the report. She stated that

she had a job coming up in a couple of weeks and until that time wondered if he could send anything to her. He stated no he could not send anything. She said she only had $2.00 whereupon he said he did not care if she had only 2¢. She said the baby had to have something to eat and he said that it was her own fault.[6]

In desperation, two of the women attempted to abandon their babies so that Muhammad would be forced to admit that they were his children and care for them. On the evening of July 13, 1962, they approached Muhammad's house on South Woodlawn Avenue in Chicago and "created a disturbance," according to the FBI. "The two women had their babies with them and abandoned the children at Muhammad's residence." Raymond Sharrieff, the Supreme Captain of the Fruit of Islam and husband of Muhammad's daughter, was at Muhammad's house at the time and decided to call the Chicago police to settle the matter. Upon the orders of someone in Muhammad's family, the police took custody of the children while they searched for the mothers. When the two women discovered that Elijah Muhammad had let his children be taken into custody by the police, "they indicated extreme disgust and [said] they would take further action against Muhammad."[7]

One FBI document, dated April 26, 1962, contains some of the most explicit evidence that the FBI was seeking more information concerning Muhammad's adultery. Through "an investigation conducted by Chicago and Phoenix" the FBI concluded that "Elijah Muhammad is engaging in extramarital activities with at least five female members of the Nation of Islam (NOI)." Although it is sparse in details about the adultery or the FBI's knowledge of Muhammad's actions, the document continues to outline the new information that the Bureau offices in Chicago and Phoenix had discovered:

> This information indicates Muhammad has fathered some children by these women and that his wife, Clara, has become aware of his infidelity which has resulted in domestic strife. Apparently, Muhammad is furnishing financial support to at least some of these women and their children and contemplates a nursery to get his illegitimate children under one roof.[8]

The document further discusses other information that could be embarrassing to the movement, such as the various "manifestations of affluence" that had grown around the Messenger's use of his followers' money, including the purchase of "expensive cars and homes for him." The significance of this document is not in its revelation of the secrets of the movement, which can be researched in far greater detail in other sources, but rather its importance is that it contains some of the first recommendations that the FBI had ever made in terms of interfering with the internal affairs of the Nation of Islam. Although the recommendations seem rather innocuous, it represented the first time in the Bureau's relationship with the Nation of Islam that it had crossed the line from being an investigatory body to an agency that was actively involved in targeting and eliminating organizations that were supposedly antithetical to the general beliefs of the American populace. It was noted in the report that

> these paradoxes in the character of Elijah Muhammad make him extremely vulnerable to criticism by his followers. He wields absolute power in the hegemony of the NOI and any successful attack on his character or reputation might be disastrous to his reputation. . . . Consideration should be given to additional investigation to corroborate and verify information furnished by the above-listed sources so that such information could be used without jeopardising [sic] these highly confidential investigative techniques. Finally, Chicago and Phoenix should make recommendations concerning the use of information thus obtained to discredit Elijah Muhammad with his followers.[9]

When the FBI discovered the incident in which the two women abandoned their babies at Muhammad's residence, they decided that the information could be "capitalized on to create dissension in the NOI through exposure of Elijah Muhammad's extramarital activity."[10] It is clear from Malcolm X's later discoveries that the FBI was successful in its mission. It had managed, by "planting the seeds of deception through anonymous letters and/or telephone calls," to discredit Muhammad before a significant number of his own followers. The loss of membership in the Chicago mosque and the growing rumor among Muslims across the country was no doubt encouraged by the FBI. While these FBI tactics do not implicate its agents in further activities against the Nation of Islam, the document certainly demonstrates that the FBI might have been an active participant in the diminution of Muhammad's flock.[11] The spread of this information worked better than the FBI could have imagined, as Muhammad's most visible spokesperson in the movement, Malcolm X, gradually became aware of the adultery and was subsequently cast from the

Muslim ranks, presenting the Nation of Islam with the potential for a major rift in its membership.

The rumors of adultery were not Malcolm X's only weapon against his former colleagues. One of the allegations that plagued the Nation of Islam for a number of years was that it was receiving financial assistance from whites. Receiving such assistance would have been against the basic philosophies of the movement. One of the Muslims' prime criticisms against organizations such as the NAACP was that they were primarily funded—and therefore directed—by white patrons. On a number of occasions Elijah Muhammad and his ministers denied that such outside funding existed, but the scuttlebutt persisted, particularly one vague rumor that a Texas millionaire had donated large sums of money to Elijah Muhammad. Another rumor claimed that the Nation of Islam had received funding from the head of the Hunt food corporation. The claims have at least some plausibility; the Nation of Islam was a wealthy organization, at one time proposing to spend $20 million to build a Chicago Islamic Center, but the bulk of its membership was on the verge of poverty. Near the end of his life, Malcolm X apparently finally conceded that the rumor was true in talking to a former member of the Los Angeles mosque. Although the authenticity of the conversation cannot be verified, Malcolm X allegedly told the Muslim that

there is a long story about how the Muslims get money. I remember when I used to work for the Messenger in Chicago, one of the jobs I had was keeping some of the books. I remember saying one day to Elijah ... "Holy Apostle, you really have to be a man of God. I am counting the donations from around the nation and I really don't see how you can keep the Nation of Islam functioning. The money is not even. There isn't enough to support the Nation ... yet it exists!" ... There is a Texas millionaire who supports not only Elijah Muhammad but the Minutemen and the John Birch Society.[12]

Malcolm X went on to tell the name of the man from Texas, whom he then said was a billionaire who had made his money in oil. His belief in racial separation apparently was the impetus for donating large sums of money to the Muslims. "When I found [this] out I didn't do anything about them at the time because I felt that these were things that I just didn't understand. . . . I was that hypnotized," Malcolm X said.[13] Whether or not this conversation is genuine, it does demonstrate that Malcolm X possessed information that would be highly embarrassing to the Muslims, if revealed. This information alone—that Elijah Muhammad was on the payroll of a white man from Texas—would have created a deep schism in the Muslim communities. The hypocrisy of criticizing other organizations for accepting money from whites and then secretly doing the same thing would have been too much for many Muslims. These disaffected blacks might have turned to Malcolm X's organization and allowed him to triumph over his former leader.

Another similar scandal that Malcolm X tried to ignite was the connection between Elijah Muhammad and the American Nazi Party leader George Lincoln Rockwell. Although the two leaders occupied opposite sides of the political spectrum, they shared views on the separation of the races, and Rockwell wanted to forge a political alliance between the two organizations. Elijah Muhammad realized the potential benefits that such an alliance could bring to the Nation's fight for separation, but the costs were extraordinary. Revelations of an alliance between the extreme right and the Nation of Islam could have had severe ramifications on the memberships of both organizations. Muhammad's policy on an alliance remained ambivalent, as he conducted secret meetings with the Nazi leader but remained aloof from a formal alliance. Although they agreed to cooperate with each other, the relationship was loose enough to satisfy both sides. In April 1962, Rockwell, apparently at the invitation of Elijah Muhammad, took advantage of an open microphone at a Muslim annual meeting, and told the assembled Muslims that he desired the same goals as they did. Dressed in full Nazi regalia, he declared that no white person wanted to live with blacks, and that all other whites agreed with him but were being hypocritical in hiding their inner desires. Muhammad made no official response.[14] But Rockwell heaped praise on the Muslim leader. In a letter to his followers, Rockwell exclaimed that

> I have just had a meeting with the most extraordinary black man in America: The Honorable Elijah Muhammad, leader of the Nation of Islam. I was amazed to learn how much they and I agree on things; they think that blacks should get out of this country and go back to Africa or to some other place and so do we. They want to get black men to leave white women alone, and white men to leave black women alone, and so do we. The Honorable Elijah Muhammad and I have worked out an agreement of mutual assistance in which they will help us on some things and we will help them on others.[15]

According to James Farmer, who later asked Malcolm X about the meeting that Rockwell referred to, the Muslim minister replied, "I give you my word, Brother James, that I knew nothing of any such meeting, but I will check into it. If such a meeting did take place, I promise you that there will be hell to pay within the Nation of Islam."[16] To Malcolm X and countless other Muslims, even a single meeting with a fascist such as Rockwell was unforgivable, and a cooperative agreement between the two organizations would have created broad dissension within the Muslim movement. After Malcolm X broke with Elijah Muhammad, his newfound knowledge of the ties between Muhammad and Rockwell became a weapon that he wielded against his former leader. The charge that Elijah Muhammad had associated himself with Rockwell never stuck to the Muslim leader, but it was one of many thorns that Malcolm X held in his side.

Although the Rockwell secret never proved to be an important weapon against Elijah Muhammad, Malcolm X's revelations of a meeting with the Ku Klux Klan in which he participated under orders from the Messenger held greater potential. The clandestine meeting took place on January 28, 1961 in Atlanta. The reason for the meeting was to institute a nonaggression pact between the two groups since they were both, after all, fighting for the same goal: the separation of the races. The pact was formalized, and the KKK agreed to help the Muslims in their goal of setting aside a couple of states for their homeland after they were freed from the laws of the United States government. The existence of the pact or of the meeting between Muslims and the KKK was never acknowledged formally by Elijah Muhammad and the Nation of Islam. Although the alliance may have had tactical benefits, it was a public-relations nightmare for the Muslims and, as such, Elijah Muhammad wanted to keep it as quiet as he could.

But, despite the secrecy, the FBI found out of the meeting only two days after it took place, almost certainly from some of their sources in the KKK rather than from Muslims. In fact, the FBI provides the only available account of the meeting, although their information relates primarily to the actions of Malcolm X. According to the FBI, during the meeting Malcolm X "claimed to have a hundred seventy-five thousand followers who were complete separationists, were interested in land and were soliciting the aid of the Klan to obtain land." Malcolm X went on to attack Jews, whom he said were "behind the integration movement, using the Negro as a tool." And, in some surprising statements, he showed some sympathy with the Klan's position on integration and even with the violent tactics that they used. According to the FBI, Malcolm X "stated that if his people were faced with the situation that the white people of Georgia now face, that traitors, meaning those who assisted integration leaders, would be eliminated."[17]

Malcolm X later said he regretted the fact that he had participated in such a meeting, but insisted that he was under orders from Elijah Muhammad and had private qualms about the potential for a pact between the Muslims and the Klan. And, after Malcolm X broke from the Muslims, he attempted to make a public issue of the Klan meeting, hoping to embarrass Elijah Muhammad and divide his movement. He tried to give the impression that Muhammad was in league with the KKK and the American Nazi Party and actively cooperated with them. The charge, of course, was not quite true, but an alliance was at least contemplated by the Muslim hierarchy, and even this revelation would have caused tremendous damage to the Muslims. Even a radical group like the Nation of Islam could not associate with the Ku Klux Klan and emerge unscathed. Muslims would have been outraged had they known at the time, and the media would have had a field day denouncing the hypocrisy of Elijah Muhammad. But when Malcolm X began reporting it in 1964, the press reacted to it as a partisan attack rather than the revealed knowledge of an insider, and thus the allegation presented the Muslims with only a major annoyance rather than a crisis.

One of the most damaging secrets that Malcolm X possessed was the information that he gained when he tabulated the finances of the Nation. While he probably did not realize the extent to which the Nation's money was being embezzled by those in charge of the treasury, he certainly knew enough so that he could make an issue of it if necessary. The Muhammad family certainly had a good deal to hide when it came to their expenses.[18] Revelations of corruption in the Nation of Islam would certainly have endangered the tax-exempt status that the Nation enjoyed as a religious organization. Almost their entire income came directly from the contributions of their followers, and they made no pretense of their incredible wealth. Elijah Muhammad and his family had accumulated a vast personal estate over the course of several years, using the funds of the Nation of Islam. Muhammad's personal holdings included his mansion and an apartment in Chicago, a large house and five other properties in Phoenix, a "palatial" home in Mexico, his familiar $150,000 jewel-encrusted fez, several Cadillacs, and several million dollars in bank deposits. In addition, much of the real estate that was bought by and for the Nation of Islam was purchased in the name of Elijah Muhammad and became a portion of his personal estate after he died in 1975. His sons and daughters also possessed large homes and fancy cars, purchased with money from the Nation of Islam. According to the FBI,

> [Muhammad] has permitted his followers to purchase expensive cars and homes for him; to provide him with bodyguards and servants; and to give him other manifestations of affluence. These luxuries have been obtained at the expense of his followers who are, in the main, extremely poor and who are continually harassed by NOI officials for greater and greater contributions.[19]

Much of the Nation of Islam's money came from profits on their newspaper, *Muhammad Speaks*. Muslims were forced to sell their quota of the newspaper and pay for the copies that they were not able to sell, leaving scores of Muslims in debt with thousands of copies of *Muhammad Speaks* piling up in their homes. One of the difficulties in selling the newspaper was that it never gained significant circulation among non-Muslims, and this led to mutinies of Muslims across the country who were unable to continue sacrificing their own well-being for the sake of Elijah Muhammad. Members of some mosques were forced to buy up to five hundred copies of the newspaper twice a month at 15 cents per copy, and the chances of recouping their losses by selling their quota were minimal. But this was a very profitable business for the Nation's leadership, as the newspaper brought in over $2 million a year. But this money came at a severe cost to the Nation, as Muslims across the United States became disillusioned with the leadership in Chicago and resentful over what they perceived as extortion by Muslim leaders.

Before Malcolm X broke with Elijah Muhammad, the

Nation of Islam resembled a corrupt corporation more than a religious group. The Nation maintained an account called the "Number Two Poor Treasury" that was established to aid those in the Nation who had been fighting poverty. But rather than being used to help the poor, Elijah Muhammad reportedly called the fund "my checking account." According to one of Malcolm X's biographers, Bruce Perry, some Muslims quipped that "Number Two Poor make Number One rich."[20] There is even information that officials in the Philadelphia mosque created an alliance with local gangs in the black community in order to raise money for Chicago. The "Muslim mob" allegedly engaged in extortion, drug running, and petty theft, and the money eventually made its way to Elijah Muhammad. Meanwhile, the planned $20 million Islamic Center that Muhammad had publicized never broke ground, and the $3 million that had been raised for the project vanished. Muhammad and those around him prospered while the Muslim membership came increasingly closer to poverty.

Benjamin Goodman, the Black Muslim from New York who followed Malcolm X out of the Nation of Islam, gave further evidence of the corruption of the Black Muslim leadership. In a 1990 interview, he stated:

> There was a lot of money floating around and a lot of people were spending money in areas where it shouldn't be spent. . . . When Mr. Muhammad died, Abdul, who was the Secretary of the Nation of Islam at the time, had $19,000 in his closet, in change, in bags. And then [Wallace] Muhammad asked him why he hadn't taken it to the bank and he said it was too heavy.[21]

While Malcolm X did not understand the full extent of the problem, his sources in Chicago alerted him to some of the diversions of funds. His knowledge of this mismanagement posed perhaps the greatest threat to the Muslims. Had his revelations about the finances of the Nation been heard by many of the Muslims, he could have had a significant effect on the numbers that followed Muhammad. He attempted to raise the issue a number of times, once on a radio interview on June 4, 1964, in which the FBI quoted him as saying that John Ali, the National Secretary, "is running the organization for one purpose and that is to get all the money out of it that he possibly can."[22] He also attacked other Muslim officials, including Elijah Muhammad, for making themselves wealthy from money from the pockets of poor people. Malcolm X "began to speak out against some of the expenses of the family members who were buying fur coats, spending a lot of money in nightclubs, wearing diamonds and other expensive jewelry—from donated money, not earned."[23] According to Goodman, who now goes by the name Karim, "Malcolm was a threat to [the Muslim officials'] access to money and living well."[24]

A few weeks before his death, Malcolm X presented the Nation of Islam with an enormous challenge as he agreed to testify for an investigation that the Illinois Attorney General's office was conducting on the tax-exempt status of the NOI. If Malcolm X had lived to testify, his information would have been used in the case of *Thomas Cooper v. State of Illinois*, which dealt with the right of Muslims to practice their religion within state prisons. But Malcolm X's testimony could have meant something far greater to the Nation of Islam: the loss of their tax-exempt status. Such a loss would have cost them millions of dollars in taxes to the state and federal governments. But, fortunately for the Nation of Islam, Malcolm X was murdered within a month of his first meeting with the attorney general's office, and he never got to testify.

The Nation of Islam had a long list of reasons why they wanted to see Malcolm X dead. From his threat as minister of a rival Muslim mosque to his potential for splitting the Muslims with his revelations of the Nation's secrets, Malcolm X represented Elijah Muhammad's worst nightmare. His threat to the movement had not been seen since Allah in the person of Wallace D. Fard disappeared mysteriously in 1933, leaving Elijah Muhammad to consolidate

Fard's followers. As in the case of the assassination of Malcolm X, the threat to the early movement was resolved with violence, leaving Elijah Muhammad in undisputed control of the Muslims. Violence was often used as tool for many Muslims, and Malcolm X was only one of many victims of the Muslims' wrath. The primary motivations for violence against the enemies of the movement were to seek revenge and to remove a threat to the Nation of Islam and Elijah Muhammad. The assassination of Malcolm X, at the hands of the Muslims, fits both these categories.

CHAPTER TEN

The Means

"The morals had gone out of the leadership [of the Fruit of Islam]. It became a political order. And it was hooligans; it became nothing but a hooligan outfit, a hoodlum outfit, of men who were just playing politics and playing revolution. Not a revolution that carried its attack outside; a revolution that kept its attack inside. Directed at leaders that showed a future. That showed promise that maybe they would become the leader. And directed at well-meaning, innocent people in the community."

—*Wallace D. Muhammad*

On Wednesday evening, January 6, 1965, six weeks before Malcolm X was assassinated, Benjamin Brown was shot from behind as he left the Islamic temple that he had established in New York. Brown was a former New York City corrections officer and a Muslim who had broken with the Nation of Islam, although he still invoked the name of Elijah Muhammad in his teachings. Despite his break from the Nation of Islam, Brown still professed his support for Elijah Muhammad, and he even hung a portrait of the Messenger in the front window of his "Universal Peace" mosque on 1473 Boston Road in the Bronx. Two hours before he was shot, Brown was approached by three Muslims, who asked that the picture be removed since Brown was not a member of the Nation of Islam and his independent mosque was not endorsed by Elijah Muhammad. When Brown refused, the Muslims left the temple, apparently only to return later with a .22-caliber rifle. The single bullet entered his chest and collapsed his right lung; Brown was immediately hospitalized at Jacobi Hospital in the Bronx, where he soon recovered from his wound. His three alleged assailants, all members of the Nation of Islam, were arrested hours later by the New York Police Department after Brown related his story of a confrontation that he had had with the Muslims hours before.

The police arrested a 47-year-old Housing Authority employee from Brooklyn, Willie 8X Gaines, along with 26-year-old Norman 3X Butler and a 29-year-old Thomas 15X Johnson, who told the police that they were a student and a painter, respectively. A .22-caliber rifle was found in Johnson's house that had apparently jammed after firing the first shot at Brown. Butler, a master of martial arts whose reputation was known to the police, was arrested by Detective John Kilroy, who later helped to investigate Malcolm X's murder. Kilroy and his police colleagues covered their faces with steel masks as they arrested Butler in recognition of his martial-arts abilities. Their caution paid off as Kilroy was hit by a karate chop to the head as he rushed in to arrest Butler. "When Kilroy got the mask off later, according to department legend, there was a deep crease in it."[1]

Butler and Johnson both maintain that they are innocent of the shooting of Benjamin Brown, as well as that of Malcolm X. In fact, they never were convicted of the Brown assault; the charges were dropped after several years, before the case went to trial. According to Johnson, he had approached Brown that day in an attempt to convince him to remove Elijah Muhammad's picture from his window. But the conversation was pleasant rather than contentious, and he had no motivation for returning with a rifle to finish the job. Even Brown admitted that the conversation was pleasant in a subsequent letter to Elijah Muhammad. Johnson maintains that the rifle was in his house because the Muslims who actually did commit the crime—he still will not admit who it was—asked him to hide the weapon so they would not be caught with it. Butler also contends that he is innocent, specifically arguing with the story that he fought with the police when he was arrested. "I'd have been dead," he said. "I couldn't [resist arrest]. There were too many guns." But regardless of the specific identities of those who shot Benjamin Brown, it is clear that they were Muslims who wanted to teach Brown a lesson for going against the teachings of the Honorable Elijah Muhammad.

Minister James X, the new leader of Muhammad's Temple Number Seven, characteristically denied any Muslim involvement in the shooting in an interview with the *Amsterdam News*. "The followers of Elijah Muhammad or so-called Black Muslims are not aggressive," he declared. "We are taught not to carry firearms, and only fight when we are attacked. I have no knowledge of the alleged altercation in the Bronx. I am looking into it."[2] It is, of course, entirely reasonable that Minister James was telling the truth about his ignorance of the event and the noninvolvement of the Nation of Islam. The act could easily have been the responsibility of renegade Muslims who were not acting under the auspices of the Nation of Islam and whose actions would have been condemned by the Muslim leadership. He was also quite correct that it is the doctrine of the Nation of Islam that firearms should not be carried and that self-defense is the only appropriate use of violence. But regardless of the involvement of the Muslim hierarchy, it is clear that this act of violence belonged to a pattern in which Muslims attacked their enemies. These acts were clearly fostered by the environment of the Black Muslim world, even if the specific acts were not ordered by the Muslim leadership.

Rather than being an isolated instance of violence, the assassination of Malcolm X was part of this pattern of violence initiated by members of the Nation of Islam. Malcolm X, Brown, and a number of other former Muslims were attacked in 1964 and 1965 for leaving the Nation. The outbreak of violence left several people badly injured and at least two people dead.[3] Much of the argument of conspiracy theorists rests on the proposition that the Nation of Islam was incapable of committing the assassination of Malcolm X. But a detailed analysis of a pattern of violent actions against enemies of the Black Muslim movement reveals that the Muslims were not only capable of such an action, but that they actually perpetrated a number of similar acts of violence. This does not necessarily indicate that they were responsible for the violence that killed Malcolm X. But it does demonstrate their ability to do so and adds to the growing mountain of evidence against the Black Muslims that implicates them in Malcolm X's murder. The motivation for all the beatings and killings was the same: the need to silence potential rivals and to punish those who had chosen to oppose the Messenger of Allah.

Contrary to most accounts of the group in the media, the Nation of Islam as an organization was not violent, nor did it advocate armed aggression. But the Nation did possess a number of unique characteristics that unwittingly encouraged certain members of the group to perpetrate acts of violence against the Nation's enemies. Only a small fraction of the entire membership participated in the violence, and it is even doubtful that a substantial portion of the Muslims even knew of these acts; but they did occur, and the responsibility for them lay within the Nation. Without the testimony of those who participated in this aggression, it is impossible to determine whether instances of violence, such as that against Benjamin Brown, were the result of a hierarchical decision from above or the work of renegade Muslims who deviated from the guidance of their superiors. In some instances, which will be detailed later, the violence was initiated by officials within the Nation of Islam—more specifically, the captain of the Fruit of Islam at the Boston mosque—but whether this was always the case, particularly with regard to the shooting of Malcolm X, cannot be determined.

One of the factors that made certain members of the Nation of Islam particularly prone to committing acts of violence against the perceived "enemies" of the movement was their dogged loyalty to the Nation's leadership and their determination to protect those leaders from outside attack. Their virulent defense of Islam and the Nation created the willingness of many Muslims, particularly those in the Fruit of Islam whose duty it was to protect their organization, to use violent tactics in order to minimize outside attacks. This may not have been the common response to outside attacks, but there are a number of documented cases in which it did occur. The conception of Elijah Muhammad as the prophet of Allah, rather than just an ordinary man, made the need to protect him even more important. According to one Muslim, members of the Nation "seem to worship [Elijah Muhammad] rather than Allah."[4] Attacks against him, whether physical or verbal, presented him with a danger that his ardent followers felt they needed to eliminate—by violence, if necessary.

The devotion of Black Muslims to Islam was also extraordinary, and attacks against the religion often brought about violent retaliation. The attitude toward Islam is demonstrated in this response by a Muslim in an interview with the Nigerian scholar E. U. Essien-Udom:

> My friends used to come here [to the store] to visit me. They are used to going to night clubs. I broke away with all of them and no longer associate with them. I rejected the nightclub. One friend continued to visit me at the store, but I decided that I could not maintain associations with kids who do not think like I do and have no love for Allah. My whole life is devoted to Islam.[5]

Such devotion to the religion and the Nation of Islam as a representation of that religion increased the willingness of some Muslims to protect them with force, even if that force violated the principles of the Nation. Even as Malcolm X's loyalty to the Muslim leadership in Chicago was waning in his final year as a member of the Nation of Islam, he still demonstrated the capacity to become violent as a result of an attack against Elijah Muhammad, although he could not follow through because he reluctantly believed that the insult was true.

Backstage at the Apollo Theater in Harlem one day, the comedian Dick Gregory looked at me. "Man," he said. "Muhammad's nothing but a . . ."—I can't say the word he used. *Bam!* Just like that. My Muslim instincts said to attack Dick—but, instead, I felt weak and hollow.[6]

There is even some evidence that implicates Elijah Muhammad in a number of violent acts, particularly during the time in which he was attempting to consolidate his leadership of the Muslims after the disappearance of W. D. Fard. One unidentified person approached the FBI in early 1964 with one such story. According to the report, the individual called the New York FBI office and told an agent that Muhammad "committed a murder in Detroit, Michigan, in 1928 and has been avoiding justice until the present time." The informant "seemed to be obsessed with this subject and indicated he had been in touch with the Senate Internal Security Subcommittee, the House Committee on Un-American Activities, various members of Congress, and has written a lengthy letter in the past to the President." And, although the Bureau decided not to take this information seriously because of the unconfirmed credibility of the witness, they received "information implicating Elijah Muhammad in at least five murders and information associating him with a Japanese espionage agent during World War II."[7] Although the allegations of murder are unconfirmed, the story of the Japanese agent is quite true, although exaggerated.[8] It is difficult to determine whether or not these claims should be taken seriously. Indeed, there is some evidence that suggests that Muhammad's rise to the leadership of the Muslims was somewhat bloody, and that he personally participated in a number of acts of violence. But that evidence is unconfirmed, since no serious research has been conducted on the early years of the Nation of Islam.

Violence was not a new concept to many Muslims. Since the bulk of the membership of the Nation of Islam came from the urban working poor, many of them having been converted in prison, a substantial percentage of the Black Muslims had become hardened to the realities of a violent life. Conditions in the ghettos were inexorably linked to violence, as frustrations and anger against the discrimination from white society and the seeming hopelessness of their situations boiled over. Elijah Muhammad and his ministers, with good reason, were generally proud of the fact that many of their followers were once criminals who were swayed into a more respectable life once they heard the "truth" that the Nation preached. "Many of my followers— and ministers—were once criminals, but I changed all that by giving them knowledge of *self*. Once they discovered who the devil was and who God was, their lives were changed." Malcolm X was one of the best examples of this trend, himself a former drug pusher and burglar who saw the wisdom of Elijah Muhammad's teachings while in a Massachusetts penitentiary. And Malcolm X shared Mr. Muhammad's admiration for the Muslim's constituency:

At the bottom of the social heap is the black man in the big-city ghetto. He lives night and day with the rats and cockroaches and drowns himself with alcohol and anesthetizes himself with dope, to try and forget where and what he is. That Negro has given up all hope. He's the hardest one for us to reach, because he's the deepest in the mud. But when you get him, you've got the best kind of Muslim. Because he makes the most drastic change. He's the most fearless. He will stand the longest. He has nothing to lose, even his life, because he didn't have that in the first place. I look upon myself, sir, as a prime example of this category—and as graphic an example as you could find of the salvation of the black man.[9]

While this reformed criminal element in the Nation of Islam was certainly one of its strengths, as it served to amplify the positive effects of becoming a Muslim, perhaps this tendency of the Muslim membership also made retaliatory acts against the enemies of the Muslims more likely. Since many of the Muslims had lived most of their lives in violent cities and a few had even participated in violence before they had converted to Islam, the possibilities for such acts against Muslim enemies increased. When coupled with such other factors as the existence of a paramilitary wing of the Muslim movement and the fierce loyalty to Elijah Muhammad, the likelihood of violence increased dramatically, particularly if the Messenger were challenged as he was when Malcolm X attempted to break from the Nation of Islam and start his own movement. Indeed, the tendency toward violence within the movement manifested itself on a number of occasions, although more often against Muslims and former Muslims than against the professed "enemies" of the movement.

Even in the days before it was accused of specific acts of violence, the Nation of Islam was continually characterized by the press, the government, and mainstream society as a radical organization that would use violent means to achieve its goals. The philosophy of armed self-defense was distinctly different from the labels that were placed on the Black Muslims by the press, but a white society, paranoid at the thought of armed African-American activists, did not explore the niceties of whether armed self-defense actually equated the aggressive use of violence. The Federal Bureau of Investigation, whose paranoia in racial matters generally eclipsed that of the rest of the white society, characterized the speeches of Malcolm as being "violent in nature wherein he attacks the United States and the white race."[10] As early as 1956, the FBI wrote to the attorney general that "allegations have been received that [the Nation of Islam's] members may resort to acts of violence in carrying out its avowed purpose of destroying non-Muslims and Christianity," even though the government did not have evidence of a single instance in which Black Muslims used violence.[11] The press was equally unquestioning in the differentiation between the Muslims' armed self-defense and aggressive violence. In his 1959 report on the Nation of Islam, Mike Wallace, along with Louis Lomax, condemned the Muslims as "hate merchants" and "hate mongers" with violent overtones.[12] Even *Playboy* magazine felt the need to condemn the teachings of the Nation of Islam before it presented a "cross-examination" of Malcolm X in 1963. The interview was not a forum for Malcolm X and the Black Muslims; instead it was a "damning self-indictment of one noxious facet of rampant racism."[13]

Malcolm X was generally able to skillfully finesse charges of violent tendencies within the Black Muslim movement as he sought to put the onus of blame for a violent society on whites. First, he pointed out the numerous examples of the use of violence by white society and the government that represents it. In particular, he pointed to the bombing of a Birmingham church in 1963, "where they bomb a church and murder in cold blood, not some grownups, but four little girls while they were praying to the same god the white man taught them to pray to, and you and I see the government go down and can't find who did it." "Uncle Sam's hands are dripping with blood, dripping with the blood of the black man in this country."[14] he declared in his famous "Ballot or the Bullet" speech. When confronted by the idea that the Muslims were hateful toward white society, Malcolm X deflected the criticism by answering that the Muslims had so much love for African-Americans that there was none left for anyone else. "The white man isn't important enough for the Honorable Elijah Muhammad and his followers to spend any time hating him," Malcolm declared in 1963.

Although the violent tendencies of the Nation of Islam were wildly exaggerated by non-Muslims, the basic philosophies of the Black Muslim movement could have increased the probability that some Muslims would commit acts of violence against the enemies of the Nation of Islam. One of the difficulties that the Muslims faced was the lack of a defined policy on the difference between armed self-defense and violent aggression. Malcolm X was often contradictory in his preachings of self-defense. "The Negro is justified to take any steps at all to achieve his equality. . . . There can be no revolution without bloodshed," he announced as he told the world of his plans to leave the Nation of Islam and found his own mosque. This statement implied that the limits of self-defense were no longer applicable.[15] On several occasions, Malcolm X went farther in his belief that violence was sometimes necessary in the fight for equality. "The Negroes should not wait for white investigators [to punish violence against blacks]. They should find the guilty ones themselves and execute them on the spot," he told *The New York Times* in 1964.[16] Generally statements such as these were regulated by a more cautious approach to the delicate issue:

> I wasn't advocating that Negroes go out and buy rifles and become involved in some kind of militia designed to initiate acts of aggression. . . . I've never said go out and initiate acts of violence or acts of aggression only to defend. And I also pointed out that this was necessary only in instances and in areas where the government itself has failed to protect the Negro. Actually, the burden is on the government. If the government doesn't want Negroes buying rifles, then let the government do its job.[17]

Technically, this response is quite true. Malcolm X and the Black Muslims never did publicly cross the line and advocate the use of aggressive violence against whites. While they may have delighted in "divine" acts such as the downing of the aircraft over France soon after a Muslim from Los Angeles was killed, the Muslims never publicly moved far from their line of armed self-defense. But this is largely a matter of semantics. The difficulty here is that the line between self-defense and aggression was never clearly defined. After he left the Muslims, Malcolm X differentiated between the legality and the morality of an action, arguing that armed aggression was morally justified, but illegal. After a discussion of the Constitutional right to bear arms, he added, "This doesn't mean that you're going to get a rifle and form battalions and go out looking for white folks, although you'd be within your rights—I mean, you'd be justified; but that would be illegal and we don't do anything illegal."[18]

The Muslims often ran up against this same paradox that Malcolm X outlined. While Muslims were supposedly entitled to gain their freedom "by any means necessary," a phrase used often by Malcolm X in his final year, they were still bound by the law and a respect for authority, according to the Nation of Islam's teachings. But when faced with this contradiction, a minority of Muslims were eventually forced to forsake their belief in upholding the laws of society in favor of what they saw as furthering the goals of the Nation of Islam.

But where exactly is the line between armed self-defense and unacceptable acts of aggression? The Nation of Islam did not institute specific rules of engagement that clarified the difference between these two concepts, leaving many Muslims without clear guidelines. It is easy to see that protecting oneself against armed aggression is acceptable under the rules of the Nation of Islam, as well as the laws of the United States, but what about cases in which opponents of the Muslims verbally attacked the Nation of Islam, or the Messenger himself? Although such attacks, whether they came from Malcolm X or any other former Muslims, clearly did not represent the endangerment of Elijah Muhammad's life, they did possibly represent the endangerment of his well-being and the well-being of the Nation of Islam. Under this interpretation, violence against the enemies of the Muslims could be entirely justified as self-defense, even though such actions would seem to be aggressive acts of violence. Individual Black Muslims could use this as a justification for violent actions that were technically not in self-defense in the legalistic sense of the phrase. Despite protests from the Black Muslims about the media's characterization of their organization as violent, the Nation of Islam had an ambivalent policy concerning the use of violence. The vague nature of the policy, and the heated rhetoric issued by Muslim ministers, allowed for continual violations of the doctrine by individual Muslims. The Muslims did not *advocate* violence, as the media continually charged, but they did create the conditions under which violence became a tool for some Muslims within the Fruit of Islam, such as in the case of the shooting of Benjamin Brown. Although they did not preach violence, the Nation of Islam made themselves into an organization far more prone to violent activities than, for example, explicitly non-violent civil rights organizations across the country.

Another difficulty in the implementation of the self-defense policy was the failure of the Nation's officers to reprimand those who had violated it. Clarence X Gill, for example, the captain of the Fruit of Islam in the Boston mosque, was responsible for at least two beatings of Muslims who had left the Nation of Islam. But Minister Louis X of the Boston mosque and his superiors in Chicago never took any action against Gill to discourage future episodes of violence and serve as a model for other potential instigators of violence. Gill was once punished by Minister Louis, not because he was violent, but because his marriage broke up after a mere three days. Since this provided a poor role model to an organization that put a premium on the family, Clarence X was forced to remain away from his Muslim brothers until he resolved his marital problems. While the Muslims put a great deal of effort into weeding out those within the movement who violated rules concerning the moral issues of using drugs or alcohol or committing adultery, they did not put the same energy into ensuring that the policy of self-defense was stringently maintained. This failure to regulate the policy exacerbated the violent tendencies that some Muslims exhibited. While those within the Nation of Islam who engaged in violent activities were a very distinct minority, their numbers were sufficient to give the Muslims a reputation for violence and to make it possible for them to contemplate—and execute—the assassination of Malcolm X.

Another aspect of the Black Muslim experience that drove a number of the most militant members into committing acts of violence was the basic characterization of the enemies of the Nation of Islam. Much of the philosophy of the Muslims, like most religious philosophies, was drawn in terms of good versus evil, a black-and-white case in which the enemy of the Nation was, by definition, evil. The righteousness of the Black Muslims was as much of a given as the evil nature of the enemy, regardless of who the enemy was. One of the central tenets in the Nation of Islam's philosophy was that the "so-called Negro" was a member of the Original People, descended from the tribe of Shabazz, and that whites were a mutagenic creation of the evil scientist Yacub. In these terms, the white race was a collection of sadistic devils in comparison to the Original People, which encompassed the entirety of the nonwhite world.

Even those African-Americans who sided with the majority white population, or more moderate Blacks who were against the philosophies of the Nation of Islam, were castigated by the Nation. Prominent civil rights leaders were focused upon and attacked for their integrationist goals and nonviolent tactics. Martin Luther King, Jr. was the recipient of many of the Muslim attacks, generally referred to as one of the "so-called Negro leaders." Although the Nation of Islam made a number of attempts to reach out to more moderate civil rights leaders, usually by inviting them to various Muslim events, Muhammad and Malcolm X viciously attacked them, calling them "house Negroes" and "Uncle Toms," and the New York minister even singled out King as being "a chump, not a champ."[19] He even derided Urban League director Whitney Young as "Whitey" Young because of his contact with whites. By defining the enemies of the Muslim movement in this way, the Nation of Islam brought the Muslims to the point where violence against enemies of the movement seemed imminent, despite Muhammad's preachings against preemptive attacks.

These attacks against whites and those blacks whom they deemed to be supporting white society created an enemy that could unify the Muslims. The Nation of Islam was unified into a coherent organization not so much by its exhortations of the valor of the black race, but by the definition and characterization of its enemies. The Nation gave its individual members a direction to focus its hatred and used this hatred to create a close-knit bond between its members and a fierce loyalty toward the leadership of the Nation, primarily Elijah Muhammad. This tactic was so effective primarily because "common hatred unites the most heterogeneous elements."[20] By creating a devil in the white man and an enemy in both whites and the blacks that followed them, the Nation established a background against which the Muslims could define themselves. "Mass movements can rise and spread without belief in a God, but never without belief in a devil. Usually the strength of a mass movement is proportionate to the vividness and tangibility of its devil."[21]

After Malcolm X adopted Islam as his religion in 1948 and was released from prison in late 1952, he quickly rose through the ranks of the Nation of Islam's hierarchy, eventually becoming the minister of the Harlem mosque and the movement's National Minister. Malcolm X's entire role and future in the movement depended upon his personal relationship with Elijah Muhammad, and as soon as tensions developed between the two leaders, Malcolm X soon found himself increasingly isolated from his fellow Muslims. His suspension from the Nation in December 1963, and his subsequent break from the movement on March 18, 1964, rapidly turned Malcolm X from the movement's greatest success story to its greatest enemy. The anger that Malcolm X had successfully directed toward white society and the "so-called Negro leaders" soon became intensely directed at him. As the animosities developed between the Nation and its former spokesperson, Malcolm X demonstrated exactly how dangerous an enemy he could be by methodically revealing the secrets of the Nation, including the extramarital affairs of Elijah Muhammad.

By June 1964, the Nation of Islam clearly had a new enemy with whom to contend, one who threatened the continued growth and maturation of the Muslim movement. Malcolm X represented a far greater threat than any other enemy to the Nation of Islam. The white "devils" had little contact with the Muslims and never constituted a threat beyond the discrimination that had always been present in society. But Malcolm X was one of their own who had betrayed them, and he possessed an intimate knowledge of the internal affairs of the Muslims, so the threat to the movement was magnified. The subsequent anger of the Muslims was similarly magnified, as Malcolm X was castigated in the pages of *Muhammad Speaks* and in the mosques as the "chief hypocrite" and enemy of the movement. Every minister in the Nation of Islam denounced his former mentor, and even Malcolm X's own brothers were paraded before the annual convention to attack him. The transfer of anger from the old enemies to the new intensified the emotions on both sides of the conflict and brought them to a level where violence seemed to be the inevitable result.

Another aspect of the Nation of Islam that made it particularly prone to violent activities during the time of the assassination of Malcolm X was the change in the basic nature of the Fruit of Islam. The FOI was the paramilitary arm of the Nation and was composed of the male members of the mosques. The Fruit of Islam members attended weekly meetings in which they received training in self-defense, the use of weapons, and other areas such as personal hygiene. The FOI learned judo and became skilled in the use of knives in the defense of its members. Each mosque was assigned a captain of the FOI that reported not to the minister of that mosque, but to the Supreme Captain of the FOI in Chicago, Raymond Sharrieff, a son-in-law of Elijah Muhammad. The FOI was established in the first few years of the movement as a means of protecting the Muslims from attacks by the police or other whites. The

FOI was also created in order to serve as the vanguard of the imminent War of Armageddon against white society, and the military training, even in small firearms in the beginning years, was instituted in order to prepare the FOI for this task.

Although the duty of serving as the Nation's vanguard of a black revolution was deemphasized in later years, the FOI retained its task of providing security for its members. Before every meeting in the various mosques, the Fruit painstakingly searched every Muslim and visitor before they entered. Patting down women as well as men, they confiscated illicit items, including weapons, cigarettes, alcohol, and even such items as women's makeup, which was regarded as frivolous. Visits from Elijah Muhammad elicited special attention from the local Fruit of Islam, as they provided the Messenger with scores of bodyguards. The FOI regularly surrounded Elijah Muhammad with an impenetrable wall of bodyguards, including cars filled with FOI members when he was traveling, attentive FOI patrolmen lining the roads looking for any conceivable assassination attempt, and guards roving inside and outside the mosques where the frail leader was speaking. In many cases, Muhammad's small, slight frame would be unseen behind the six-foot wall of bodyguards.

Over the years, the Fruit of Islam gained another task other than that of providing security for its members: that of enforcers for the rules of the Nation, ensuring that each member lived by the letter of the Nation's laws and punishing those who violated them. The FOI thus became a police force that would protect the Muslim community and also enforce the laws of that community, giving it a special power over other Muslims that could often lead to abusive behavior. Muslims led a rigorous life of self-discipline, denying themselves the excesses that the rest of the population enjoyed and devoting themselves fully to the maintenance of the Nation. The rules of the Nation were as exacting as they were numerous. Members of the Nation could be punished by the Nation for not selling their quota of the Nation's newspaper, *Muhammad Speaks*, for not bringing enough Lost-Founds (non-Muslims) to the weekly meetings, for not attending meetings themselves, or for using alcohol or drugs. Muslims were also expected to eat only one meal a day, sleep only the necessary number of hours, contribute regularly to the local mosque, attend several Muslim meetings per week, pray five times a day, and avoid frivolity, which included movies, theaters, sporting events, and any activities sponsored by civil rights organizations. According to writer Louis E. Lomax:

> Indeed, it is around the widely known and deeply admired morality of Malcolm X that one of the few pieces of humor about the Muslim movement came into being. The story is that Malcolm was attempting to convert a Negro Baptist to the teaching of Islam.
> "What are the rules of your organization?" the Negro asked.
> "Well," Malcolm said, "my brother, you have to stop drinking, stop swearing, stop gambling, stop using dope, and stop cheating on your wife!"
> "Hell," the convert replied, "I think I had better remain a Christian."[22]

C. Eric Lincoln, who conducted some of the first scholarly research on the Nation of Islam, identified the Fruit of Islam as a source of tension within the movement that would manifest itself in a possible struggle for power after the expected death of Elijah Muhammad. "The FOI no longer dedicates itself solely to guarding the Black Nation against 'trouble with the unbelievers, especially with the police.' It now acts also as a police force and judiciary—or, more exactly, a constabulary and court-martial—to root out and punish any hint of heterodoxy or any slackening of obedience," Lincoln wrote in 1961.[23] This change in the role of the FOI increased its power within the movement and made future changes in the Nation's leadership contingent upon an alliance with the Nation's paramilitary branch.

The evolution of the Fruit of Islam was also significant because of the increasing tendency for the FOI to use its force against members or former members of the Nation rather than against the enemies of the movement. Although the original justification of having a paramilitary wing to the Nation of Islam was to serve as the vanguard against Euro-American society, there were no major cases of reported violence between the FOI and whites, although there are countless instances in which the FOI instigated violence against those blacks who supposedly betrayed the movement. Indeed, in the two situations in which violence between the Fruit of Islam and police seemed imminent, the Nation reined in the FOI and prevented them from retaliating. That they were able to do this is in large measure a result of the extraordinary discipline required of Muslims and the unusual degree of loyalty that the Muslims held toward their leaders.

One situation where violence became imminent between blacks and whites was the 1962 shooting of Ronald Stokes by a police officer in Los Angeles. But despite the clear injustice that was perpetrated by whites against the Muslims, Elijah Muhammad ordered his flock to remain docile and stay aloof from violent retribution. This was a clear case in which the Muslims did not match their rhetoric of armed self-defense with their actions, and this failure led to a mild insurrection in the Los Angeles Muslim mosque. A second situation in which violence seemed possible between whites and the Muslims occurred in Harlem on April 14, 1957. Police were called to the scene of a fight between two men. In the course of clearing the crowd away from the fight, they happened upon two men who declined the policemen's invitation to leave the scene. One of the men, Hinton Johnson, engaged in a verbal exchange with a policeman, who knocked him to the ground with a nightstick. As Brother Hinton X, as he was known in the Nation of Islam, lay on the ground with his head split open, his companion, another Muslim, ran to a telephone to notify Malcolm X and the Fruit of Islam that help was needed. Malcolm X ran to the scene, was rebuffed by the police, and then returned to his Harlem mosque to round up some Muslim enforcers. "In less than half an hour about fifty of Temple Seven's men of the Fruit of Islam were standing in ranks-formation outside the police precinct house" where Johnson was being held.[24] Malcolm X presented himself to the police and went inside the station with his Muslim bodyguards to negotiate with the police.

Finally, the police allowed Malcolm X to see his Muslim brother and, when Malcolm saw the semiconscious Johnson he demanded that the police call an ambulance immediately and send Johnson to a hospital. When the police complied and the ambulance arrived, Malcolm X gave the word and the perfectly disciplined FOI disappeared, only to reappear at the hospital where Johnson was being treated. "The crowd was big, and angry, behind the Muslims in front of Harlem Hospital. Harlem's black people were long since sick and tired of police brutality."[25] When Malcolm gave the word that Johnson was receiving adequate treatment, he motioned for the Muslims to leave, and the incensed crowd quickly dispersed, averting a possible riot. "This is too much power for one man to have," a policeman told James Hicks, the editor of the *Amsterdam News*. "He meant one *black* man. I'll never forget that," Hicks recalled.[26]

The Johnson case was resolved when doctors put a steel plate in his head to fix his cracked skull and a jury awarded him $70,000 as a result of the beating. The performance of the Muslims, and particularly the Fruit of Islam, was the break that Malcolm X was looking for, as the discipline of the Muslims and the willingness to stand up to the police was conveyed in dramatic form to the rest of the New York community. The Muslims had flexed their muscles in front of the New York authorities, but at the same time stopped short of escalating the confrontation into violence. At numerous points during the encounter, violence between blacks and whites seemed imminent, but the Muslims demonstrated their power without pushing the point too far and inciting a riot. The tremendous discipline of the Fruit of Islam and the loyalty of the FOI to Malcolm X had successfully escalated and then defused the situation, and the Muslims won the non-violent battle against the police.

It is significant, however, that the Muslims chose not to escalate the tense situation into a riot against the New York Police Department. Rather than resorting to violence, the Nation of Islam opted to pursue legal means against the police by suing them for brutality, eventually winning what was then the largest cash settlement in history against the New York police. For the Nation of Islam, which regarded itself as obeying a higher authority—Allah—than the white man's laws or court system, it is interesting that the judicial tactics of the NAACP were chosen over the retaliatory path that the Muslims preached. A primary tenet of the Black Muslim philosophy, and one that differentiated them the most from civil rights organizations, is that violence is acceptable and even necessary when it comes to defending oneself and one's fellow Muslims from the white authorities. This failure to live up to the philosophy that the Nation of Islam preached led to the criticism that was later echoed by Malcolm X when he broke from Elijah Muhammad that "those Muslims talk tough, but they never *do* anything."[27]

The significance of two instances of racial conflict between the Muslims and the police—the beating of Hinton Johnson in Harlem and the shooting of Ronald Stokes in Los Angeles—is that neither of them resulted in the Armageddon that Elijah Muhammad had predicted. Contrary to their philosophies, the Muslims decided to seek justice in the government's courtrooms rather than in open battle with the police. This also seems to be the usual pattern in the Nation of Islam, as Elijah Muhammad often sought mediation from the white society's justice system, suing police departments for brutality, penitentiaries for refusing to allow the practice of Islam inside prisons, and even the grocery chain Safeway for discrimination. While Elijah Muhammad sought to prevent the Muslims from initiating full-scale war with white society, a similar battle was brewing between the Black Muslims and their enemies in the black communities, in which the Muslims *did* resort to violence.

While there are almost no documented cases in which the Muslims channeled their energies into retaliation against whites, which was a basis of their philosophy, there were a number of cases in which individual Black Muslims used tactics of violence against "Originals," the Nation of Islam's term for those who were members of the original tribe of Shabazz. Violent retribution seemed to be the method of choice for dealing with those Muslims who defected from the Nation or those who in some way directly challenged the well-being of the movement or its leader, Elijah Muhammad. It is difficult to determine in these cases whether orders were issued by the leadership in Chicago or individual ministers or Fruit of Islam captains, or whether the initiative came from individual Muslims without approval from above. Certainly there was no public acceptance from the Muslim leadership that such acts of violence were committed by Muslims, and Elijah Muhammad made every effort to distance the Nation of Islam from such acts. "We have never resorted to such a thing as violence," Muhammad declared on the day after Malcolm X was killed, adding that "we have never resorted to arms."[28]

The hostilities of Muslim against Muslim erupted into what *The New York Times* called "a mounting pattern of violence," resulting in a number of beatings and at least one death, although a number of other killings, including that of Malcolm X, can be linked to the Black Muslims. The Fruit of Islam, unable to demonstrate its power against the white society that it had been trained to hate, turned its attention—and its violence—against its own kind. Many of the victims of the Muslims were physically beaten for their challenges to the Nation of Islam, and a few faced Muslim weapons that Elijah Muhammad said the Muslims did not own. Most of the victims were Black Muslims who renounced their membership publicly, and threatened to become an embarrassment to the Nation of Islam by setting up rival movements. Whether these former Muslims actually posed a genuine threat to the movement is irrelevant to the Nation of Islam. A more important point is that the victims challenged the Prophet Elijah Muhammad and his teachings, thereby setting themselves up for violent retribution.

One case was that of Willie Eugene Greer, an unemployed long-shoreman who was 31 years old in 1965 when he was beaten for remarks that he made the summer before. During the Nation of Islam's annual convention, held on February 28, 1965, at the Chicago Coliseum, Greer was able to sneak past the heavy FOI security without being recognized. However, once inside, Greer reported being attacked by "a hundred of the elite security guards" who repeatedly kicked and hit him.[29] Greer managed to crawl out of the convention hall and was immediately hospitalized for his extensive cuts and bruises. Greer's beating was the result of comments that he made almost a year before during a meeting of the Black Muslims at Washington Park in New York City, where Greer said he climbed to the podium and told the crowd that "Muhammad should move out."[30] Even such an innocuous comment as that represented a direct threat to The Honorable Elijah Muhammad in the eyes of the Muslims, and the Fruit of Islam, whose duty it was to protect the Messenger of Allah from harm, responded with violence in order to minimize the threat.

In October 1964, another Muslim was attacked for leaving the Nation of Islam. Details of the beating are scarce, but it seems to fit the same pattern of other acts of violence against Muslims who left the Nation of Islam. But this time the victim was beaten so badly that he died from his injuries. Kenneth Morton was a New York painter who joined Harlem Temple Number Seven while Malcolm X was the minister. But late in 1964, Morton began distancing himself from the Muslims and subsequently was beaten by members of the Fruit of Islam for straying too far from the flock. Finally, in October 1964, he decided to leave the Nation of Islam. But soon after he left, Morton was attacked by two Muslims in front of his home. He was hospitalized for his injuries and told police the story of his beating, including the names of the Muslims who were involved. But Morton finally died from his injuries on November 5, 1964. According to the *Amsterdam News*, Alvin Jennings and Elenger Grey, both Muslims from New York, were arrested and charged with Kenneth Morton's death.

Leon Ameer, one of Malcolm's lieutenants, also fell victim to violence from the Black Muslims. He was assaulted in Boston after leaving the Nation of Islam. Ameer was born in New York City in 1933, but soon moved to the Virgin Islands before returning to New York at age 15. He received an honorable discharge from the Marines after enlisting at age 18 and worked at odd jobs before he joined the Nation of Islam in 1955. In the final few months of Malcolm X's life, Ameer served as the Organization of Afro-American Unity's Boston representative, and Ameer has been used by conspiracy theorists as a key piece of evidence that the government was involved in the murder. According to those theorists, Ameer was killed by government agents immediately before he was to divulge the truth about Malcolm X's assassination. Whether or not this is the case, one particular beating that he suffered at the hands of the Black Muslims serves as further evidence in a pattern of Muslim violence. Ameer was actually beaten not once but twice on Christmas Day, 1964, leaving him unconscious after the second assault. The beatings apparently were in retaliation for his decision to leave the Nation of Islam and join Malcolm X's Organization of Afro-American Unity, where he became the Boston OAAU representative and a contender for the leadership after Malcolm X died.

Before the beatings, Ameer, a muscular karate and judo expert who often performed at the Muslim annual conventions, was charged by the Nation of Islam with adultery and thievery. The first beating came on Christmas Day in the Sherry-Biltmore Hotel in Boston. Ameer, the former captain of the New Haven Fruit of Islam and a former press secretary of Muhammad Ali, was attacked by four Muslims from the Boston mosque in the lobby of the hotel. A passing police officer, Detective James Kilday, stopped the fight and arrested the four attackers, among them Clarence X Gill, The captain of the Boston Fruit of Islam. Gill had become known for his role in a beating of Aubrey Barnette, an officer in the Boston mosque who left the Muslims in 1964. Ameer testified against the Muslims, who included Gill, Joseph Smott, and brothers Roy and Ronald Thompson, in early February 1965, before the Boston Municipal Court. Ameer announced to the court that he would be filing a civil suit against the Nation of Islam for its attacks against him. All four of the Black Muslim suspects were convicted of the assault and fined $100 by the court.

The second beating that Ameer suffered happened within hours of the first, as he was attacked again by his former associates that night in his hotel room. He was not found until the next day, as police detectives discovered Ameer's unconscious body in his bathtub after Ameer failed to show up in court to file a complaint against Clarence X and the rest of his assailants. He was taken immediately to Boston City Hospital and could not be revived from his coma for three days. He remained in the hospital for fifteen days before he was allowed to go home. Even after his beatings, Ameer continued to receive threatening phone calls, and "on two occasions escaped further attack only on the strength of the chain on his hotel room door."[31] The assassination of Malcolm X only confirmed for Ameer that the Muslims were capable of murder. "I know that my life is worth nothing," Ameer declared soon after Malcolm X was killed. Malcolm X agreed with that assessment before he died: "If my life is worth three cents, then Leon's is worth two cents," he said in early February.

Despite the obvious threat to Ameer's life from the Nation of Islam, conspiracy theorists have taken his case as further evidence that it was the government—and not the Muslims—that carried out the murder of Malcolm X. Within a short time of his mentor's assassination, Ameer began to change his opinion about who was responsible for the violence. According to Eric Norden, who published probably the best argument for a government conspiracy in *The Realist* magazine in 1967, Ameer was killed for getting too close to the real reason why Malcolm X was assassinated. "I have facts in my possession as to who *really* killed Malcolm," Ameer told a Boston branch of the Socialist Workers Party on March 13, 1965. "They aren't from Chicago. They're from Washington."[32] "This is probably the last time you will see me," he announced to the audience.[33] According to Norden, "the next morning his dead body was discovered by a chambermaid in his room at Boston's Sherry-Biltmore Hotel. He had died of strangulation."[34]

Actually, the cause of Ameer's death remains unknown. On the day of his death, even before he was able to conduct an autopsy, Medical Examiner Richard Ford announced: "There is no evidence of any injuries at present. I understand he was an epileptic. He was found dead with froth on his mouth. This is possibly indicative of an epileptic attack or even a heart attack."[35] However, Ameer's wife, a loyal Black Muslim who had left her husband when he joined Malcolm X's Organization of Afro-American Unity in December 1964, claimed that her husband did not have epilepsy or heart trouble. Norden and other conspiracy theorists grabbed this statement as evidence that the coroner claimed that Ameer's death was from natural causes only in order to conceal the fact that the government murdered Ameer. But Mrs. Ameer did tell the Associated Press on the day of her husband's death that he was worried about a blood clot in the brain that developed after the beatings on Christmas Day. "I don't know," she said [about her husband's death]. "He was afraid of being killed, but I'm not accusing anyone."[36]

A further incident of violence against the enemies of the Black Muslim movement came in the summer of 1964. Tensions between the followers of Malcolm X and those of Elijah Muhammad came to a momentary peak when the Nation of Islam leader ventured to New York for the first time in three years. The visit to New York proved to be a bitter confrontation between the two former allies as death threats were circulated against both leaders. In the end, Elijah Muhammad assembled over 6,500 supporters at the 369th Armory, including a large number of out-of-town Muslims. Muhammad Ali, the recently crowned heavyweight champion of the world, was on hand for the rally and presented the Messenger with a gold model of a mosque that he received on his trip to Africa. Meanwhile, Malcolm X held a meeting before 1,000 supporters in order to announce the formation of his Organization of Afro-American Unity and to announce the goals of his new, secular organization. Answering a question after his rally, Malcolm X attacked his former mentor in a clear game of tit for tat. "Elijah spends his time denouncing white persons and my followers. Why doesn't he denounce the Ku Klux Klan and the White Citizens Council?"

Elijah Muhammad's rally was marred by two different outbreaks of violence, both of them made almost inevitable by the high degree of tension at the rally and the death threats that had been circulated against the Messenger. The first example involved a man named Jesus Emanuel, who referred to himself at the time as a "blood son of the original Mother and Father Divine." For several hours before the beginning of the rally, Emanuel circulated literature through Harlem that attacked Elijah Muhammad, but luckily he did not incur the wrath of the Muslims. During the actual rally, however, Emanuel produced a sign that called the Messenger a "mix bred phony." This was apparently too much for the Black Muslims to endure, and Emanuel was set upon by a number of them. He wound up with a broken nose and two missing teeth, but left the rally without pressing charges against the Muslims who had attacked him.

The second attack was a beating by several members of the Fruit of Islam and brought the police in direct conflict with the Muslim security organization. The victim was a 21-year-old named David Wetstone, who lived in the

Bronx. Although he did nothing to provoke the ire of the Muslims, apparently he was recognized by the Black Muslims as a follower of Malcolm X. Given the animosity between the Muslims and their former minister in New York, Wetstone was immediately attacked as he entered the rally. The police, who saw the beating, moved in to stop the rout, but the Fruit of Islam, in ranks formation, intervened and pushed the police back almost 25 yards. The policemen were backed up by some of the other 100 police that were on hand at the Armory in case of violence. The tense situation was defused by the additional policemen, who barely avoided an all-out war with the angry Muslims. If the FOI was willing to assault one of Malcolm X's followers and risk an all-out war with the police, then they certainly would have no qualms with taking a lesser risk and reaping greater benefits, as they did with the assassination of Malcolm X.

The beating of Aubrey Barnette proved to be one of the most embarrassing events for the Nation of Islam, as it led to the publication of "The Black Muslims Are a Fraud," an article with a headline in bold letters printed in the *Saturday Evening Post* soon after Malcolm X was killed. In his article, written with Edward Linn, Barnett, a 5′6″, slightly built college graduate, detailed his beating at the hands of thirteen well-built men whom he recognized as "members of the Muslim terror squad," the Fruit of Islam. Barnette was a recent graduate of Boston University with a degree in business administration when he first joined the Muslims, attracted by the Muslim program for economic uplift. But rather than improving his financial condition, his long hours of labor at the Boston's Temple No. 11 forced him to quit his overtime hours at the post office, and contributions to the temple consumed almost one-fifth of his remaining income. Barnette reported that this was a fairly common experience among Muslims; whereas many Muslims were originally businessmen, they were forced to sell their businesses as a result of their investment of time and effort in the Nation of Islam. Barnette also discussed the use of the

Fruit of Islam as enforcers rather than protectors when he told of one incident in the temple:

> Once Captain Clarence [of the Fruit of Islam] received information that the brother and brother-in-law of Minister Louis's wife had entered the Y.M.C.A., which is as out-of-bounds as a Muslim can possibly get. The investigator discovered that the two were going to the "Y" regularly to study the self-defense technique called karate. Clarence concluded that if they were secretly studying karate it could only be for use against the Muslims. The two men were hustled down to the basement of the mosque for questioning while a temple meeting was in progress. Instead of confessing, however, they insisted that they had only been trying to find out whether karate was worth teaching to the rest of the F.O.I. Clarence didn't believe them and had his lieutenants beat them.[27]

In his article, Barnette also discussed another use of violence by the Fruit of Islam, this time against the members of the mosque. One of the businesses that the Nation of Islam initiated, under the guidance of Malcolm X, was the newspaper, *Muhammad Speaks*. Although it began as an internal organ to report the news of the Nation, it soon became an instrument of profit, as each member of the mosque was given a quota of newspapers to sell. Since members were expected to pay for all the newspapers allotted, even if they could not sell them, many members had to pay a substantial amount of money to the mosque. And, according to Barnette, "when a brother fell too far behind [in sales of newspapers], members of the terror squad [the Fruit of Islam] would pay him a night visit. If he still wouldn't—or couldn't get up the money, they would invite him out for a ride, drive him to Franklin Park and work them over." This policy precipitated a major crisis in the Boston mosque as the Muslim businessmen—who were the victims of many of the beatings since they did not have time to hawk the newspapers—began to leave the mosque en masse in outrage over the beatings, never to return.

A similar defection occurred at the Chicago mosque in 1964, inviting potential violence between the mosque officers and the Muslims who complained about the policy of selling *Muhammad Speaks*. According to FBI reports, seven members of the mosque approached the Bureau office in Chicago on June 11, 1964, asking for protection from other Muslims, who had threatened them with physical violence. Wade X, the spokesperson for the group of seven, said that Muslim officials "had threatened them with bodily harm and possibly death." He went on to tell the FBI that

> They all admired Elijah Muhammad very much and did not hold him responsible for the fact they believed members of the NOI at MTI #2 [Muslim Temple of Islam #2 in Chicago] were being exploited by officials of that temple. He said that their main grievance was the pressure put on members by the officials for selling the NOI paper "Muhammad Speaks," greed on the part of those officials, their expensive living, coupled with their "superior attitude."[38]

It was at this point that Barnette decided to leave the mosque as well. He was verbally attacked by Minister Louis X, the former calypso singer who became minister of the Boston mosque, as a "bourgeois Negro" after he joined an organization to protest police brutality, a major offense to a religion that bans involvement of its members in civil rights organizations. In a 1963 letter to the mosque, Barnette announced his decision to leave the mosque, "lest my unhappiness infect the others." Nine months later, Barnette found himself in the wrong place at the wrong time when he went to the Boston airport only fifteen minutes after an attempt was made on Malcolm X's life by the Muslims. Malcolm X was scheduled to be in a car heading to the airport (actually he had sent four of his lieutenants while he remained in New York during the incident), when a car of armed Muslims cut them off. One of Malcolm X's allies waved the shotgun he was carrying, and the other car disappeared. When Malcolm X's men arrived at the airport, they walked toward their gate, shotgun brandished to prevent other attacks. The police were immediately called, who began arresting "anybody who looked suspicious, which in this case meant almost any Negro." This included Barnette, who was detained briefly by the police.

Barnette was beaten soon after this incident, presumably because the Muslims who saw him with the police assumed that he was testifying against them. At the time of the beating, Barnette was driving through Roxbury, a Boston ghetto, with John Thimas, also a former member of the Boston mosque, when a pink Cadillac filled with Fruit of Islam members cut them off and forced them to stop. Thimas was dragged from the car first and attacked with karate chops. Barnette was then removed from the car and surrounded by Muslims, who began punching and kicking him. Since the beating occurred in the middle of a busy street, traffic piled up and drivers from other cars finally came to help the victims. Barnette was hospitalized with a broken ankle, ribs, vertebrae, and internal bleeding. "I was in the hospital for a week, in bed at home for another week and out of work for a total of three weeks. My ankle was in a cast for a month."[39]

Barnette called his beating "an act of revenge" for daring to quit the Nation of Islam. Although he hardly represented a genuine threat to the Muslim movement, Barnette did have specific details of the movement that would have been of interest to the FBI and others who were enemies of the Muslim movement. "I believe we were beaten as punishment for quitting and also as a warning to us to keep our mouths shut."[40] The attempt to prevent Barnette from going to the press with his experiences clearly backfired and even gave him a new example of the corruption of the Muslims as he recounted the story of his beating. Barnette gave increased credence to the theory that Malcolm X's death represented a "mounting pattern of violence" rather than an isolated case of an attack by the Muslims.

Even Elijah Muhammad's son Wallace was not immune from threats of retribution from the Fruit of Islam. After he split with the Nation in 1963, he reported receiving death threats from NOI officials. Wallace broke publicly from the Nation of Islam in 1963 after learning of his father's adultery and other examples of corruption in the movement. Until his break from the Nation, Wallace was seen as the front-runner to succeed Elijah Muhammad since Wallace was, as Malcolm X put it, "Mr. Muhammad's most strongly spiritual son, the son with the most objective outlook."[41] But it was apparently this objectivity that made him question the teachings and the sincerity of the Nation of Islam. Wallace, along with his brother Akbar, who studied orthodox Islam at Al-Azhar University in Cairo, began to see the contradictions between Islam and the religion that their father preached as Islam. They also saw weaknesses in their father. According to Malcolm X's autobiography, it was Wallace who first confirmed his father's adultery to Malcolm X. "Wallace said he didn't feel that his father would welcome any effort to help him," the New York minister and NOI National Minister reported.[42] According to the *Chicago Daily Defender* newspaper:

The son of the Muslim leader said that his disenchantment with the movement began in Jan. 1963, when he was released from prison after serving a term for violation of draft laws. "When I came out of [of prison], I was told by members of the family that the organization was in 'bad shape' and that there was an 'explosive situation' in the private quarters of my father," he said. Wallace said he wrote twice to the elder Muhammad, only to be told to "stay out of my [Muhammad's] business." The younger man said appeals to his father's "basic goodness and decency" proved useless.[43]

According to Wallace Muhammad, the threats came from "officers" of the movement in Chicago, although he did not specify which officers he meant. "The leadership in Chicago is ruthless and frantic" and "they will kill you," Muhammad told the *Defender*. "They said they would beat me up. Then they began to make threats on my life. I know they are fanatics and will kill you." The death threats finally stopped after he went publicly to the FBI, the local police, and his parole officer[44] and reported them. "The members of my father's staff are guilty of some or all of these evils [that are banned by the Nation, such as adultery and drinking]. There have been beatings, lies and hypocrisy; they have presented my father as a holy image, and misused thousands of dollars," Wallace Muhammad said. Ironically, Wallace Muhammad recanted these statements publicly at the annual Muslim convention held only days after Malcolm X was assassinated, but later reaffirmed them when his father was dead, leaving him in a position to inherit the leadership of the movement.

Wallace Muhammad made himself the perfect candidate for violence against him from the Fruit of Islam, according to the pattern apparent in other cases. He was an official in the movement, the son of the Messenger, and the future leader of the entire religion. But when he disavowed his belief in his father as the Prophet of Islam and spread information concerning Elijah Muhammad's adultery, he set himself up for a confrontation with the Fruit of Islam. Luckily, Wallace became the victim only of threats and not violence, although an explanation for this would be pure speculation. Certainly he did not represent the threat that Malcolm X posed when he left the Nation. Unlike Wallace, Malcolm X had tremendous support and popularity across the country, with a name recognition that easily surpassed that of the Messenger he represented. Wallace would not have been able to start his own organization that could compete with the Muslims for membership and attention, as Malcolm X did. He also did not attempt to go public with accusations against Elijah Muhammad and the Nation of Islam that would easily discredit the movement, as Malcolm X did. Wallace may have also been saved by his name. Perhaps the Fruit of Islam did not want to harm the son of the Prophet, or were given specific orders not to harm him from officials in the movement. The important point, however, in terms of trying to establish a pattern in the cases of violence against enemies of the Nation of Islam, was that the Fruit of Islam, according to Wallace, targeted him with threats of violence, even though these threats were never carried out.

From these examples of violence and threats of violence, the pattern seems clear. Members of the Fruit of Islam were dispatched to deal with those who had abandoned the movement and in some way challenged the authority of the Nation of Islam's leadership. Although at least two victims were killed, it does not seem as if it was the intention of the Muslims to murder their victims. Rather, it seems that the displays of violence were used primarily as a means of intimidation. The shooting of Benjamin Brown and the assassination of Malcolm X are certainly exceptions to this basic rule. All of these victims of Muslim violence represented either a potential or an actual threat to the Black Muslim movement or, more specifically, a threat to Elijah Muhammad. While it is difficult to believe that someone like Willie Greer could have posed a threat to the movement, he still represented a challenge to the teachings of the Honorable Elijah Muhammad, and he was amply paid back for his sin of degrading the Messenger.

Using these examples as the context surrounding the assassination of Malcolm X, it becomes far more plausible that it was individuals within the Black Muslim movement who performed the murder, a possibility that conspiracy theorists seem intent on dismissing. They insist that the Black Muslims would not have killed one of their own, and it therefore must have been the government that conspired against the black nationalist. According to these theorists, the government was the only one capable of actions ranging from poisoning him in Cairo, barring him from France, and burning down his house in a manner that suggested that Malcolm X had actually set the fire. While these three incidents make an interesting conspiracy theory when tied together and slightly manipulated, there is no evidence that any of these three incidents had anything whatsoever to do with the assassination. There is, however, a great deal of evidence that links the Nation of Islam to the crime, whether it be individual members or the group as a whole. The pattern of violence, the previous attempts on Malcolm X's life, and the blatantly clear motive all serve to place the Muslims in the forefront of responsibility for the assassination.

These examples of violence do not show that the Black Muslims, whether individually or as a group, were responsible for the death of Malcolm X. Rather, it simply demonstrates that the Muslims were capable of such an act. While it is still not clear whether these beatings were enacted under orders from higher-ups in the Nation or whether they were individual deviations from official Muslim policy, it is clear that they had the ability and the capacity to carry out the crime. They had a highly developed motive that included a long list of reasons why they would want to see Malcolm X dead. Even Malcolm X was quite aware of the threat that he faced in the final year of his life. "I'm a marked man," he told Alex Haley one day. "I've had highly placed people tell me to be careful every move I make."[45] And he often revealed what he considered the source of the threat to his life in a highly quotable line that showed both his own immodesty and his fear of the Muslims. "There is no group in the United States more able to carry out this threat than the Black Muslims. I know, because I taught them myself."[46]

CHAPTER ELEVEN

The Aftermath

"Dear Daddy, I love you so. O dear, O dear, I wish you wasn't dead."
> —*Malcolm X's young daughter, Attilah,*
> *shortly after her father's murder.*

The violence that characterized the Nation of Islam during the final year of the life of Malcolm X did not stop when Brother Malcolm was gunned down in the Audubon Ballroom. Malcolm X was just one of many victims of the violence of the Nation of Islam during the 1960s and 1970s, murdered because he disagreed with the politics of the Messenger of Allah, the Honorable Elijah Muhammad. Malcolm X got caught in the Muslims' politics of retaliation, which proclaimed that the ultimate sin was not to attack African-Americans, but to attack Elijah Muhammad. In the case of Malcolm X, such a sin required the punishment of death. The murders, such as the one on February 21, 1965, continued at a regular pace, but escalated in the early 1970s, when Elijah Muhammad's tight control over the strings of power began to fade. As it became clear that Muhammad was soon to die, the discipline among the Muslims also began to wither, and gun battles and involvement in organized crime began to take the place of the traditional Muslim austerity.

The year 1973, two years before Elijah Muhammad finally passed away, was a particularly violent one for the Nation of Islam. The internal strife within the Nation was compounded by external struggles with other Muslim groups across the country. Disagreements with other Muslim groups often turned into violence, as the internecine warfare in the American Muslim community grew more vicious. One Muslim group, the Hanafi community, was particularly critical of the Nation of Islam and Elijah Muhammad. Their leader, Hamaas Abdul Khaalis, began attacking Elijah Muhammad as a false prophet who taught his followers a version of Islam that perverted the true religion. Hamaas wrote letters to ministers of the Nation of Islam in different parts of the country in an attempt to convince them that their Messenger was misleading them and that they should renounce the Nation. Soon after he sent the letters, he began receiving death threats, followed by a beating that he and his son-in-law suffered in Washington, D.C.

The confrontation between the Hanafis and the Black Muslims turned deadly on January 17, 1973, as seven members of the Hanafi community were executed at the former house of basketball player Kareem Abdul-Jabbar, who was a member of the Hanafis. The three-story mansion was being used at the time as the headquarters for the Hanafis when several black men, identified as members of the Nation of Islam, broke in and killed two adults and five children, four of whom were drowned in a bathtub. One of the survivors identified the men as Black Muslims. Hamaas immediately blamed the Black Muslims for the murders and called for the overthrow of Elijah Muhammad as the leader of the Nation of Islam. According to Abdul-Jabbar, "apparently, [the Black Muslims] were so threatened, they had to take the lives of children. It must have been some fanatical person, someone very sick and ill."[1] Although the Nation of Islam denied any part in the murders, at least six members of the Nation of Islam were later arrested by police for their part in the murders.[2]

Later that year, more factional battles between the Black

Muslims and other Muslim communities took the life of James Shabazz, the minister of Muhammad's Newark Mosque Number 25. Shabazz was gunned down in his driveway as he was entering his car on September 4, 1973. Eleven men were arrested for the crime, all of them members of the New World of Islam, which had been trying to take over the Nation of Islam's Newark Mosque.[3] The bodies of two decapitated Black Muslims were discovered the next month near the site of the Shabazz slaying; the heads were found four miles away. Police almost immediately linked the killings with the Shabazz murder the month before.[4] The Nation of Islam also found itself in turf battles with such non-Muslim nationalist organizations as the Black Panther Party. One 100-person brawl between the Muslims and the Panthers exploded in Atlanta over the rights to sell newspapers at a particular street corner.[5] In another outbreak of violence, Hakim Jamal, who wrote a memoir of his time with Malcolm X, was murdered in May 1973, in front of his wife and child, apparently for his "loose-lipped" attacks against Elijah Muhammad.[6]

However, the Nation of Islam faced far more problems in the early 1970s than factional battles with other organizations. Elijah Muhammad's health had deteriorated to the point of what one observer called "senility," and his control over the Muslims diminished. "He sometimes goes into a state of senility and the worst is expected at any time. But things could go on like that for some time." As Muhammad struggled to stay in command of the Nation, the group's finances dwindled. The "thriving business empire" estimated at $70 million that Muhammad built from the collections of his followers fell into "jeopardy of crumbling for lack of cash flow and technical and managerial skills," *The New York Times* reported in late 1973.[7] The newspaper also reported that the Nation of Islam had attempted to search for money in grants from Arab countries. The Muslims were successful in obtaining $3 million from Libya's Muammar Khadafi, although all other nations turned down the request. Even Libya refused to offer a second monetary gift because of the internal strife within the Muslims and the internecine killings that had recently taken place. Some Muslims also allegedly turned to organized crime, especially in cities on the East Coast, according to an investigation by the *Times*. According to one Philadelphia source, "a lot of guys went back to their old ways. Remember, the Muslims were big recruiters in the jails and prisons. And Philadelphia has a history of gangs, so it was rather easy for the gang members to take on the trappings of the religion, change their names and keep on operating as they had."[8]

The Honorable Elijah Muhammad finally passed away in early 1975, almost ten years after Malcolm X had been assassinated. The Nation of Islam underwent dramatic changes after the death of their leader. Under the new direction of Wallace D. Muhammad, who changed his first name to Warith, the Muslims moved away from the fiery antiwhite rhetoric toward a more moderate—even conservative—religious stance. Orthodox Islam supplanted Elijah Muhammad's hybrid form of racially motivated Islam, and the focus of the Muslims on economic growth waned in favor of spiritual growth. Wallace Muhammad, driven by the same religious ideas that had caused his expulsion from the Nation of Islam ten years earlier, was now in a position to implement them with the death of his father. Before he was expelled from the Muslims in 1964, he had firsthand knowledge of orthodox Islam and knew that the religion that his father sold as Islam was nothing even close. After the death of Malcolm X, he rejoined the Nation, apparently intent on making the changes from inside rather than from the outside.

When he finally got his chance in 1975, Wallace purged the Nation of many of the false ideas that ran counter to the actual beliefs of Islam. Gone were the ideas of racial separation, the divine nature of W. D. Fard and Elijah Muhammad, and the notion of a coming Armageddon that would set the darker world against the whites in a battle to the death. Even many of the symbols of the old days were gone. The rigid dress code that mandated long white dresses for the women and suits and ties for the men was abolished. Wallace Muhammad renamed the Nation of Islam, calling it the World Community of Islam in the West (WCIW). Similarly, he changed the name of *Muhammad Speaks* to *Bilalian News*, after a 14th-century Muslim. Even the numerous businesses that had been the foundation of the Nation of Islam under Elijah Muhammad, began to be sold to pay off the Nation's various debts. The Muslim restaurants, bakeries, clothing stores, and dry-cleaning establishments quickly dwindled as Wallace Muhammad moved the focus of the Nation away from economics. The Fruit of Islam—which Wallace Muhammad called the "punch your teeth out" wing of the Nation of Islam—was similarly disbanded in order to relieve the Nation of the violence that had afflicted it in the past. And, in a symbolic gesture to try to heal the wounds of the past, Wallace Muhammad renamed the Harlem Mosque Number Seven in honor of Malcolm X.

In the place of the antiwhite, militant Nation of Islam with its own paramilitary Fruit of Islam grew a more docile religious group that looked to Mecca rather than Chicago for spiritual rejuvenation. The younger Muhammad even ceded his day-to-day control over the organization to a council of advisors so that he could focus more on the religious aspects of the group, although he still essentially controlled the major operations. In one of the most remarkable—and controversial—departures from his father's teachings, Wallace Muhammad announced that whites would finally be allowed to join his Islamic mosques. The notion that whites were the devils, created from a mutant strain by an evil scientist, was replaced by the Islamic belief that people of all races were brothers and sisters. Wallace even struck up an alliance with the United States Labor Alliance, a predominantly white middle-class organization. In another surprising turn for the former Nation of Islam, Wallace downgraded his father from the status of Messenger to that of an ordinary human. Instead of being divinely guided, Elijah Muhammad was "misguided," his son admitted. The truth of Malcolm X's charges of adultery against Muhammad was also conceded, and all of Muhammad's children—legitimate and illegitimate—were given a share of the inheritance.

Wallace even guided his World Community of Islam in the West into mainstream politics, allowing his followers to join civil rights and community-based organizations. This overturned his father's insistence that the Muslims belong to only one organization, the Nation of Islam. As a result of the new policy, Muslims in New Orleans teamed up with others to fight for changes in the public-school system, and scores of Muslims across the country joined civil rights groups that they had been forbidden to join under Elijah Muhammad. Muhammad himself joined the Black Leadership Forum, where he met with Benjamin Hooks of the NAACP and other major civil rights leaders. Muhammad even endorsed President Jimmy Carter for his actions on civil rights and attacked Hooks publicly when Hooks criticized Carter. Clearly, the Nation of Islam had changed. In the eyes of some, the new World Community of Islam in the West—the former Nation of Islam—had grown even more conservative than the NAACP. "I condemn the flag-waving and patriotism by Wallace," one Muslim said, "and I think they have become more conservative than the NAACP. It's ironic. Back in the 1960s, we condemned the NAACP because it was too conservative; we were the militants. But now the tables have turned."

Dissatisfaction with the new order in the Nation of Islam grew tremendously and increased with every change that Wallace Muhammad made. Just as Malcolm X's followers became disenchanted when he returned from Mecca with a new outlook on racial matters, so, too, did the Muslims grow weary of the dizzying changes made by Wallace Muhammad. Many felt that nothing was wrong with the Nation of Islam as it was under the Messenger and that Wallace was betraying his father's memory. The militancy, the homogeneity, the religious zeal—all of which Wallace changed in his new organization—were positive aspects of the Nation, some argued, and should not be changed. Even some of those who agreed with many of the changes that Muhammad made yearned for the days when the Nation was a group to be feared by the white community and where the power was entirely in the hands of blacks.

A number of smaller groups across the country attempted to revive the old days of the Nation of Islam under the Honorable Elijah Muhammad. The Elijah Muhammad Mosque in St. Louis continued to display a mural of the Messenger in honor of his divine nature. At least two independent *Muhammad Speaks* newspapers appeared in defiance of Wallace Muhammad's *Bilalian News*. But the most serious challenge came from Louis X, the minister of the Boston mosque who had succeeded Malcolm X in the Harlem temple when Malcolm X was killed. Louis X, who changed his name to Abdul Haleem Farrakhan but called himself Louis Farrakhan, rose in the Nation of Islam under the Messenger and became the movement's National Minister, a position which Malcolm X also held.

At first Louis Farrakhan accepted the changes that had taken place in the former Nation of Islam after the Honorable Elijah Muhammad died. Even if he didn't like the direction that the organization was taking, he had little power to change the situation. He played the role of dutiful minister and accepted the fact that Wallace Muhammad had supreme control over the Muslims. "No other man holds the key to divinity," Farrakhan declared after the Messenger died. "There is no one wise enough to approach the shoelace of Wallace D. Muhammad." But when Wallace Muhammad found his new World Community of Islam in the West in financial troubles after he sold many of the thriving businesses that kept the Nation of Islam afloat, Farrakhan made his move. Deciding the Elijah Muhammad's methods of organization were right all the time and that Wallace was damaging to his father's memory, Farrakhan split from the movement and reinstated the Nation of Islam.

His first step was to consolidate some of the original structures of the Nation of Islam, including the Chicago Mosque Number Two and Elijah Muhammad's Hyde Park mansion. Wallace was only too happy to sell these symbolic trophies to Farrakhan—a total cost of almost $3 million—in order to pay the debts of his WCIW. Farrakhan installed himself in the Messenger's former seat of power in Hyde Park, then reestablished the Nation of Islam under the same rules that had governed the organization while the Messenger was still alive. The Fruit of Islam was recreated, the dress code reinstituted, and the divinity of Elijah Muhammad reaffirmed. Farrakhan could not attract nearly as many adherents as the Nation had during the 1960s, but he defended the besmirched honor of Elijah Muhammad and returned the Nation to its original state. The two offshoots of the Nation of Islam—Wallace Muhammad's WCIW and Farrakhan's new NOI—grew along separate, but not amicable, lines during the 1980s, although Farrakhan had not matched the membership of the WCIW, which was again renamed, this time as the American Muslim Mission.

Although he has figured prominently in the Nation of Islam since the early 1970s, Louis Farrakhan has been in the national spotlight only since 1984, when he waded into presidential politics and endorsed Rev. Jesse Jackson for the Democratic nomination. Farrakhan initially made headlines when he allegedly threatened Milton Coleman, a *Washington Post* reporter who disclosed Jesse Jackson's reference to New York City as "Hymietown." Farrakhan reportedly said that "we're going to make an example of Milton Coleman. One day soon, we will punish you by death, because you are interfering with the future of our babies—for white people and against the good of yourself and your own people. This is a fitting punishment for such dogs."[9] Farrakhan has denied making the comment.

Since his initial foray into national politics, Farrakhan has tried desperately to dispel the notion that he is anti-Semitic, a charge that has surfaced repeatedly in his career because of his statements attacking Zionism. But Farrakhan has never been able to shake the anti-Semitic label, in large part because every time that he attempts to clear his name, he winds up making statements that are as offensive as the ones that he is trying to explain. His statements that "Judaism is a dirty religion" and that "Hitler was a great man," both reveal his personal convictions about Jews. According to *The New Republic* magazine, which has been a critic of Farrakhan's, "After a long explanation of how the 'dirty religion' remark was taken out of context, he accused Jewish people of 'using God's holy name as a shield for your dirty religion.' "[10]

But despite the charges against him, Farrakhan has had remarkable success in limited skirmishes against the drug trade, which he argues has been tearing apart the foundations of the United States. The war against drugs, he maintains, has been an excuse for the government to declare war on African-Americans. "There is a war being planned against black youth by the government of the United States under the guise of a war against drugs and gangs and violence," he said.[11] Farrakhan has been as vocal as Malcolm X in his own war against the evils of drugs and advocates a moral reformation for African-Americans across the country. In an effort to control the drug trade, members of the Nation of Islam in Washington, D.C., began patrolling certain housing projects in 1990 in order to remove the drugs from the buildings. As a result, the drug trade was almost eliminated from two projects, Mayfair Mansions and Paradise Manor.

Much of Farrakhan's success depends upon his oratorical skills, which allow him to inspire raw emotions in his listeners. According to one observer, "for many the act of consuming [a speech from Farrakhan] is the principal gratification.

In that sense going to a Farrakhan speech is identical to going to an M.C. Hammer concert; it is the happening place to be at the moment. Farrakhan is a masterful per-

former and spellbinding orator. He offers his audience a
safely contained catharsis: visceral rebellion without dangerous consequences, an instant, painless inversion of
power and status relations. As a talented demagogue,
Farrakhan mingles banalities, half-truths, distortions and
falsehoods to buttress simplistic and wacky theories. The
result is a narrative in which he takes on the role of racial conscience and, in Malcolm's old phrase, "tells it
like it is." He cajoles, berates, exhorts, instructs and
consoles—all reassuringly, without upsetting the framework of conservative petit-bourgeois convention.[12]

Farrakhan has also been plagued by charges that he encouraged the assassination of Malcolm X, while some have
asserted that Farrakhan took an active role in ordering it or
planning it. In a 1985 interview with NBC, Malcolm X's
widow, Betty Shabazz, criticized Farrakhan for his actions
after Malcolm X broke from the Nation of Islam. She went
on to say that she regretted the day that she ever met Louis
Farrakhan. According to Farrakhan, "as a member of the
Nation of Islam, who was a contemporary of Malcolm, who
disagreed with Malcolm in his vilification of the Honorable
Elijah Muhammad and forthrightly spoke against Malcolm—naturally Mrs. Shabazz could not have any warm,
tender feelings for me, given the whole scenario."[13]
Farrakhan has argued that the only reason for the claim
that he was involved in Malcolm X's assassination was his
growing popularity, so that "every effort of the establishment media to rupture that popularity has been taken. Now,
to take Malcolm as a hero of the Black struggle and in
some way attempt to make Louis Farrakhan guilty for
Malcolm's assassination is really a blow that is not just
low; it strikes you at the ankles if someone is shooting for
your stomach. That is as low as you can get." Farrakhan
vehemently denies any role, directly or indirectly, in the assassination of Malcolm X, arguing that neither he nor the
Honorable Elijah Muhammad gave any orders to kill their
former colleague. "I have never been investigated for any

part or complicity in the assassination of Malcolm X. I have never been mentioned in the early writings on Malcolm's assassination. My name never came up, because I was not a major player in the Nation of Islam."[14]

But when Farrakhan claims that he has never been investigated for the assassination, he misses the point of arguments that he encouraged the assassination. In fact, only one of the five assassins has been investigated, but that does not prove the other four innocent. Farrakhan's claims that he never gave an order to kill Malcolm X are also misguided. It seems unlikely that Farrakhan actually did have any direct involvement in the murder. The five assassins were from the mosque in Newark, while Farrakhan's home base was Boston. Although it remains unknown whether the assassins were working on their own or under orders from their superiors in the movement, the potential for Farrakhan, then a self-admittedly minor player in the Nation, being involved in the decision-making process was slim. But the argument that Farrakhan was indirectly involved in the assassination is valid. His scathing articles in *Muhammad Speaks* and his vitriolic attacks on Malcolm X inside and outside his own mosque were certainly contributing factors in the assassination.

Farrakhan helped create the climate of hatred that finally killed Malcolm X. His editorials were the most direct attacks of any that were printed in the Nation's newspapers during this time, and his prediction that "the die is set, and Malcolm shall not escape" helped convince the Muslims that Malcolm X should be killed. The assassination of Malcolm X was not a simple act of violence that was conceived and executed within a matter of seconds. Rather, it was a complicated process of establishing an environment that was ripe for murder. First, the members of the Nation of Islam had to believe that Malcolm was "worthy of death," as Farrakhan wrote in *Muhammad Speaks*. Second, individual members of the Nation of Islam had to be convinced to actually carry out the execution. The final step, of course, was the actual assassination. While Farrakhan almost certainly played little or no role in the actual planning of the assassination, he was instrumental in providing the context for the murder.

This is not to say that Farrakhan's actions during 1964 and 1965 were intended to bring about Malcolm X's assassination. In a murder trial, it is unnecessary for the prosecution to prove that the defendant actually wanted to kill the victim, or that the defendant actually set out to kill. The only relevant fact is whether the defendant actually did commit murder. Similarly, it is not germane—nor is it simple to discover—whether Farrakhan actually intended to create an environment in which the death of Malcolm X was certain. The fact is that he did help to create the climate, and therefore he must share some of the responsibility for the assassination.

But Farrakhan is not alone in this respect. Elijah Muhammad and other Chicago officials must certainly bear a sizable portion of the responsibility for the murder. They served to hasten Malcolm X's departure from the Nation of Islam and to ensure that Malcolm X's subsequent relationship with the Muslims would be one of opposition rather than cooperation. All those Muslims who violently castigated Malcolm X through *Muhammad Speaks* or through the Muslim pulpit must share in the blame, as well as those who silently allowed the talk of violence and revenge to proceed without opposition. And even Malcolm X should be faulted, since it was he who encouraged the idea of violent retribution against the enemies of the Nation of Islam while he was still a member. As a prominent Muslim minister, he almost certainly realized the violent potential of the Fruit of Islam, but he never tried to discourage that violence until he became its target.

The assassination of Malcolm X provides a vivid illustration of the need for a greater understanding of the internal and external pressures on the movement of African-American liberation. Malcolm X was certainly the victim of external interference from the FBI and other government and media organizations that sought to limit his appeal to African-Americans. But he was also the victim—and the instigator—of a complex web of animosities that were indigenous to his segment of the movement. The perception that the civil rights movement was a unified collection of groups and individuals who were besieged from hostile outside forces is quite true, although somewhat incomplete. It is true that civil rights workers were bitterly opposed by entrenched racists and those who were fond of the status quo. It is true that the FBI and other law-enforcement officials often took sides in the struggle, most often on the side of the white communities whose beliefs were being threatened by a new concept of American equality. It is also true that the battle for human and civil rights in the 1960s achieved a unity of purpose that rarely had been seen before in America, in large part because of the unique, violent character of the opposition to African-American equality. But this unity should not diminish the often-overlooked fact that outside opposition was not the only difficulty that the movement was forced to overcome in its quest for justice. As in other movements, while the civil rights struggle was viciously attacked from the outside, it was also being challenged by internal dissension that was far less visible, but just as destructive.

Although common folklore provides a picture of Dr. Martin Luther King, Jr., as the unquestioned leader of a great movement, the truth was not that simple. While King led the most visible and effective portion of the struggle during the early phases of the movement, he was far from immune from criticism and opposition from within him movement. In small communities such as Albany, Georgia, which he visited in a sincere effort to help, he retreated under fire from local black leaders who felt that King had done more harm than good. In battlegrounds such as Albany and Chicago, where he was defeated by Mayor Richard Daley's machine politics, King's efforts were hampered by internal and external opposition, both of which combined to force his retreat back to his home in Atlanta. As the 1960s wore on, criticism of King grew from within his Southern Christian Leadership Conference and from such other civil rights organizations as the Student Nonviolent Coordinating Committee, which was taking an increasingly militant position. The Nation of Islam also severely criticized King and other civil rights leaders, calling them impediments to African-American freedom.

Just as King received his share of internal criticism, the Nation of Islam also took a beating from both outside sources such as the government and the white-dominated media, as well as from internal sources. Despite the Nation's philosophy that dissent was anathema to the movement, internal opposition to the policies made in Chicago was not uncommon, although it generally did not last long. Those who disagreed with the Messenger, even on small, insignificant points, were subject to possible banishment from the Nation, physical abuse from the nation's paramilitary wing, or both. This internal opposition, from such sources as Wallace D. Muhammad and eventually Malcolm X, was indigenous and was not produced by external pressures. Although conspiracy theorists argue that the government created and encouraged internal opposition through the politics of division, much of this opposition, at least in the Nation of Islam, was natural and unaffected by outsiders.

It is important for historians and modern-day activists to understand that it is naïve to believe that hostility from the government and defenders of the status quo was the only reason for the failure of the civil rights movement to accomplish many of its goals. The movement was not free from the natural process that molds all successful organizations working together for a common goal. Policies are developed and implemented, then modified to fit unique circumstances or conditions that were not anticipated in the formulation of policy. This process is characterized by diversity of opinion that can create as many pressures, and develop as many problems, as criticism from the outside. The Nation of Islam, although not a democratic organization, was still plagued—or aided—by internal differences of opinion, a fact that many historians who try to romanticize the civil rights era fail to realize.

Malcolm X's feud with Elijah Muhammad and his exodus from the Nation of Islam was part of a natural process, largely unfettered by government culpability. Assertions to the contrary are based on faulty assumptions of capabilities and motivations, as well as an incomplete knowledge of history. While the government—particularly the FBI—did intervene in many organizations, such as SNCC and the Black Panther Party for Self Defense, in the later 1960s, the government had little reason or inclination to involve itself in the internal disputes of the Nation of Islam. The assassination of Malcolm X must be viewed as the culmination of a system of violent retribution that was endemic to the Nation of Islam. While the government authorities did not directly involve themselves in or encourage the activities of the Nation of Islam, they also refrained from curtailing the violence of the Nation, at least so long as it did not affect the white communities to which most of the authority figures belonged.

In his book, *To Kill a Black Man*, about the lives of Malcolm X and Martin Luther King, Jr., journalist Louis E. Lomax writes:

> This society, this violent and corrupt American society, this racist American society assassinated both Malcolm X and Martin Luther King, Jr. The men arrested may have pulled the trigger, but they by no means acted alone; American society was not only in concert with the assassins but there is every evidence that they were the hired killers.[15]

In a certain sense, Lomax is correct in his assessment. American society was guilty in ignoring the desperate pleas for understanding from Malcolm X. His lengthy orations on the seemingly hopeless plight of African-Americans in the United States were largely ignored, and even scorned by

most of America. Similarly, his cries for help in his final
year, when his life was constantly in danger of being extinguished by the Nation of Islam, were also readily dismissed, without even the consideration that his life might
be worth protecting. But Lomax means far more than this
by his accusation, implying that the government or other
forces outside the Muslim community actively conspired to
murder Malcolm X. By making such a statement, he makes
the naïve mistake of assuming that the problems of the
Muslim community, or of the civil rights movement, were
the result of outside, deleterious interference.

It is clear that many of the problems of African-
American communities in the United States have been
caused by the racial hierarchy of power in this country. Internal violence, drug abuse, and the general sense of hopelessness that fuel these problems can all be attributed
directly or indirectly to the larger white society that serves
to constrain the ambitions of the black minority and rob
them of a sense of dignity and self-worth that is essential in
a law-abiding society. But this does not indicate that all
problems in African-American communities can find their
roots in the larger racial balance. Internal dissent and factional battles are natural attributes of all human societies,
and the struggle between Malcolm X and Elijah Muhammad was a natural manifestation of that conflict. Lomax's
statement may have some validity in that resorting to violence rather than negotiation may have been an imposed
factor in the controversy. But his larger implications are
overstated and distribute blame unnecessarily to communities that had no effect on the assassination of Malcolm X.

It is impossible to determine what effects Malcolm X could
have had on the civil rights struggle if he had remained
alive long enough to solidify his position and fight for civil
rights in his own way. By the end of his life, he knew that
he wanted to become more involved in the movement, but
had not yet been able to define his role in it. Perhaps his
role would have paralleled the position that he took when

he visited the Selma, Alabama, civil rights struggle that was being led by Dr. King and his Southern Christian Leadership Conference. Although Malcolm X did not meet with Dr. King, who was in jail at the time, he did give a speech at a mass meeting of Selma citizens. As he was waiting to speak, he leaned over to Coretta Scott King and reassured her that he was only there to help. According to Mrs. King, "he said he wanted to present an alternative; that it might be easier for whites to accept Martin's proposals after hearing him [Malcolm X]." Malcolm X then gave a speech in which he presented the doctrine of self-defense, telling the audience that "I don't advocate violence, but if a man steps on my toes, I'll step on his." Later in the speech, he made the observation that "whites better be glad Martin Luther King is rallying the people because other forces are waiting to take over if he fails."[16]

Malcolm X's role, as he explained it in Selma, Alabama, would be to prod along government leaders and local whites who were conspiring to dampen the effects of the civil rights movement. By presenting these leaders with a choice of peaceful change or violent upheaval, Malcolm X apparently believed that they would rationally choose the former alternative. But it is doubtful that Malcolm X would have allowed himself to be used as an idle threat for long. He had far too much pride and ambition for that. Malcolm X's dynamic personality suited him to a leadership role in the movement, rather than a cheerleader on the sidelines or a ruffian who would threaten to abuse those who hindered the movement. Malcolm X would have defined his own movement, which may or may not have complemented the civil rights movement in the Southern states.

Malcolm X was a black nationalist, dedicated to the notion that blacks should be in charge of the communities in which they lived. He recognized that African-Americans had to control their own economies and their own politics if they could truly break free from America's rigid racial hierarchy. He also realized that the recognition and acceptance of African-American culture was a crucial factor in the struggle for freedom. It is likely that he would have raised the banner of black consciousness, much as Steven Biko did in South Africa before he was killed. Although Malcolm X desired to be a part of the mainstream civil rights movement and wanted to foster it as much as he could, there is no evidence to believe that he would have become a colleague of such people as King, James Farmer, Whitney Young, and Roy Wilkins. By nature, Malcolm X was an outsider to the movement, a nationalist among integrationists. His brash style and uncompromising attitude would never have allowed his to agree fully with the integrationists. The most he probably would have done was to refrain from attacking them, insisting that they probably thought they were doing what was right.

Much has been made of the apparent congruence of opinion that Malcolm X and Martin Luther King, Jr. were approaching toward the end of their lives. Their respective deaths, it is argued, ended what would have evolved into an agreement by the two men on their basic approaches to the civil rights movement. But to accept this hypothetical situation as fact would be to overestimate the evolution of beliefs in each of the two men and to romanticize the civil rights struggle unnecessarily. Both men clearly were moving away from their original positions and had gained a greater flexibility in their beliefs, but this does not indicate that they had begun to follow an unalterable path toward concurring opinions. Their backgrounds, religious affiliation and beliefs, and political philosophy were all radically different; while they were unquestionably breaking down some of the barriers between them, the obstacles were too great to overcome.

Malcolm X focused much of his time in his final year fighting toward a dual goal: bringing the United States up on charges of racism before the United Nations and linking the African struggle for independence with the African-American struggle for independence. It is doubtful that he would have enjoyed any success in his quest to charge the United States with human-rights abuses had he lived long enough to continue his efforts. As he discovered during his African trip during the summer of 1964, most African nations were too busy establishing themselves as independent nations to worry about their long-lost brothers and sisters in North America. Even if he had been successful in raising the consciousness of African leaders as to the plight of their American relatives, it is doubtful that the American "dollarism" that Malcolm X castigated could have been overcome. Newly emergent African nations desperately needed the support of the United States, and forcing the issue of the American government's resistance to the civil rights movement would have forced them to make sacrifices that they were unwilling to make.

It is possible that Malcolm X would have enjoyed greater success in culturally linking the black Africans and their brothers and sisters in the United States. Islam, which Malcolm X hailed as the "natural" religion for blacks across the globe, was gaining strength in America, not just through the Nation of Islam but through other Muslim organizations such as the Hanafis as well. The civil rights movement was headed in a pan-Africanist direction anyway, and Malcolm X would have accelerated its course. The cultural linkage between the descendants of American slaves and the home of their ancestors in Africa had been shattered by hundreds of years of oppression and cultural denial in America, but Malcolm X fought, with some success, to remove the negative stigma attached to Africa and Africanisms. Had he remained alive longer, Malcolm X certainly would have continued his work and undoubtedly made further progress in linking African and American blacks.

But, of course, any talk of what Malcolm X would have done if he had lived is pure speculation. As it was, in death Malcolm X gained more fame and acceptance than he ever did when he was alive. He was hailed instantly as a hero and a martyr of the movement, although throughout most of his life he had attacked the movement as a farce. The legacy of Malcolm X has been a confusing one, largely because Malcolm X was unable to consolidate his beliefs before he was murdered. Political groups from all across the spectrum have been able to seize portions of Malcolm X's beliefs and claim them as their own, telling the world that they are the true inheritors of Malcolm X's legacy. The Socialist Workers Party, a predominantly white leftist organization, was able to take his criticisms of capitalism and use them to show that Malcolm X was irreversibly headed in the direction of socialism. The Black Panther Party for Self Defense, under Huey Newton and Bobby Seale, claimed that they had exclusive rights to Malcolm X's legacy, as they formed self-defense units that "policed the police" to make sure that the law-enforcement authorities did not abuse African-Americans. Even President Richard Nixon, who was on the opposite side of the political spectrum from Malcolm X, trumpeted Malcolm X's ideas of black capitalism as the natural route toward self sufficiency for African-Americans. Even today, the struggle for Malcolm X's beliefs goes on, as Vice-President Dan Quayle publicly made it known that he was reading Malcolm X's autobiography in the days after the 1992 Los Angeles uprising in an attempt to show that he was in tune with the issues that faced urban blacks.

In the words of historian John Henrik Clarke, the assassination of Malcolm X extinguished "the brightest light we had produced in the twentieth century, and our movement was set back a generation."[17] According to Dr. C. Eric Lincoln, the author of the first book on the Nation of Islam, "for the Negroes in America, the death of Malcolm X is the most portentous event since the deportation of Marcus Garvey in the 1920s."[18] Malcolm X clearly represented the ideas, concerns, and frustrations of the inner cities of America. His loud, strong voice enunciated the message of urban distress. It was a message that African-Americans needed immediate help, a message that was not being addressed by the civil rights leaders in the South. In many ways, his call for black control of black communities was overshadowed by Dr. King and his Southern movement, but his call for the collective self-improvement of African-Americans gained him the love and respect of millions of African-Americans. Although his assassination forever ended his role in American politics, the voice of Malcolm X is still alive today through the admiration of those who follow him and the grudging respect of those who oppose him.

Appendix

Author's Note:
The following affidavit was filed by Talmadge Hayer in November, 1977. He signed the original, handwritten document with the name Thomas Hagan, which was considered to be his official name in the New York State Correctional system. The document appears here exactly as written, with all spelling and grammatical errors intact.

State of New York
County of Ulster

  I, Thomas Hagan, being duly sworn, dispose and says:

1) I am one of the persons indicted for the murder of Malcolm X at the Audubon Ballroom, N. York, N.Y. Feb. 21 1965.

2) That I have been sentenced to life in prison for my part in the crime.

3) That I am now incarcerated at Eastern Correctional Facility.

4) That I am writing this affidavit in the hope that it will clear my co defendants of the charges against them in this case. My co defendants are Thomas 15X Johnson and Norman 3X Butler.

  That sometime in 1964 Malcolm X was said to have gone against the Leader of the Nation of Islam, the Hon. Elijah Muhammad.

  By the following year Malcolm X was declared a hypocrite by the Nation of Islam.

  That in the summer of 1965 I was contacted by a Brother named Lee and another Bro. named Ben.

  These brothers asked me what I thought about the situation with Mal. X? I said I thought it was very bad for anyone to go against the teachings of the Hon. Elijah, then known as the Last Messenger of God. I was told that Muslims should more or less be willing to fight against hypocrites and I agreed w/ that. There was no money payed to me for my part in this. I thought I was fighting for truth & right. There was a few meetings held concerning this. Sometimes these were held in a car driving around. Bro. Lee, Bro. Ben, a Brother named Willie X, the other Brother's name was Willbour or a name like it. From these meetings it was decided that the only place that Mal X. was sure to be was the Audubon Ballroom on Feb. 21, 1965. Therefore the plan was to kill this person there. On Feb. 21st 1965 we met at Bens house Sunday morning. On Feb. 20th 1965 we had gone to the Ballroom to check it out.

One Sunday morning we, the above named, got in this Bro. Wilbour's car and drove to N.Y.C. We parked the car a few blocks away and two at a time drifted into the Ballroom early. Me and Bro. Lee took sets down front in the first row.

Bro. Willie and Ben sat right behind us, and Bro. Willbour took a set far in the back. It was his to throw the fire bomb & pretend that someone was picking his pocket. I used a 45 weapon. Bro. Lee had a lugar and Willie X had the shot gun. The plan was that when the shooting started people would be running all over the place & with this we could get out of the Ballroom.

So when the shotgun went off Bro. Lee & me fired our guns at Mal X. & ran for the door. I was shot in the right leg but was able to keep moving on just one leg. I was able to get down stairs by sliding down railing to the floor. I was captured right outside Ballroom by a police officer.

This affidavit is factural to the best of my knowledge. Thomas 15 Johnson and Norman 3X Butler had no thing to do with this crime whatsoever.

Thomas Hagan

Sworn to before me
this 30th day of November, 1977
William M. Kunstler

Author's Note:
This second affidavit was filed in February 1978 and goes into more detail than the original affidavit. Again, all spelling and grammatical errors have been retained. The full names and addresses of Hayer's accomplices, however, have been deleted.

State of New York
County of Ulster

I, Thomas Hagan, being duly sworn, disposes and says:

That this affidavit is an addition to my first affidavit. And that the statements made herein are more in detail and hopefully will clear up any doubt as to what took place in the killing of Malcolm X and the innocents of Norman Butler and Thomas Johnson.

It was some time in the summer of 1964 that I was approached concerning the killing of Malcolm X. The time must of been a month or so before the Hon. Elijah Muhammad spoke in New York City in 1964.

I was walking in down town Paterson when two brothers, both Muslims, was driving by in their car. I knew these men well. They asked me to get in the car. They wanted to talk to me. Both of these men knew that I had a great love, respect and admiration for the Hon. Elijah Muhammad.

They started talking about what was going on with Malcolm X and how this man was defaming the Hon. Elijah Muhammad. This was the feelings of most men in the N.O.I. at that time.

I know that it was Ben who spoke to Leon first and then they spoke to me. I learned from them that word was out that Malcolm X should be killed. I can't say for I don't know who passed that word on. But I thought that Ben knew.

We soon got together with two more men. Both lived in Newark, N.J. Ones name was William X. . . . I never knew his last name.

The other man was a Bro. named Wilbur or Kinly. I don't know his full name. But we used his car on Feb. 21, 1965.

We met a few times to discuss how to carry out this killing. Some times we talked while driving around. Or at Bens or Lees house. Some times we drove around for hours.

We tryed to get as must information on the movements of Mal. X as we could.

We, the people above stated, drove out to Mal X. house one night to see what security was there. We found it heavyly guarded. We soon decided that the only place that Mal X would be was at the Ball Room where he was making speeches to the people there. In fact we attened one of these meetings to see what security was there. We learned that no one was searching at the door for weapons. This was in the winter of 1964-65.

We talked about this on the way back to Jersey. We drove back in Ben's car. We knew that the only place that Mal X was sure to be was at that Ball Room. And we decided that with a crowd there we had a good chance of getting in there and out after the move was made, the shoting that is.

We decided to visit the Ball Room the night before the killing to set this up. It was a dance that night and we came there like everyone alse, got a ticket went in and looked the place over. This was Feb. 20, 1965.

This night we used Bens car and on the way home we discussed what everyone thought. Everyone agreed that we would do this the next day Feb. 21, 1965. The next morning we would meet at Leons house and Bens to go over our plane. We decided after looking at the place that we would get there early. Drift in and take sets. Leon and me up front and left side facing stage. Ben and William right behind us. I had the 45 auto. Leon the Luger. William had the shotgun. Wilbur or Kinly had the set in the back of the place. His job was to accuse someone of picking his pocket and throw the smoke bom. This was timed to happen when Mal X started to greet the people. Almost at the same time William would fire the shotgun and Leon and I would fire our guns at Mal X. and run for the door.

On Feb. 21, 1965, we drove to N.Y.C. in Wilbur or Kinly's car, a blue Cat., about 1962 or so. We parked a few blacks from the Ball Room on a street heading for George Was. bridge. We figure that with all the people there we could make it out in the crowd.

As for the weapons I got them from a man who had them for sale I bought them from him. This person had nothing to do with the crime. I made the smoke bom that was used. I, Thomas Hagan have written this affidavit in the hope that the information wold exonerate Thomas Johnson and Norman Butler of the crime that they did not commit. This affidavit is factual to the best of my knowledge. And I am willing to state what took place in the matter before any court of law.

                                                              Thomas Hagan

Sworn to before me   Witnessed by
this 25th day of February, 1978   Nurriden Faiz

Notes

Chapter One

[1] Malcolm X, with Alex Haley, *The Autobiography of Malcolm X* (New York: Ballantine Books, 1965), p. 2.

[2] Malcolm X was born with the name Malcolm Little and earned the nickname "Big Red" on the streets because of his height and his reddish complexion. He took the surname "X" when he was admitted to the Nation of Islam to represent the unknown African name that was stripped from him by the white slave owners. All Black Muslims are required to shed their "slave" name until a new name is given to them by Elijah Muhammad, the leader of the Nation of Islam. Malcolm X was eventually given the Islamic name Malik El-Shabazz.

[3] Malcolm X, *Autobiography*, p. 428.

[4] Ibid., p. 426.

[5] Ibid., p. 138.

[6] David Gallen, *Malcolm X: As They Knew Him* (New York: Carroll & Graf, 1992), pp. 30–31.

[7] Although he proclaimed himself to be the final prophet of Allah and urged his followers to learn Arabic, the primary Islamic language, Muhammad could never speak or read Arabic.

[8] Erdmann Doane Benyon, "The Voodoo Cult Among Negro Migrants in Detroit," in *American Journal of Sociology*. May 1938. Volume XLIII, Number 6, pp. 895–96.

[9] Muhammad's rise to the top, however, did not come without difficulties, and there are numerous rumors about the violent battles between Muhammad's followers and those who followed others who wished to succeed W. D. Fard. Muhammad emerged triumphant, but he was forced to move the headquarters of the new Nation of Islam from Detroit to Chicago in order to avoid further violence.

[10] Malcolm X, *Autobiography*, p. 317.

[11] Dr. Betty Shabazz is currently Director of Communications and Public Relations at the Medgar Evers College in Brooklyn.

[12] Betty Shabazz, "Malcolm: Betty Shabazz on Loving and Losing Him," *Essence*. (February, 1992), p. 50.

[13]Peter Goldman, *The Death and Life of Malcolm X*, 2d edition (Urbana: University of Illinois Press, 1979), p. 261. This remains the best biography written on Malcolm X, in large part because of the brilliance of Goldman's writing and his ability to express the remarkable qualities of Malcolm X to the reader.

[14]Malcolm X, *Autobiography*, p. 432.

[15]Goldman, *Death and Life*, p. 297.

[16]Ibid., p. 295.

[17]Ibid.

[18]Malcolm X, *Autobiography*, p. 433.

[19]Ibid.

[20]Roberts went on to infiltrate the New York chapter of the Black Panther Party and provided the police with valuable information on its leadership. He finally surfaced as an undercover police agent in late 1970, when he testified against thirteen Black Panthers who were arrested on charges of trying to destroy several New York department stores.

[21]Goldman, *Death and Life*, p. 322.

[22]*New York Times*, 22 February 1965.

[23]John Henrik Clarke, ed., *Malcolm X: The Man and his Times* (Trenton: Africa World Press, Inc., 1990), p. xii.

Chapter Two

[1]Roy Wilkins, "No Time for Avengers," *New York Amsterdam News*. 6 March 1965.

[2]*New York Times*, 23 February 1965.

[3]Ibid.

[4]*Time*, 5 March 1965.

[5]Ibid.

[6]This James Shabazz should not be confused with the James Shabazz who remained loyal to Elijah Muhammad. Many Muslims—including Malcolm X—adopted the surname Shabazz, named after the original tribe of blacks.

[7]*New York Amsterdam News*, 6 March 1965, p. 3.

[8]*New York Times*, 24 February 1965.

[9]*New York Amsterdam News*, 27 February 1965, p. 1.

[10]*Time*, 5 March 1965.

[11]The Black Muslim philosophy includes all people who are not of European descent in the "darker majority" of the world. According to the Muslims, when Armageddon comes, the dark world will rise up and kill the white "devils" and assume control of the world.

[12]*New York Times*, 25 February 1965.

[13]Ibid., 26 February 1965.

[14]*New York Amsterdam News*, 6 March 1965.

[15]*New York Times*, 24 February 1965.

[16]King Papers Project.

[17]*New York Times*, 27 February 1965.

[18]Transcript of *People v. Hayer*, 23 February 1966, p. 2685.

[19]Paul Hoffman, *Tiger in the Court* (Chicago: Playboy Press, 1973), p. 27.

[20]See Hoffman for more information on Stern.

[21]*New York Times*, 24 February 1965.

[22]All Muslims, upon admission to the Nation of Islam, are given the new last name of X. Thomas Johnson was the fifteenth man named Thomas in the Harlem mosque, so he was given the name Thomas 15X. Similarly, Norman 3X was the third man named Norman in the New York mosque.

[23]Goldman, *Death and Life*, p. 320. One of the limitations of Goldman's biography of Malcolm X is his adoption of the persona of a policeman when discussing the investigation into Malcolm's death. Unsurprisingly, he comes to the same conclusion that the police forwarded: Hayer, Butler, and Johnson were the three murderers. In 1978, when new evidence about the assassination came to light, Goldman wrote an addendum to his book and announced his conversion to the new interpretation.

[24]Interview between Peter Goldman and Muhammad Abdul-Aziz (Norman Butler) at Sing Sing Prison in New York on April 16, 1979.

[25]*New York Times*, 27 February 1965.

[26]Ibid.

[27]*New York Amsterdam News*, 13 March 1965, p. 1.

[28]Interview between Peter Goldman and Khalil Islam (Thomas Johnson) in Dannemora Prison on May 21, 1979.

[29]*New York Times*, 4 March 1965.

[30]Interview with Herbert Stern.

Chapter Three

[1]Although he admitted during the trial that the person in the pictures looked somewhat like him, Hayer strenuously denied that he was in the picture. He also denied that he had ever taken karate or had any knowledge of any martial art. However, many years later, he confessed that it was he in the photographs.

[2]*People v. Hayer*, Opening statement of Peter L. F. Sabbatino, p. 188.

[3]*People v. Hayer*, Testimony of Ronald Timberlake, pp. 1322–23.

[4]*People v. Hayer*, pp. 2407–08.

[5]The Nation of Islam owned a number of businesses around the country, including restaurants, bakeries, and dry-cleaning establishments.

[6]*People v. Hayer*, Testimony of Talmadge Hayer, February 23, 1966, p. 2680.

[7]Ibid., p. 2684.

[8]The Muslims argued against using the term "Black Muslim" ever since it was coined by C. Eric Lincoln in his 1959 book, *The Black Muslims of America*. "From Mr. Muhammad on down, the name 'Black Muslims' distressed everyone in the Nation of Islam," Malcolm X wrote in his autobiography. "I tried for at least two years to kill off that 'Black Muslims.' Every newspaper and magazine writer and microphone I got close to: 'No! We are black *people* here in America. Our *religion* is Islam. We are prop-

erly called Muslims!' But that 'Black Muslims' name never got dislodged." (*Autobiography*, p. 247)

⁹*People v. Hayer.* Testimony of Talmadge Hayer, February 28, 1966, p. 3146.

¹⁰Interview with Thomas Johnson, 21 May 1979, and with Norman Butler, 16 April 1979. Conducted by Peter Goldman.

¹¹*People v. Hayer.* Testimony of Talmadge Hayer, February 28, 1966, p. 3159.

¹²*New York Times*, 8 March 1966.

¹³*People v. Hayer*, Testimony of Talmadge Hayer, February 28, 1966, p. 3156.

¹⁴*People v. Hayer.* 7 March 1966, p. 3716.

¹⁵Ibid. 19 January, 1966. p. 264.

¹⁶*People v. Hayer*, p. 250.

¹⁷Ibid. 14 April, 1966. pp. 4208–209.

Chapter Four

¹Louis E. Lomax, *To Kill A Black Man.* (Los Angeles: Holloway House Publishing Co., 1968), p. 249.

²One of the best books on the subject of the JFK assassination is *Reasonable Doubt* by Henry Hurt (New York: Henry Holt and Company, 1985). A thorough investigation into the Martin Luther King, Jr., murder can be found in *The Martin Luther King Assassination* by Dr. Philip H. Melanson (New York: Shapolsky Publishers, Inc., 1991).

³*San Francisco Chronicle*, 8 April 1992.

⁴Autobiography, pp. 430–31.

⁵*New York Times*, 24 February 1965.

⁶Hakim Abdullah Jamal, *From the Dead Level* (New York: Random House, 1972), p. 195. It is difficult to determine how accurate Malcolm X's quotes are in Jamal's book, since they are almost entirely from personal recollection rather than from research. Therefore, his quotes from this book must be regarded with some skepticism. However, this particular quote, if not verbatim, certainly represents the feelings of Malcolm X and seems like something that he would say.

⁷James Farmer, *Lay Bare the Heart* (New York: Arbor House, 1985), p. 233.

⁸The Freedom Rides were initiated in 1960 by CORE in order to desegregate Southern interstate transportation facilities by riding integrated buses through the Deep South. Some of the most harrowing and inspirational tales of the entire civil rights movement have come out of the Freedom Rides, during which the riders were harassed and beaten and the buses bombed.

⁹Interview with James Farmer, February 16, 1992.

¹⁰Farmer, *Lay Bare the Heart*, p. 233.

¹¹A number of socialist authors, including Breitman (see Note 13) and Norden (see Note 12), have gone to great lengths to try to prove that

Malcolm X had adopted a socialist society as his model for the emerging nations in Africa and also as a future system for the United States. But Malcolm X made only a few vague statements in his final year concerning the merits of socialism and, given the confusion in his political philosophies during this time, they cannot be viewed accurately as a definite conversion to Marxist principles.

[12]Eric Norden, "The Murder of Malcolm X," *The Realist*, February 1967, p. 15.

[13]George Breitman, Herman Porter, and Baxter Smith, *The Assassination of Malcolm X* (New York: Pathfinder Press, 1976), p. 54.

[14]Goldman, *Death and Life*, p. 301.

[15]*New York Amsterdam News*, 13 March 1965.

[16]Norden, "Murder," p. 10. There is no further confirmation from Malcolm X that he actually believed that the CIA was behind the "poisoning." All that is left is the word of his half-sister that he made a statement to this effect.

[17]Goldman, *Death and Life*, p. 230.

[18]*New York Amsterdam News*, "Malcolm X Denies He Is Bomber," 20 February 1965.

[19]Norden, "Murder," p. 12.

[20]Ibid.

[21]Ibid.

[22]Ibid., p. 10.

[23]Ibid.

[24]Ibid., p. 8.

[25]Ibid.

[26]Ibid., pp. 8–9.

[27]Ibid., p. 11.

[28]Malcolm X's FBI file, Section 1, 4 May 1953.

[29]Kenneth O'Reilly, *"Racial Matters"* (New York: The Free Press, 1989), p. 9. This book is perhaps the best on the relationship between the FBI and the civil rights movement. For more specific information on the FBI's relations with individual leaders, see *The FBI and Martin Luther King, Jr.* by David Garrow (New York: Penguin Books, 1981) and *Malcolm X: The FBI File* by Clayborne Carson (New York: Carroll & Graf, 1991).

[30]Ibid., p. 178.

[31]Ibid., p. 127.

[32]Ibid.

[33]David J. Garrow, *The FBI and Martin Luther King, Jr.* (New York: Penguin Books, 1981), pp. 125–26.

[34]Report of the Church Committee Hearings, p. 57.

[35]The Black Panther Party for Self Defense, founded by Huey P. Newton and Bobby Seale in Oakland, California, was far more aggressive in its approach to the authorities, and it attracted far more attention from the FBI than did the Nation of Islam. Whereas the Nation was never really a target for the FBI while Malcolm X was alive, the BPP became a target for dirty

tricks since its inception in 1967. The FBI continually harassed the Panthers, and at one time declared them to be the greatest threat to the internal security of the United States, in large part because the BPP backed up its rhetoric of armed self-defense with violence. Members of the Nation of Islam, however, were never engaged in the actual practice of armed self-defense, and were forbidden to carry weapons. As such, they never represented the threat that the Black Panthers did.

[36]Ward Churchill and Jim Vanderwall, *The COINTELPRO Papers.* (Boston: South End Press, 1990).

[37]Malcolm X's FBI file, Section 8, 4 February 1963.

[38]Elijah Muhammad's FBI file, 26 April 1962.

[39]*New York Times*, 13 May 1978.

[40]The FBI went far beyond this point in its efforts to combat the Nation of Islam after the formal initiation of COINTELPRO in 1967. One plan was the dissemination of a comic book written by agents of the New York Bureau office to all the members of the New York mosques. The comic book explained how much money the Nation was taking from its membership and how Elijah Muhammad and the New York ministers used the money to buy themselves fancy cars and extravagant clothes. Permission was quickly given by Washington, and the comic book was sent to the New York Muslims in order to stir up dissension within the movement.

[41]Memo from J. Walter Yeagley, Assistant Attorney General, to Director, FBI. Dated 26 September 1960.

[38]Nelson Blackstock, *COINTELPRO: The FBI's Secret War on Political Freedom* (New York: Vintage Books, 1976), p. 113.

[39]Goldman, *Death and Life*, p. 3.

[40]Herb Boyd, "Hero or Charlie Bad Guy," *Class* (January, 1992), p. 55.

[41]Goldman, *Death and Life*, p. 77.

[42]George Breitman, ed., *Malcolm X Speaks* (New York: Grove Press, 1965), p. 4.

[43]Ibid., p. 22.

Chapter Five

[1]Peter Goldman, "Malcolm X: An Unfinished Story?," *The New York Times Magazine*, 19 August 1979, pp. 26–32, 62–63.

[2]Hayer mistakenly wrote that the plot began in the summer of 1965 rather than 1964.

[3]Wallace is now known as Warith D. Muhammad.

[4]Goldman, *Death and Life*, p. 412.

[5]Ibid., p. 413.

[6]Goldman published an article in *The New York Times Magazine* (see Note 1), and also an epilogue for the second edition of his book, *The Death and Life of Malcolm X*, in which he discussed the new evidence as well as his interviews with Hayer and the other two men convicted of the assassination.

[7]*New York Times*, 7 December 1977.

[8]Goldman, *Death and Life*, p. 421.

[9]Malcolm X's FBI file, Section 19, 29 May 1980. Letter from Congressman William J. Hughes to FBI Director William Webster. When asked about the letter that he wrote to the FBI, Congressman Hughes said, in a January 2, 1992 letter to the author, that he had no knowledge of ever writing to the FBI on this matter. "I went back and checked the records of my correspondence during the year of 1980," he wrote. "I found no record of having written a letter to the FBI on the subject, and have no recollection of sending such a letter."

[10]Malcolm X's FBI file, Section 19, 20 June 1980. Letter from FBI Assistant Director Revell to Congressman Hughes.

[11]This quotation, as well as all subsequent quotations from Thomas Johnson, except where specifically noted, are from an interview conducted by Peter Goldman with Johnson in Dannemora Prison on May 21, 1979.

[12]This quotation, as well as all subsequent quotations from Norman Butler, except where specifically noted, are from an interview conducted by Peter Goldman with Butler in Sing Sing Prison on April 16, 1979.

[13]Goldman, *Death and Life*, p. 424.

Chapter Six

[1]Specific information on the assassination, except where otherwise identified, are taken from two affidavits filed by Talmadge Hayer (called Thomas Hagan, and now known as Mujahid Halim) to the State of New York on November 30, 1977 and on February 25, 1978. These affidavits are reproduced in the Appendix.

[2]This quote and all others from Talmadge Hayer except where specifically identified come from an interview between Hayer and author Peter Goldman. Goldman interviewed Hayer in 1979 in Napanoch Prison, and this remains the only interview of Hayer. I am indebted to Peter Goldman for furnishing the transcript of the interview.

[3]Malcolm X, *Autobiography*, p. 36.

[4]Goldman, *Death and Life*, p. 415.

Chapter Seven

[1]Malcolm X, *Autobiography*, p. 152.

[2]Ibid., p. 169.

[3]Ibid., p. 196.

[4]Ibid., p. 197.

[5]Ibid.

[6]Ibid., p. 198.

[7]Louis E. Lomax, *When the Word Is Given* (Cleveland: The World Publishing Company, 1963), p. 93.

[8]E. U. Essien-Udom, *Black Nationalism: A Search for an Identity in America* (Chicago: University of Chicago Press, 1962), p. 101.

[9]Ibid., p. 177.

[10]Bruce Perry, *Malcolm* (New York: Station Hill, 1991), p. 163.
[11]Malcolm X, *Autobiography*, p. 296.
[12]Ibid., p. 297.
[13]Haley in *Autobiography*, p. 404.
[14]Essien-Udom, *Black Nationalism*, p. 71.
[15]Malcolm X, *Autobiography*, p. 296.
[16]Ibid., p. 289.
[17]*Los Angeles Herald Dispatch*, 17 May 1962.
[18]Malcolm X's FBI file, Section 8, 16 November 1962, p. 2.
[19]Perry, *Malcolm*, p. 192.
[20]Jamal, *From the Dead Level*, p. 196.
[21]Ibid., p. 200.
[22]Ibid., p. 201.
[23]Goldman, *Death and Life*, p. 106.
[24]Jamal, *From the Dead Level*, p. 195.
[25]Ibid., p. 217.
[26]Goldman, *Death and Life*, p. 108.
[27]Ibid.
[28]Breitman, *Malcolm X Speaks*, p. 20.
[29]Louis Lomax in Goldman, *Death and Life*, p. 116.
[30]Malcolm X's FBI file, Section 9, 15 November 1963, p. 4.
[31]Malcolm X, *Autobiography*, p. 290.
[32]Malcolm X began the Muslim newspaper with help of the staff at the *Los Angeles Herald Dispatch*, who showed him the technical aspects of running a newspaper, and the aid of journalist Louis E. Lomax, who teamed up with CBS newsman Mike Wallace in 1959 to present the documentary, "The Hate That Hate Produced" on the Nation of Islam. The piece brought nationwide notoriety to the movement, and made Malcolm X and Lomax friends. Lomax then showed Malcolm X the subtleties of reporting, which the Muslim put to work as he wrote the articles and took most of the pictures for the initial editions of *Muhammad Speaks*.
[33]Malcolm X, *Autobiography*, p. 292.
[34]Elijah Muhammad's FBI file, 23 January 1964, p. 4.
[35]Malcolm X's FBI file. Section 6, 17 November 1960.
[36]Elijah Muhammad's FBI file. Undated, p. 2b.
[37]Malcolm X's FBI file, Section 8, 16 November 1962, pp. 7–8.
[38]Ibid.
[39]Ibid., p. 7.
[40]Malcolm X, *Autobiography*, p. 298.
[41]Malcolm X's FBI file, 15 November 1963.
[42]Malcolm X, *Autobiography*, p. 295.
[43]Dr. Shabazz presumably meant Chicago, not Detroit. Muhammad's primary residence was in Chicago.
[44]Shabazz, "Malcolm," p. 109.
[45]Malcolm X, *Autobiography*, p. 294.
[46]Elijah Muhammad's FBI file. Undated, p. 23.

[47]Ibid., p. 22.
[48]Shabazz, "Malcolm," p. 109.
[49]Malcolm X, *Autobiography*, p. 297.
[50]Ibid.
[51]Ibid., p. 299.
[52]Ibid.

Chapter Eight

[1]Clarke, *Malcolm X*, pp. 284–85.
[2]Malcolm X, *Autobiography*, p. 300.
[3]*New York Times*, 2 December 1963.
[4]R. W. Apple, "Malcolm X Silenced for Remarks on Assassination of Kennedy," *New York Times*, 5 December 1963.
[5]Malcolm X, *Autobiography*, p. 302.
[6]*New York Times*, 5 December 1963.
[7]*New York Times*, "Malcolm Expected to Be Replaced," 6 December 1963, p. 27.
[8]Ibid.
[9]*New York Times*, 5 December 1963.
[10]*Newsweek*, 16 December 1963.
[11]*New York Amsterdam News*, 7 December 1963.
[12]*New York Times*, 5 December 1963.
[13]Malcolm X, *Autobiography*, p. 302.
[14]Raymond Sharrieff was Muhammad's son-in-law and Supreme Captain of the Fruit of Islam. John Ali was an officer in the New York mosque and originally one of Malcolm X's friends. He later became National Secretary in charge of the Nation of Islam's finances.
[15]Elijah Muhammad's FBI file, 27 January 1964.
[16]Malcolm X, *Autobiography*, p. 303.
[17]Elijah Muhammad, *Message to the Blackman in America* (Chicago: Muhammad Mosque of Islam No. 2, 1965), p. 246.
[18]Henry Hampton and Steve Fayer, *Voices of Freedom* (New York: Bantam Books, 1990), p. 257.
[19]Malcolm X, *Autobiography*, p. 304–05.
[20]Thomas Hauser, *Muhammad Ali* (New York: Simon & Schuster, 1991).
[21]*New York Times*, 9 March 1964.
[22]Gertrude Samuels, "Feud Within the Black Muslims," *New York Times Magazine*, 22 March 1964, Section 6.
[23]*New York Times*, 9 March 1964.
[24]Malcolm X's FBI file, Section 11, 18 June 1964.
[25]Ibid.
[26]Breitman, *Malcolm X Speaks*, pp. 20–22.
[27]Ibid.
[28]Ibid.
[29]*Muhammad Speaks*, 10 April 1964, p. 3.
[30]Malcolm X, *Autobiography*, pp. 308–09.

[31] Bruce Perry writes in *Malcolm*, his biography of Malcolm X, that the demolition expert was a Muslim named Langston X, and that Captain Joseph, the leader of the New York Fruit of Islam was involved in the planning. But this information is unconfirmed.

[32] Malcolm X, *Autobiography*, p. 303.

[33] Ibid., p. 309.

[34] Ibid., p. 316.

[35] *New York Times*, 7 April 1964.

[36] Breitman, *Malcolm X Speaks*, p. 20.

[37] Malcolm X, *Autobiography*, p. 317.

[38] Breitman, *Malcolm X Speaks*, p. 60.

[39] Ibid., pp. 59–60.

[40] According to the theories of the Nation of Islam, the white race had its origins in a mad scientist named Yacub, who was exiled from the original tribe of Shabazz to the island Patmos. He created the "devil" race over thousands of years by interbreeding the lightest of the island's inhabitants, and murdering those who had darker skin. Eventually after six thousand years, the inhabitants became progressively lighter, and weaker, until they became a race of evil blue-eyed devils.

[41] Breitman, *Malcolm X Speaks*, p. 21.

[42] *Muhammad Speaks*, 10 April 1964, p. 9.

[43] Citation from the Koran (Chapter 4, Verse 115) in *Muhammad Speaks*, 24 April 1964, p. 3.

[44] "Divine Messenger Must Be Obeyed," *Muhammad Speaks*, 10 April 1964.

[45] Elijah Muhammad in *Muhammad Speaks*, 5 June 1964, p. 1. Citation is taken from the Koran (Chapter 9, Verse 73).

[46] Elijah Muhammad in *Muhammad Speaks*, 10 April 1964, p. 8.

[47] Now known as Louis Farrakhan.

[48] *Muhammad Speaks*, 8 May 1964.

[49] Malcolm X's FBI file, Section 11, 18 June 1964.

[50] Goldman, *Death and Life*, p. 173.

[51] Ibid., p. 215.

[52] *Muhammad Speaks*, 19 June 1964.

[53] "Malcolm X Calls for Muslim Peace," *New York Times*, 27 June 1964, p. 9.

[54] "Malcolm X Repeats Call for Negro Unity on Rights," *New York Times*, 29 June 1964, p. 32.

[55] *Muhammad Speaks* later reported that 15,000 of Muhammad's followers had attended and withdrew its claim that the rally was "the largest gathering of black people ever assembled in America." Rather, the meeting was "the largest concentration" of blacks, which is a far different claim.

[56] "Elijah Muhammad Rallies His Followers in Harlem," *New York Times*, 29 June 1964, p. 32.

[57] Goldman, *Death and Life*, p. 211.

[58] Ibid., p. 22.

[59]"Islam's Gift to Him: Useful Life," *Muhammad Speaks*, 25 August 1964, p. 9.

[60]*Muhammad Speaks*, 3 July 1964, p. 9. Facial hair was forbidden by the Nation of Islam.

[61]"Cites 20-Year Association with Messenger of Allah," *Muhammad Speaks*, 11 September 1964, p. 4.

[62]*Muhammad Speaks*, 31 July 1964, p. 1.

[63]*Muhammad Speaks*, 23 October 1964, p. 8.

[64]Alex Haley in *Autobiography*, p. 419.

[65]Malcolm X's FBI file, Section 13, 15 December 1964, p. 1.

[66]There are even some rumors that Minister Louis was bought off by Chicago, as they offered him a Boston house in return for his continued loyalty to the Nation of Islam. These rumors, however, are unconfirmed.

[67]*Muhammad Speaks*, 4 December 1964.

[68]Jamal refers to Bradley as "Edmund Bradley" in *From the Dead Level*.

[69]Jamal, *From the Dead Level*, p. 242.

[70]Ibid., p. 216.

[71]Ibid., p. 225.

[72]Ibid., p. 226.

[73]Edward Bradley, as told to Louis E. Lomax, "Driver Tells How Malcolm X Escaped Death in Chase," in *The Washington Star*, 24 February 1965, p. 1.

[74]Ibid.

[75]Ibid.

[76]Ibid.

Chapter Nine

[1]Despite its name, the University of Islam was a grade school for Muslim children. The Nation had plans to enlarge the school when the $20 million Islamic Center was built, so that it would include a high school, university, and graduate school. However, the Islamic Center was never built, and the highly praised "University of Islam" remained a small grammar school.

[2]Elijah Muhammad's FBI file, 9 October 1964, p. 21.

[3]Malcolm X's FBI file, Section 14, 20 January 1965, p. 5.

[4]Goldman, *Death and Life*, p. 222.

[5]Elijah Muhammad's FBI file, 31 December 1956.

[6]Ibid., 19 June 1962.

[7]Ibid., 14 July 1962.

[8]Ibid., 26 April 1962, p. 1.

[9]Ibid.

[10]Ibid., 14 July 1962.

[11]There is often a wide gulf between the FBI's claims and its actual achievements. Just because the Agency contemplated an action does not indicate that the action was effected. Any counterintelligence actions against domestic groups had to be approved in Washington before being implemented, and there is no evidence that the actions discussed in these

documents were approved and implemented, particularly with the success that the Bureau claims.

[12]Jamal, *From the Dead Level*, p. 218.

[13]Ibid., p. 219.

[14]*Muhammad Speaks*. April 1962. Volume II, Number 6, p. 3.

[15]Farmer, *Lay Bare the Heart*, p. 226.

[16]Ibid.

[17]Malcolm X's FBI file, 17 May 1961.

[18]See Perry, *Malcolm*, for more information concerning the finances of the Nation of Islam.

[19]Malcolm X's FBI file, 26 April 1962.

[20]Perry, *Malcolm*, p. 223.

[21]Interview with Benjamin Karim by Clayborne Carson, February 27, 1990.

[22]Malcolm X's FBI file, Section 14, 20 January 1965, p. 7.

[23]Interview with Benjamin Karim.

[24]Ibid.

Chapter Ten

[1]Goldman, *Death and Life*, p. 272. In a 1978 interview with Goldman, Butler denied that he resisted arrest, instead asserting that he had been unnecessarily abused by the police.

[2]*New York Amsterdam News*, 16 January 1965.

[3]In an interview, Wallace Muhammad told Goldman that he knows of at least ten people who were killed by the Muslims.

[4]Essien-Udom, *Black Nationalism*, p. 79.

[5]Ibid., p. 108.

[6]Malcolm X, *Autobiography*, p. 296.

[7]Elijah Muhammad's FBI file, 23 January 1964.

[8]For more information, see the books by E.U. Essien-Udom and C. Eric Lincoln.

[9]G. Barry Golson, ed. *The Playboy Interview* (New York: Playboy Press, 1981), p. 47.

[10]Malcolm X's FBI file, 2 January 1958.

[11]Elijah Muhammad's FBI file, 31 December 1956.

[12]Malcolm X's FBI files, 21 July 1959, pp. 22–29.

[13]Golson, *Playboy Interview*, p. 39.

[14]Breitman, *Malcolm X Speaks*, "Ballot or the Bullet" speech.

[15]"Brother Malcolm: His Theme Now is Violence," in *US News and World Report*. Volume LVI, No. 12. 23 March 1964, p. 19.

[16]*New York Times*, 22 March 1964.

[17]Goldman, *Death and Life*, p. 168.

[18]Breitman, *Malcolm X Speaks*, "Ballot or the Bullet" speech.

[19]Lomax, *When the Word is Given*, p. 85.

[20]Hoffer in Lincoln, *The Black Muslims in America*. p. 106.

[21]Ibid.

[22]Lomax, *When the Word is Given*, p. 58.

[23]Lincoln, *The Black Muslims in America*.

[24]Malcolm X, *Autobiography*, p. 233.

[25]Ibid., p. 234.

[26]Goldman, *Death and Life*, p. 59.

[27]Malcolm X, *Autobiography*, p. 289.

[28]*New York Times*, 23 February 1965, p. 1.

[29]*New York Times*, 1 March 1965.

[30]Ibid.

[31]*New York Times*, 22 February 1965.

[32]Norden, "Murder," p. 16.

[33]*New York Times*, 14 March 1965.

[34]Norden, "Murder," p. 16.

[35]"Malcolm X Aide Dead in Boston," *New York Times*, 14 March 1965, p. 57.

[36]*New York Times*, 14 March 1965.

[37]Aubrey Barnette, "The Black Muslims Are a Fraud," *Saturday Evening Post*, 27 February 1965, pp. 23–29.

[38]Elijah Muhammad's FBI file, Undated, p. 20.

[39]Barnette, "Black Muslims," p. 24.

[40]Ibid.

[41]Malcolm X, *Autobiography*, p. 297

[42]Ibid.

[43]"Muhammad Son Says Muslims Threatened Him," *Chicago Daily Defender*, 8 July 1964, p. 3.

[44]Wallace Muhammad reported to a parole officer because of his conviction for refusing to register for the draft. Black Muslims as a rule refused to register because of their objection to fighting in America's wars.

[45]Malcolm X, *Autobiography*, p. 411.

[46]Ibid., p. 422.

Chapter Eleven

[1]John Kifner, "Jabbar Talks of Islamic Strife Linked to Slayings," *New York Times*, 25 January 1973, p. 57.

[2]Donald Janson, "Coxson Murder Suspect Fails to Show Up in Court," *New York Times*, 22 August 1973, p. 79.

[3]Richard Phalon, "11 Sect Members Arrested in Newark Muslim Slaying," *New York Times*, 25 October 1973, p. 32.

[4]Wechsler, Philip. "Decapitated Bodies of Two Found in Newark Park," *New York Times*, 19 October 1973, p. 47.

[5]Adolph Reed, Jr., "The Rise of Louis Farrakhan," *The Nation*, 21 January 1991, p. 52.

[6]*New York Times*, "Black Leader Slain By Boston Gunmen; Muslim Feud Hinted," 3 May 1973, p. 26.

[7]Paul Delaney, "Black Muslim Group in Trouble from Financial Problems," *New York Times*, 6 December 1973, p. 37.

[8]Ibid.

[9]Reed, "Rise of Louis Farrakhan," p. 56.

[10]David Kurapka, "Hate Story," *The New Republic*, 30 May 1988, pp. 19–20.

[11]Lynda Wright, "Farrakhan's Mission," *Newsweek*, 19 March 1990, p. 25.

[12]Adolph Reed, Jr., "All for One and None for All," *The Nation*, 28 January 1991, p. 87.

[13]Michael Hardy and William Pleasant, *The Honorable Louis Farrakhan: A Minister for Progress.* New York: New Alliance Publications, 1988.

[14]Ibid.

[15]Louis E. Lomax, *To Kill a Black Man* (Los Angeles: Holloway House Publishing Co., 1968), p. 249.

[16]Malcolm X, *Autobiography*, p. 427.

[17]David Gallen, *Malcolm X: As They Knew Him.* (New York, Carroll & Graf Publishers, Inc. 1992), p. 30.

[18]Malcolm X, *Autobiography*, p. 444.

Selected Bibliography

Books:

Baldwin, James. *One Day, When I Was Lost*. New York: Bantam Doubleday Dell Publishing Group, Inc., 1972.

Baldwin, James. *The Fire Next Time*. New York: Bantam Doubleday Dell Publishing Group, Inc., 1963.

Blackstock, Nelson. *COINTELPRO: The FBI's Secret War on Political Freedom*. New York: Vintage Books, 1975.

Bontemps, Arna and Conroy, Jack. *Anyplace But Here*. New York: Hill and Wang, 1966.

Breitman, George. *The Evolution of an Revolutionary*. New York: Pathfinder Press, 1967.

Breitman, George, ed. *Malcolm X Speaks*. New York: Grove Press, 1965.

Breitman, George; Porter, Herman, and Smith, Baxter. *The Assassination of Malcolm X*. New York: Pathfinder, 1976.

Carson, Clayborne. *Malcolm X: The FBI File*. New York: Carroll & Graf Publishers, Inc., 1991.

Churchill, Ward and Vander Wall, Jim. *The COINTELPRO Papers*. Boston: South End Press, 1990.

Clark, Kenneth B., ed. *King, Malcolm, Baldwin*. Middletown, Connecticut: Wesleyan University Press, 1963.

Clarke, John Henrik. *Malcolm X: The Man and His Times*. Trenton: Africa World Press, Inc., 1990.

Cleaver, Eldridge. *Soul on Ice*. New York: Dell Publishing Co., Inc., 1968.

Cone, James H. *Martin & Malcolm & America*. New York: Orbis Books, 1991.

Crotty, William J., ed. *Assassinations and the Political Order*. New York, Harper & Row, Publishers, 1971.

Curtis, Richard. *The Life of Malcolm X*. Philadelphia: Macrae Smith Company, 1971.

Essien-Udom, E. U. *Black Nationalism: A Search for an Identity in America*. Chicago: University of Chicago Press, 1962.

Farmer, James. *Freedom—When?*. New York: Random House, 1965.

Farmer, James. *Lay Bare the Heart*. New York: Arbor House, 1985.

Farrakhan, Louis. *Back Where We Belong.* Philadelphia: PC International Press, 1989.

Gallen, David. *Malcolm X: As They Knew Him.* New York: Carroll & Graf, 1992.

Garrow, David J. *The FBI and Martin Luther King, Jr.* New York: Penguin Books, 1981.

Goldman, Peter. *The Death and Life of Malcolm X.* New York: Harper and Row, Publishers, 1974.

Haley, Alex and Malcolm X. *The Autobiography of Malcolm X.* New York: Ballantine Books, 1965.

Hampton, Henry and Fayer, Steve. *Voices of Freedom.* New York: Bantam Books, 1990.

Hardy, Michael and Pleasant, William. *The Honorable Louis Farrakhan: A Minister for Progress.* New York: New Alliance Publications, 1988.

Hauser, Thomas. *The Life and Times of Muhammad Ali.* New York: Simon & Schuster, 1991.

Hoffman, Paul. *Tiger in the Court.* Chicago: Playboy Press, 1973.

Independent Black Leadership in America. New York: Castillo International Publications, 1990.

Jamal, Hakim Abdullah. *From the Dead Level.* New York: Random House, 1972.

Kly, Y.N., ed. *The Black Book: The True Political Philosophy of Malcolm X.* Atlanta: Clarity Press, 1986.

Lincoln, C. Eric. *My Face Is Black.* Boston, Beacon Press, 1964.

Lincoln, C. Eric. *The Black Muslims in America.* Boston: Beacon Press, 1961.

Lomax, Louis E. *The Negro Revolt.* New York: Harper & Row, Publishers, 1962.

Lomax, Louis E. *To Kill A Black Man.* Los Angeles: Holloway House Publishing Co., 1968.

Lomax, Louis E. *When the Word Is Given.* Cleveland: The World Publishing Company, 1963.

Luellen, David Elmer. *Ministers and Martyrs: Malcolm X and Martin Luther King, Jr.* Ann Arbor: University Microfilms, 1972.

Melanson, Philip H. *The Martin Luther King Assassination.* New York: Shapolsky Publishers, Inc., 1991.

Muhammad, Elijah. *Message to the Blackman in America.* Chicago: Muhammad Mosque of Islam No. 2, 1965.

Muhammad, Elijah. *The Fall of America.* Chicago: Muhammad Temple of Islam No. 2, 1973.

Onwubu, Chukwuemeka. *Black Ideologies and the Sociology of Knowledge: The Public Response to the Protest Thoughts and Teachings of Martin Luther King, Jr., and Malcolm X.* Ann Arbor: University Microfilms, 1975.

O'Reilly, Kenneth. *"Racial Matters."* New York: The Free Press, 1989.

Parks, Gordon. *Voices in the Mirror.* New York: Doubleday, 1990.

Perry, Bruce. *Malcolm*. New York: Station Hill, 1991.

T'Shaka, Oba. *The Political Legacy of Malcolm X*. Richmond, California: Pan Afrikan Publications, 1983.

Ulasewicz, Tony. *The President's Private Eye*. Westport, Connecticut: MACSAM Publishing Company, Inc., 1990.

Wolfenstein, Eugene Victor. *The Victims of Democracy: Malcolm X and the Black Revolution*. London: Free Association Books, 1989.

Articles:

Baldwin, Lewis. "A Reassessment of the Relationship Between Malcolm X and Martin Luther King, Jr." *The Western Journal of Black Studies* (1989): pp. 103–10.

Balk, Alfred and Haley, Alex. "Black Merchants of Hate." *Saturday Evening Post*, 26 January 1963, pp. 71–74.

Barnes, Fred. "Farrakhan Frenzy." *The New Republic*, 28 October 1985, pp. 13–15.

Barnette, Aubrey. "The Black Muslims Are a Fraud," *Saturday Evening Post*, 27 February 1965, pp. 23–29.

Benyon, Erdmann Doane. "The Voodoo Cult Among Negro Migrants in Detroit." *American Journal of Sociology* (1938): 894–907.

"Black Supremacy Cult in U.S.—How Much of a Threat?" *U.S. News & World Report*, 9 November 1959, pp. 112–14.

"The Black Supremacists." *Time*, 10 August 1959, pp. 24–25.

Boyd, Herb. "Hero or Charlie Bad Guy." *Class*, 13 (1992): pp. 54–57.

Bradley, Edward, as told to Lomax, Louis E. "Driver Tells How Malcolm X Escaped Death in Chase." *The Washington Star*, 24 February 1965, p. 1.

Branch, Taylor. "The Uncivil War" *Esquire*, May 1989.

Crawford, Marc. "The Ominous Malcolm X Exits from the Muslims." in *Life*, 20 March 1964.

Goldman, Peter "Malcolm X. An Unfinished Story?" *New York Times Magazine*, 19 August 1979, pp. 26–32, 62–63.

Goldman, Peter. "Who Killed Malcolm X?" *Newsweek*, 7 May 1979, p. 39.

Golson, G. Barry, ed. *The Playboy Interview*. New York: Playboy Press, 1981. pp. 37–53.

Goodheart, Lawrence B. "The Odyssey of Malcolm X: An Eriksonian Interpretation." *The Historian*, pp. 47–62.

Haley, Alex. "Mr. Muhammad Speaks." *Reader's Digest*, March 1960, pp. 100–104.

Haley, Alex. "The Malcolm X I Knew." *Saga*, November, 1965, pp. 37–39, 68–70.

Handler, M. S. "Assertive Spirit Stirs Negroes, Puts Vigor in Civil Rights Drive." *The New York Times*, 23 April 1963, p. 20.

Hernton, Calvin C. "Another Man Done Gone: The Death of Malcolm X."

White Paper for White Americans. New York: Doubleday & Company, Inc., 1966, pp. 97–104.

Krauthammer, Charles. "The Black Rejectionists." *Time*, 23 July 1990, p. 80.

Kurapka, David. "Hate Story: Farrakhan's Still At It." *The New Republic*, 30 May 1988, pp. 19–20.

Lester, Julius. "The Time Has Come: Farrakhan in the Flesh." *The New Republic*, 28 October 1985, pp. 11–12.

Malcolm X and Farmer, James. "Separation v. Integration," in Broderick, Francis L.; Meier, August; and Rudwick, Elliot, eds. *Black Protest Thought in the Twentieth Century.* New York: The Bobbs-Merrill Company, Inc., 1971.

Morrison, Allan. "Who Killed Malcolm X?" *Ebony*, October 1965, pp. 135–40.

"Muhammad Son Says Muslims Threatened Him." *The Chicago Daily Defender*, 8 July 1964, p. 3.

Norden, Eric. "The Murder of Malcolm X." *The Realist*, February 1967, pp. 1–22.

"Now It's a Negro Drive for Segregation." *U.S. News & World Report*, 30 March 1964, pp. 38–39.

Parks, Gordon. "The White Devil's Day Is Almost Over." *Life*, 31 May 1963, pp. 25–32.

"Recruits Behind Bars." *Time*, 31 March 1961, p. 14.

Reed, Adolph, Jr. "All for One and None for All." *The Nation*, 28 January 1991, pp. 86–92.

Reed, Adolph, Jr. "The Rise of Louis Farrakhan." *The Nation*, 21 January 1991, p. 1.

Samuels, Gertrude. "Feud Within the Black Muslim Movement." *New York Times Magazine*, 22 March 1964, p. 17.

Shabazz, Betty. "The Legacy of My Husband, Malcolm X." *Ebony*, June 1969, pp. 174–82.

Shabazz, Betty. "Loving and Losing Malcolm." *Essence*, February, 1992. pp. 50–54, 104–11.

Smith, Baxter. "New Evidence of FBI 'Disruption' Program." *The Black Scholar*, July-August 1965. Volume 6, Number 10. pp. 43–48.

Southwick, Albert B. "Malcolm X: Charismatic Demagogue." *The Christian Century*, 5 July 1963, pp. 740–41.

"The Muslim Message: All White Men Devils, All Negroes Divine." *Newsweek*, 27 August 1962, pp. 26–30.

"The Pied Piper of Harlem." *The Christian Century*, 1 April 1964.

Tucker, William. " 'X' Marks the Champ." *The Miami News*, 19 February 1964.

Vincent, Ted. "The Garveyite Parents of Malcolm X." *The Black Scholar*, April 1989, pp. 10–13.

Worthy, William. *Esquire*, February 1961. p. 102.

Wright, Lynda. "Farrakhan's Mission." *Newsweek*, 19 March 1990, p. 25.

Index

287